Advance Praise for Abounding in Kindness

"Elizabeth Johnson, CSJ, is one of my favorite contemporary theologians, and her marvelous books on God, on Jesus, on Mary, and on the saints have helped me immensely in my life as a Christian. She is that rare theologian who combines vast learning with a clear writing style and an ability to convey complex topics with consummate ease. *Abounding in Kindness*, a new collection of essays and presentations designed for the widest audience possible—that is, for the whole People of God—is the perfect introduction to her faith-filled vision. Her new book is clear, accessible, inviting, wise, provocative, and always inspiring. Highly recommended."

—**James Martin, SJ**, author, *Jesus: A Pilgrimage*

"With her characteristically clear and elegant prose, Elizabeth Johnson breathes new life into the fundamental beliefs of the Christian tradition. Those seeking a rich portrait of the Living God and a mature conversation about faith—regardless of their level of expertise—will find these essays a revelation. This volume offers an inspiring display of Johnson's theological creativity and breadth of scholarship."

—**Jamie L. Manson**, columnist, *National Catholic Reporter*

"*Abounding in Kindness* is Christian Apologetics at its best. The voice of Elizabeth Johnson helps make faith and the church credible. She presents an image of a God who is ever beyond us, but who envelops us in an empathic embrace that is deeper than human love we can understand. If you are struggling to reconcile your faith with your intellect, this is your book."

—**Ronald Rolheiser, OMI**, author, *Sacred Fire*

"Those who have followed Elizabeth Johnson over the years with gratitude and respect will find here a rich compendium of some of her more recent insights and teaching. In particular, her sections on creation are brilliant as well as avant garde, and her discussions of the Holy Spirit, superb. Both are informed as well by Johnson's signatory clarity about the positions she is taking and by the judiciousness with which she has assumed them."

—**Phyllis Tickle**, author, *The Great Emergence*

"*Abounding in Kindness* comes from the heart of one of the finest Catholic theologians of our time. It will be an inspiration to all—theologians and lay people alike—as we strive to embrace God's abundant compassion and to live it as disciples of Jesus, who so favored the least, the lost, and the last. This book reflects the amazing resource it can be 'for life to the full' when theology and spirituality are integrated by a faithful Christian and a great theologian."

—**Tom Groome**, author, *What Makes Us Catholic*

*For my colleagues at Fordham University,
with admiration and deep gratitude*

Also by Elizabeth A. Johnson

Consider Jesus: Waves of Renewal in Christology

She Who Is: The Mystery of God in Feminist Theological Discourse

Women, Earth and Creator Spirit
(Madeleva Lecture in Spirituality)

Friends of God and Prophets:
A Feminist Theological Reading of the Communion of Saints

The Church Women Want: Catholic Women in Dialogue (editor)

Truly Our Sister: A Theology of Mary in the Communion of Saints

Dangerous Memories: A Mosaic of Mary in Scripture

Quest for the Living God: Mapping Frontiers in the Theology of God

Ask the Beasts: Darwin and the God of Love

Contents

III
JESUS THE LIVING ONE

IV
KINDLE IN US THE FIRE OF DIVINE LOVE: CHURCH MATTERS

V
EPILOGUE

Introduction

This book of short pieces invites readers to muse about different aspects of the Christian faith. Created with the conviction that theology is meant for the whole people of God, it collects writings of mine that have appeared in popular journals intended to make insights accessible to a broad reading public. It also includes lectures delivered to students at colleges and universities and before adult audiences in church venues. In bringing these pieces together between two covers, my hope is that they will serve to nourish the minds and hearts of a larger pool of folk than read or heard the original, or at least give the reader something more to think about regarding God's abounding kindness, something more to question, or argue over, or imagine anew, or even pray with, and then enact.

Much of this material, including named lectures, has been previously published in the United States or abroad. The pieces have been lightly edited to remove references to particular occasions, to eliminate repetition, and to promote clarity. Their arrangement loosely follows the pattern of the Christian creed, starting with the issue of belief itself and moving through the mystery of God the Creator, Jesus Christ, and the work of the Holy Spirit, which itself diversifies into issues about justice, spirituality, and community. In no way is this book meant as a commentary on the creed or a complete discussion of the creed's various components. This is just a convenient arrangement, given the spread of subject matter.

As I reviewed these writings one theme kept emerging in various forms, namely, the overflowing compassion of the living God engaged with the struggles and suffering of the world. The book's title brings this to expression with the words of Psalm 103, which praises God who is "merciful and gracious, slow to anger and abounding in kindness" (v. 8). In picturesque language the psalm goes on to say that God knows how fragile we are, like dust, like the wildflowers that wither when the dry wind blows. Yes, we are mortal, but God surrounds the world with steadfast love greater than the height of the sky above the earth; in a culture prior to airplanes and space travel, this was a significant comparison. Yes, we transgress, but instead of dealing with us as we deserve, God removes our sins farther away than the east is from the west. This psalmist had a good geographical imagination. Greater than earth's measurable height and depth, length and width, divine compassion abides through thick and thin, from everlasting to everlasting. Remembering this, people need to keep the covenant, which the prophet Micah elsewhere describes as acting justly, loving mercy, and walking humbly with your God (6:8). No wonder the psalm ends with an outburst of praise, summoning all creation to bless such mighty goodness.

Abounding in kindness, the holy mystery of God is love beyond imagining. Not enough people seem to know this, even those who practice the Christian religion. But the drumbeat of this good news resounds throughout the history of ancient Israel where, from the start of their liberation from slavery, people encountered "a God merciful and gracious, slow to anger, and abounding in steadfast love and faithfulness" (Ex 34:6). The drumbeat becomes unmistakably intense in Jesus Christ who preached and enacted divine compassion in startling ways, all the way to the cross and beyond. Its volume ramps up in the church wherever this word is heard and practiced amid the joys and hopes, the griefs and anxieties of people of this age.

This is not a word that returns to its Maker empty. Working creatively for peace amid horrific violence; struggling for justice in the face of massive poverty and military oppression; advocating ecological wholeness for the earth's life-giving systems and stressed-out species; educating the young and the old; healing the sick and comforting those in despair; creating beauty; taking joy in nourishing children; promoting freedom for captives: the list could go on because the needs are enormous. Even a simple cup of cold water given in Christ's name symbolizes how the abounding kindness of God becomes effective in this world. While a variety of different

topics are addressed in the pieces gathered here, the compassionate love of God is the underlying theme throughout.

Heartfelt thanks go to my editor Robert Ellsberg, whose creative vision and enthusiasm for this project helped carry the work
along from its inception. I would also like to thank the editors who
over the years invited me to contribute articles to their publications, and the heads of programs in higher education, religious
communities, and church venues who invited me to lecture. Am-
plifying their invitations over the years has been the long-ago
query of my friend Mary Lou Buser CSJ, physical therapist and
community gardener. As a fledgling academic I had just happily
published three scholarly articles, when she asked, "But when are
you going to write something for *us*?" Sequestered in a university
and measuring up to its demands, I probably would not have written in this vein without these proddings.

This book enters the list as one more effort to amplify awareness of the abounding kindness and fidelity of God, to practical
and critical effect.

I
PATTERNS OF FAITH
IN A QUESTIONING TIME

1

Passing on the Faith
The Banquet of the Creed

In a sermon delivered in the fifth century Augustine presented an evocative idea. Focusing on the people before him, he mused that the early Christians in the first century had no idea that one day there would be a church in North Africa, a community of believers praising God in a language and culture very different from their own. The church that he and his congregation now formed was to those ancestors in the faith a "church of the future." He reached the challenging heart of the matter with the insight, "They weren't yet able to see it, but they were already constructing it out of their own lives" (*Sermon* 306).

This, it seems to me, is a superb description of the responsibility adult believers have to pass on the faith. Christian faith is a two-thousand-year-old phenomenon, handed down from generation to generation. It has been carried through history in a diverse community of disciples who have expressed it in vastly different cultures and climates. In eras such as medieval Europe when Christianity was culturally dominant, faith was passed on without much difficulty, the spark of belief catching hold more or less through the practices of the whole society. In other times such as our own in the more secular, pluralistic twenty-first-century, such ease is gone. But the church of the future still needs constructing, and the material is our own lives.

The task of passing on the faith involves facing some daunting obstacles in our time and place. Among the more potent are these. Even everyday thought has to grapple with the public challenge of atheism coming from the old masters of suspicion Feuerbach, Nietzsche, Marx, and Freud, along with their new postmodern heirs. Culturally the air is colored by extremes, with public attacks on religion on the one hand, rigorous Christian fundamentalisms on the other, and a certain agnosticism or comfortable indifference to religion in-between. Drawn from science and technology, assumptions about how the world works rightfully place natural rather than supernatural powers at the center of attention. Powerful consumerist values overshadow the appeal of gospel virtue. Religious pluralism embodied in colleagues, neighbors, friends, and lovers removes the absolutism of Christianity. The institutional church itself often appears as an obstacle to faith, being mediocre in preaching, numb to pressing spiritual needs, and irresponsible, even sinful, in actions taken and disastrously not taken in face of the sexual abuse of minors, misuse of church monies, and other scandals. We are in a new epoch that presents a challenge without precedent.

In this context, an insight of Karl Rahner's offers thought-provoking direction for the road ahead: "The devout Christian of the future will either be a mystic, that is, one who has experienced something, or he [she] will cease to be anything at all."[1] The Christian will be one who has *experienced* something of the beauty and love of the living God, one who has felt the attraction so that it becomes personal knowledge, or faith will be a dead fish. In the contemporary context it is crucial to note that the faith we are considering is not, first of all, assent to propositions, be they doctrinal or moral. Neo-scholastic theology defined faith this way, making it an intellectual act of the mind. Contemporary theology has rediscovered a more biblical view, seeing faith as the assent of a person's whole being to the mystery of the ineffable God who is unspeakably close in Jesus Christ through the Spirit. Faith entails committing yourself to this mystery, risking a relationship that has the power to transform your life. At the heart of it all, what does Christianity proclaim? It announces the good news that the reality of God surrounds us with forgiving, abounding kindness in the midst of our darkness, injustice, sin, and death. All the doctrines and rituals aim to unpack this basic wonder. Faith means entrusting yourself to this presence, leaning your heart on this Rock, and responding with your life's energies. This is normally done with others in a community of disciples called church.

Handing on the faith entails bringing the streaming new potential of the next generations into vibrant contact with this good news in such a way that they can experience how encounter with ineffable Love makes life meaningful, replete with goodness, actively compassionate toward others, and hopeful in the midst of struggle. For this to happen fruitfully, we who have been on earth a little bit longer have to speak and act out of the depths of our own religious experience. The lamp of the word of God burns primarily with the oil of our own lives. Conscious of the challenges of our day, we need to witness to faith creatively in word and deed so that the spark will catch among the young. As in every era, a practice of discernment helps us to figure out which elements of faith need particular emphasis. Adults in the church who treasure their faith must make deliberate decisions not only about strategies but also about emphases in what is being passed on in order to intrigue new generations into a life of relationship with the living God.

Toward that end, I propose to reflect on the Nicene Creed, hammered out in the fourth century and widely used across the divided Christian churches. Within a three-part division it narrates the story of the one God who creates the world, saves the world in Jesus Christ, and ensures the world's blessed future in the Holy Spirit. Countless commentaries have drawn out the meanings of each phrase of this cornucopia of the living tradition. I have no intention of replacing this accumulated wisdom, let alone of giving a survey of what the creed confesses. My interest turns instead to issues in our day that raise new questions and bring forth fresh insights. I will highlight two such themes under each article of the creed. As we create the church of the future out of our own lives, these emphases, I suggest, can enrich the experience of faith, allowing it to be passed on in a vibrant way.

FIRST AFFIRMATION

The creed begins: "We believe in one God," and goes on to affirm that the signature act of this indescribable Holy One is to make all that exists in heaven and on earth, whether visible or invisible. The entire dazzling universe, from the smallest particle to the most enormous galaxy, from the simplest plant and wildest animal to the most complex human being, comes from the hand of the one Maker of heaven and earth. Notice right at the outset that God is not pictured all alone in isolated splendor but as Creator, in relation to the whole world, which depends on divine graciousness for its very existence. Just as people can see in an artistic work something of the artist who created it, so too from ancient times onward, people have noted that the beauty and power of the natural world can reveal the glory of the unseen God who made it. The universe is magnificent and the creed begins by affirming that God makes and loves the whole shebang.[2]

In the context of a humble creation theology, two dimensions of faith that need to be passed on in our day are a faith that reverences the incomprehensible mystery of God and a faith that loves the earth.

Respecting God's Holy Mystery

It is a constant struggle in theology, preaching, and popular practice to understand that the one God we are confessing in human words is infinite holy mystery beyond imagining. Such has always been a central tenet of monotheistic faith. The One who is ground, support, and goal of all creation, while profoundly present, cannot be completely understood or defined. Our ignorance is not due to some reluctance on the part of God to self-reveal in a full way, nor to the sinful condition of the human race, nor even to the modern mentality of skepticism about religious matters. Rather, it is proper to God's being God and not a creature that God is beyond our human power to grasp. In Augustine's unforgettable echo of earlier Greek theology, "*Si comprehendis, non est Deus*": if you have understood, then what you have understood is not God (*Sermon* 52). We are deceiving ourselves if we think otherwise.

Paradoxical as it might seem, this very awareness is an enlivening form of knowledge. There is always more to explore, like railroad tracks that seem to the eye to meet at a distant point but that open to a yet further vista once the observer reaches that point. Augustine consistently pushes this acknowledgment of God's incomprehensible character through to its genuine religious goal, the knowing of God through love. If we wish to savor something of God, he writes, then we should attend to our loving, for God is Love. "In loving, we already possess God as known better than we do the fellow human being whom we love. Much better, in fact, because God is nearer, more present, more certain."[3] The God who pervades yet cannot be contained in creation or caught in concepts is nonetheless deeply known in human love, as love itself.

Of course, as Aquinas described it, we must take excellent qualities known from the created world and speak about God as being good, wise, loving, and so forth. These words are truly spoken and we can have a reliable sense of what they mean. The nature of this language is such, however, that whatever the words mean in an earthly setting, they have to go through the refining fire of analogy and escape into the "more" of an unknown plenitude when said of God. The Fourth Lateran Council taught this in a deliberately crafted axiom: between the Creator and creature no similarity can be said without noting that between them the dissimilarity is always ever greater.

In today's spiritual climate, Rahner has argued, this truth of the incomprehensibility of God belongs not at the margins or at the end of the road in theology but at its very heart. In the face of atheistic criticism and the arid experience of agnosticism, the darkness of divine definition opens room for faith to grow. Supported but not bound by the limits of clear concepts, people can dare to entrust their existence to the always greater holy mystery surrounding their lives with unfathomable love. Without the incomprehensible God as horizon and ultimate fulfillment, the human project itself would meet an impenetrable limit such that the human spirit would shut down, having no further depths of knowledge or love to plumb.

As adults pass on the faith to the next generation, the sense of God they convey deserves to be worthy of these young lives. The creed's magnificent affirmation of belief in "God the Father, Creator of heaven and earth," must not reduce the Creator to a puny godling, a single male-acting subject who is part of the scheme of created things. The living Source of all is not a being among other beings! Rather, the living God is the incomprehensible mystery of love beyond imagining. As Scripture so beautifully shows, this uncreated plenitude can be expressed in many images: father, of course, and also mother, midwife, shepherd, lover, artist, potter, liberator, friend, Wisdom; also hovering bird and angry mother bear; also blowing wind, blazing flame, flowing water, unapproachable light; the One in whom we live and move and have our being. But in truth the reality of God, being the uncreated Source of all, is beyond all images, goes beyond telling.

For the sake of the faith of the church of the future, we need to attend to what we mean and do *not* mean when we say God.

Loving the Earth

Contemporary science is crafting a dynamic picture of how the universe came to be. From the initial flaring forth of the Big Bang some 13.8 billion years ago, to the formation of galaxies with their billions of stars, to the shaping of our sun and its planets 5 billion years ago, to the slow evolution of life on Earth over deep eons of time, the cosmic adventure has moved toward increasing complexity and beauty. We humans who emerged from this cosmic process a mere speck of time ago are now conscious of this history. This makes us, in Rabbi Abraham Heschel's beautiful words, "the cantors of the universe," those creatures who can give praise to the Creator with and in the name of all the rest.[4]

Telling the story of the universe in this evolutionary way makes us realize that the earth is not just a backdrop for the human drama of sin and redemption. Rather, the world has its own intrinsic value, being loved by God for its own sake. With its strong interest in human affairs, theology has often forgotten this truth. Perhaps a silly question can help shift our focus: what was God the Creator doing for billions of years before we humans came along? Surely not just "waiting" for the human race to evolve so salvation history could begin. Rather, through unfathomable depths of time God was continuously empowering the cosmos's own creative emergence. In the process the natural world itself became an ever more beautiful sacrament of divine presence, a locus of divine compassion, and the bearer of a divine promise that keeps opening it up to a fresh and unexpected future.

In a terrible way our human practices are wreaking damage on the life-systems of air, water, and soil, and on the other species that share with us one community of life on this planet. Why have we who confess that God created this world not risen up en masse in its defense? One reason is that through theology's engagement with Greek philosophy, we have inherited a powerful dualism that devalues matter and the body and prizes the spirit as closer to God. The task now is to develop a life-affirming theology of earth/matter/bodies, one that will do better justice to this world that God makes and so loves. We need to realize that a moral universe limited to the human community no longer serves the future of life. Countering the sins of ecocide, biocide, geocide, we must take action on behalf of justice for the natural world, promoting care, protection, restoration, and healing, even if this goes counter to powerful economic and political interests . . . and it does.

Reflecting on these matters in 1990, Pope John Paul II made an urgently important connection. The emphasis on human dignity so typical of Catholic social teaching must cross the species line and extend to all creation. According to this radical principle, "Respect for life and for the dignity of the human person extends also to the rest of creation."[5] The reason for respect is the same in both cases. All are creatures of the one Creator whose abounding kindness excludes nary a one. If we truly believe in "one God, Maker of heaven and earth," then we will hand on to the next generation a faith that loves the earth.

SECOND AFFIRMATION

"We believe in one Lord Jesus Christ." After affirming Jesus Christ's unity with God in the great, once-disputed Greek term *homoousios* (one in being, consubstantial), the creed briefly recounts his life on earth, born of Mary, suffered under Pilate, crucified, died, buried, then risen and coming again to judge the living and the dead. Note how the two points, one to do with heaven, one with earth, shed light on each other. For the story of Jesus receives its power from the belief that here the transcendent God draws radically near by becoming incarnate in human flesh. A genuine member of the human race, living a real historical life from start to finish, "tempted in every respect as we are, yet without sinning" (Heb 4:15), Jesus is in person the divine Word expressed in finite terms. Here we are at the center of what is most identifiably *Christian* about Christian faith. The historical details, then, matter, for Jesus embodies the very ways of God with the world. What he does discloses the character of God.

Aspects of this story bring into high relief two further themes that could color the faith we hand on, namely, faith that does justice, and faith that lives in joyful compassion.

Doing Justice

Jesus' story starts out as a distressing one. He was born into a poor family, laid in a manger, and soon became a refugee fleeing a ruler's murderous violence. In Gustavo Gutiérrez's memorable words, the advent of God in Christ is "an irruption smelling of the stable."[6] Years later Jesus announced the theme of his ministry with liberating words from the scroll of Isaiah: "The Spirit of the Lord is upon me, because he has anointed me to bring good news to the poor. He has sent me to proclaim release to the captives and recovery of sight to the blind, to let the oppressed go free, to proclaim a year of favor for the Lord" (Lk 4:18–19).

What follows is indeed good news in the concrete as the prophet from Nazareth meets and transforms suffering and despair. The Messiah heals the sick, exorcizes demons, forgives sinners, and cares for those whose lives are a heavy burden. He practices table companionship so inclusive that it gives scandal: "Behold, a glutton and a drunkard, a friend of tax collectors and sinners" (Mt 11:19). Illuminated by his creative parables centered in the coming kingdom of God, these merciful actions destabilize the prevailing norms of who is first and who is last in the eyes of God. They establish beyond doubt divine solidarity with those who lack basic necessities: "I was hungry and you gave me to eat...I was hungry and you gave me no food" (Mt 25:35, 42). Neglect of "the least of these" means turning your back on God.

In historical perspective, Jesus' death on the cross is the price he paid for his prophetic ministry. And here, precisely where one would least expect to find divinity, amid torture and unjust execution by the state, the gospel locates the presence of God. *Ecce homo:* behold the suffering face of Jesus. He is risen as a pledge that there will be a blessed future for all the violated and the dead, cast off as if their lives had no meaning.

Through the centuries and continuing today, the following of Jesus has brought forth magnificent deeds of charity toward those who are suffering. In our time the global struggle of millions of people for peace, human rights, equality, and sufficient material goods for a decent life makes clear that discipleship also calls for action to establish social justice by transforming structures that create the miseries of war, oppression, and massive poverty to begin with. Here the following of Jesus raises up strong counter-cultural challenges on many fronts:

❖ How can we economically well-off Christians continue patterns of consumption that contribute to the destruction of the environment and the destitution of millions of poor people struggling for life? Renewed emphasis on Jesus' prophetic preferential option for the poor in the name of God summons our conscience to action on behalf of justice that will change oppressive structures in keeping with his loving, liberating intent. Latin American theologian José Miranda states the challenge with singular directness: "No authority can decree that everything is permitted, for justice and exploitation are not so indistinguishable. And Christ died so that we might know that not everything is permitted. But not any Christ. The Christ that cannot be co-opted by the comfortable is the historical Jesus."[7]

❖ How can we white Christians in this country continue to support attitudes, actions, and inactions that diminish the well-being of African American and other racial and ethnic groups struggling to live with full human dignity? During the time of slavery, the faith of black people understood the liberating message of Jesus better than their white masters did. An enslaved people deeply intuited his cross' connection with their suffering, which gave them hope. Following Jesus entails solidarity in the effort to ensure that human rights be honored for all God's people, whatever the color of their skin, country of origin, or legal status.

❖ How can we in this hierarchical church continue to relegate women to second-class status governed by patriarchal structures, laws, and rituals? Jesus called women disciples who followed him in Galilee, were faithful witnesses of his death, and commissioned witnesses of his resurrection. In the decades following they participated with men in founding the church. Even apart from myriad gospel examples of Jesus' beneficent relationship with women, his rejection of any relationship patterned on domination ("the rulers of the Gentiles lord it over them...but it will not be so among you," Mt 20:25-26) challenges the church to become a more inclusive community.

Divine predilection for history's lowest and least does not mean that God opts only for those marginalized by sex, race, class. Divine love is universal, not exclusive. But it does mean that the living God has a particular care for those who are hurting. Listen to Mary's song of justice, the *Magnificat*: she sings that God her savior has brought down the mighty from their thrones and lifted up the lowly; filled the hungry with good things but sent the rich away empty, all in fulfillment of the ancient promise of mercy. This is what is meant by a love that does justice, the kind of love that enacts God's *mercy* in a broken world. Handing on a faith that does justice ensures that the next generation will find a solid path of discipleship in our day.

Living with Joyful Compassion

The most recognizable Christian symbol is an instrument of torture and death, turned into the flowering tree of life, the cross. I think one of the worst ideas we have passed on is that God the Father needed and wanted the sacrifice of this bloody death in order to forgive sin. In the eleventh century Anselm took the idea of satisfaction as it was practiced under feudalism and crafted it into a powerful argument for the necessity of the cross. In truth, he meant this as a reflection on God's mercy, but in the hands of lesser preachers it soon became a toxic idea, namely, that our sins have so offended God that he demands death as recompense. Aquinas, Scotus, and others criticized this theory and the necessity that is so woven into it, but it won the day for the next thousand years.

Today, criticisms of this satisfaction theology of the cross are many. It makes it seem that the main purpose of Jesus' coming was to die, thus diminishing the importance of his ministry and robbing his life of freedom. It glorifies suffering more than joy as a path to God, leading to a masochistic piety. Liberation theology criticizes how the theory inculcates passivity in the face of unjust suffering rather than awakening the will to resist. Feminist theology criticizes how it portrays a father handing over his son to death, connecting this with domestic violence and child abuse. Underlying all of these problems is the bloodthirsty picture of a God who needs to be placated by suffering. Compare this to the idea of God present in the major parables of Jesus. It would be as if in the parable of the prodigal son the father says to the returning runaway, "No, you may not come in until you have repaid what you wasted"; the older brother offers to help; he works himself to the bone in the fields, finally dying of exhaustion; at which point the father says, "All right, you can come in now." How contradictory this is to the God Jesus knew and taught!

How then shall we understand the cross? Not as a death required by God in repayment for sin, but as an event of divine love whereby the Creator of the world entered into intimate contact with human suffering, sinfulness, and death in order to heal, redeem, and liberate from within. This view comes across in the multitude of metaphors used by the New Testament to interpret the cross. Early Christians did indeed use the cultic metaphor of sacrifice drawn from the ritual slaughter of animals in the Jerusalem temple and later pressed into service by Anselm. But as the New Testament shows, they also used business metaphors such as buying back and redeeming; legal metaphors such as justification; military metaphors such as liberation and victory over the enemy; political metaphors such as mediation, peace-making, and reconciliation; medical metaphors such as healing; family metaphors such as adoption; and even maternal metaphors such as giving birth (Jesus died so we could be "born of God": the most frequently used interpretation in the letters of John). As these metaphors work, we are subtly led away from the notion of the cross as a death required by God in repayment for sin and toward appreciation of the cross as an event of divine compassion in solidarity with human suffering, sin, and death.

Jesus did not come to die but to live and help others live in the joy of the reign of God. To put it baldly, God is not a sadistic father, and Jesus was not a passive victim of divine desire for satisfaction. Rather, his suffering, freely borne in love out of fidelity to his ministry and his God, is precisely the way our gracious God has chosen to enter into solidarity with all those who suffer and are lost in this violent world, thereby opening up the promise of new life out of the very center of death. It is in this vein that we would do well to hand on the story of Jesus, so that faith is lived in the joy of life and compassionate action with those who are suffering, rather than in prizing pain in the name of God.

THIRD AFFIRMATION

"We believe in the Holy Spirit." The creed goes on to describe what the Spirit, worshiped together with the Father and the Son, accomplishes. The Lord and Giver of life precisely gives life, inspires prophets, brings the church to life, consecrates people through baptism and the forgiveness of sins, and ensures the resurrection of the dead and the life of the world to come.

This article of the creed connects the Spirit in a particular way to the church, the community made one, holy, catholic, and apostolic by grace. Augustine used a particularly striking image to bring this point home. The Spirit is already at work among you, he preached to his congregation, cultivating you like an orchard, producing buds, strengthening your branches, clothing you with leaves, and loading you with fragrant flowers and fruit. Central to this spiritual flourishing is the eucharistic body and blood of Christ which can transform people themselves into the body of Christ: "If you receive them well, you are yourselves what you receive" (*Sermon* 227). In our day Edward Schillebeeckx has written with similar sensitivity to the way the Spirit shapes the church:

> The living community is the only real reliquary of Jesus. …By following Jesus, taking our bearings from him and allowing ourselves to be inspired by him, by sharing in his *Abba* experience and his selfless support for the "least of my brethren" (Mt 25:40), and thus entrusting our own destiny to God, we allow the history of Jesus, the living one, to continue in history as a piece of living christology, the work of the Spirit among us.[8]

The church as a piece of living christology: in the context of a Spirit-oriented ecclesiology, two dimensions of faith that our day calls for passing on are faith that reverences the presence of God in the world's religions and faith that dares to hope against hope for the resurrection of the dead.

Reverencing the World's Religions

In light of today's encounter among different religions, theology is increasingly having to think about the salvific design of God for the whole world. Christians affirm that this saving plan reaches its highest historical density and revelatory clarity in Jesus Christ with significance for all. We Christians are the bearers of this treasured knowledge; we witness and proclaim it. Yet the Word of God is not constrained by this particular history, nor is the Spirit of God limited by the church. Due to God's gracious initiative, different paths are laid down in different societies inviting people to share divine life. Thus the religions with their saving figures and sacred texts, their creeds, codes, and rituals can be considered channels of grace set up by God's providence to be ways people in different cultures encounter and respond to the Holy One. This is the teaching of Vatican II, still not widely appreciated:

The Catholic Church rejects nothing that is true and holy in these religions. She regards with sincere reverence those ways of conduct and of life, those precepts and teachings which, though differing in many aspects from the ones she holds and sets forth, nonetheless often reflect a ray of that Truth which enlightens all people.... The Church, therefore, exhorts her children, that through dialogue and collaboration with the followers of other religions, carried out with prudence and love and in witness to the Christian faith and life, they recognize, preserve and promote the good things, spiritual and moral, as well as the socio-cultural values found among these people.[9]

Put plainly, what is true and holy in the religions expresses God's presence in the world through the universal working of Word and Spirit. Such diversity in the religious sphere gives dazzling expression to the depth and breadth of God's holy mystery. It witnesses to the superabundant generosity of God who manifests divine purpose to the human race in such manifold ways.

It is odd, when you think about it, that for centuries the Christ event was used to obscure or even negate the work of God in other religions, rather than to expand appreciation of it. Christians assumed that since the Word is present here, personally incarnate in Jesus Christ, and the Spirit is present here, poured out on the church, then God is not present elsewhere, or at least not so truly and lovingly present. We saw this as an either-or scenario. But with the trinitarian God being infinite, this makes no sense. The revelation in Christ of God's will to save all people actually postulates a sweeping divine activity in the world, not only in a general sense but also in the religions that lay down explicit paths of holiness. Not to recognize this is tantamount to being ignorant of the greatness of God.

Rabbi Jonathan Sachs proposes some arresting analogies. What would faith be like if we acknowledged the presence of God in other faiths, whose truth is not our truth? It would be like feeling secure in one's own home, yet moved by the beauty of foreign places when we travel, knowing they are someone else's

home, not ours, but still part of the glory of the world that is
ours. It would be like realizing that our life is a sentence written
in the story of our own faith, yet pleased to know that there are
other lives written in the stories of other faiths, all part of the
great narrative of God's call and humanity's response. Those
who are confident in their faith are not threatened but enlarged
by the different faith of others. As we discover ever more truth
about God in each other, the dignity of difference can be a source
of blessing.[10]

In a world where violence propelled by religious differences
wreaks havoc and shatters lives, it is imperative that the religions
learn to live respectfully with one another. This does not mean reducing everything to the lowest common denominator, but rather
reframing the way we see our differences. If Christians become
aware of the work of the Spirit in the world's religions, our deepest commitments can impel us to work together in solidarity for hal-
lowing the world in peace.

Hoping for the Resurrection of the Dead

There is a powerful logic that connects the opening of the creed,
God creating heaven and earth, with the closing of the creed, the
Creator Spirit bringing about the resurrection of the dead and the
life of the world to come. In both cases we begin with virtually
nothing: no universe, no future for the dead. In the first case the
vivifying breath of the Spirit moves to create the world. In the end
case, the Spirit moves again and, in a new act of creation, keeping
hold of the beloved creature, carries a person through perishing
into new life, indeed carries the whole creation through transformation into a new heaven and a new earth. The creed traces this
logic, from the original creation through the story of Jesus Christ
to the promise of the future.

Hope in eternal life for oneself, others, and the whole cosmos,
in other words, is not some curiosity tacked on as an appendage
to faith but is faith in the living God brought to its radical conclusion. It is faith in the Creator Spirit that does not stop halfway but
follows the road consistently to the end, trusting that the God of

the beginning is also the God of the end, who utters the same word in each case: let there be life. All the biblical images of the end-time—light, banquet, harvest, wedding feast, rest, singing, homecoming, reunion, tears wiped away, seeing face to face, and knowing as we are known—point to a living communion in God's own life. We die not into nothingness but into the embrace of God. Transformation, not annihilation, is the goal. There is a reason to hope, then, even with tears of grief streaming down our cheeks. In the end there is God or there is nothing. This is a precious truth that we need to hand on.

CONCLUSION

Each age passes on the faith according to its own lights. In sharing these reflections about what is needed in our day, I am aware that there are many other suggestions that could be made. The exercise itself has left me awed by what a rich treasure the Christian heritage holds. Extrapolating from the gospel story of Jesus, Scripture dares to present the living God as fundamentally and essentially Love (1 Jn 4:8). Present through the Spirit in the world, God is the lover of this world, including us human beings, and graciously desires the well-being of all. Faith then becomes the radical experience that at the heart of the world this kind of Love exists as a reality greater than any other. We are moved to prayer, by turns silent, wildly lamenting, repenting, joyfully thanking, and praising. We are moved to compassionate praxis that corresponds to God's own heart. We are moved to these actions together, as church, as the community of disciples of Jesus, budding like an orchard.

In the biblical book of Proverbs, Holy Sophia goes to great pains to prepare a feast. After building a house, setting the table, dressing meats and fermenting wine, she sends her maidservants out around the town to invite all who will listen: "Come, eat of my bread and drink of the wine I have mixed. Lay aside immaturity, and live, and walk in the way of insight" (Prov 9:5–6). Cognizant that the future effectiveness of the word of God draws on the energies of our own lives, we adults in the church should be greatly encouraged to partake of this banquet of the creed. Then

together in the power of the Spirit we can call to future generations to come and be nourished for their own life's journey.

---

*Adapted from an address at Boston College in "The Faith That the Church
Hands On" series, 2006; published in* Prophetic Witness: Catholic Women's
Strategies for Reform, *ed. Colleen Griffith (New York: Crossroad, 2009): 6–15.*

Notes

1. Karl Rahner, "Christian Living Formerly and Today," *Theological
Investigations* Vol. 7 (New York: Crossroad, 1971), 15.

2. Timothy Ferris, *The Whole Shebang* (New York: Simon & Schuster,
1997).

3. Augustine, *On the Trinity*, 8.8.12.

4. Abraham Heschel, *Man's Quest for God* (New York: Scribner, 1954),
82; "Whose ear has ever heard how all trees sing to God? Has our reason
ever thought of calling upon the sun to praise the Lord? And yet, what
the ear fails to perceive, what reason fails to conceive, our prayer makes
clear to our souls. It is a higher truth, to be grasped by the spirit: 'All Thy
works praise Thee' (Psalms 145:10). We are not alone in our acts of
praise. Wherever there is life, there is silent worship. The world is always
on the verge of becoming one in adoration. It is man who is the cantor of
the universe, and in whose life the secret of cosmic prayer is disclosed."

5. John Paul II, "Peace with God the Creator, Peace with All of Creation," (World Day of Peace Letter, 1990), par. 16.

6. Gustavo Gutiérrez, *The God of Life* (Maryknoll, NY: Orbis, 1991), 84.

7. José Miranda, *Being and the Messiah* (Maryknoll, NY: Orbis, 1977), 9.

8. Edward Schillebeeckx, *Christ* (New York: Seabury, 1980), 641.

9. Vatican II, *Nostra Aetate* (Declaration on the Relation of the Church
to Non-Christian Religions), par. 2.

10. Jonathan Sachs, *The Dignity of Difference* (New York: Continuum,
2003).

2

Atheism and Faith
in a Secular World

Peering through the mists of time, anthropologists who study early human culture report finding indications of religious practice. It seems that from the beginning human beings lived with a sense of a numinous power which they could not control yet with which they sought to live in harmony. They saw the natural world pervaded with spirits that dwelt in every mountain and tree, river and animal, and developed rituals to commune with these spirits. The graves of Neanderthal people give evidence of this sense of the sacred. On occasion, they buried their dead with great care, smearing the body with red ochre (the tint of the living body), and flexing the body into a fetal position to prepare for new birth. Then they would enclose artifacts for future use: beads, bowls, antlers. Something more than simply the end of a life was being expressed in these burial practices. The magnificent cave paintings of animals found in southern Europe, dated twenty to thirty thousand years ago, offer another example. Some scholars now interpret these works as religious artifacts created by shamans and used in community rituals. It is not far-fetched to argue that religion emerged with tools and fire.

Over time this basic awareness of a sacred presence developed into an array of religions, organized and not so organized, which channeled human relationship to the divine. The world's religions have shown an enormous diversity of beliefs and practices. One could spend a lifetime studying their history, from the indigenous life-ways of Australian aboriginal and Native American peoples, to the polytheism of ancient Egyptian, Mesopotamian, Greek, and

Roman practices, to the Taoism of China, the Hinduism of India, Buddhism's many forms, and the monotheism of Judaism, Christianity, and Islam. Taken as a whole, the range of religions gives evidence that the search for right relationship with the sacred in some form has been a persistent activity of the human spirit, for better or worse.

The picture changes quickly in the modern period. In a partial census of the world's peoples conducted in 1900, 2 percent of the population contacted declared themselves to be atheists. In 2000, that number was 20 percent. Today it is quite possible to live a satisfying and good life without any affiliation with an organized religion and even without a "spirituality," that is, without personal beliefs and practices that put one in touch with the sacred.

This is the situation, then, in which we reflect on faith in an increasingly secular world. I invite you to consider three points. First, the background of the current situation, focusing on historical factors that have challenged religion and continue to shape our culture. Next, the meaning of faith in this setting. And finally, notions of God that, passing through atheism's purifying fire, might satisfy the longing of this age. Since I am a Catholic theologian I speak from this perspective, rather than from the perspective of Buddhism, Islam, or some other tradition, though all the religions are dealing with this problem. My point is not to prove the truth of Catholic belief nor indeed to argue that it is better than unbelief. You know as well as I do that some unbelieving folk have more moral integrity than some religious people. But on this Ash Wednesday I propose simply to reflect with you on what faith means and why it can be a beautiful and beneficial choice amid the ambiguity of this increasingly secular world.

BACKGROUND OF THE SITUATION

The first major break with the generally religious character of human life occurred in the West in sixteenth-century Europe after the Reformation. The bloody wars of religion between Protestants and Catholics led people to realize that religion could no longer be the basis for civil society. Instead, religious identity was such a source of division and mayhem that the state had to find another basis for unity among the people. Perhaps the consent of the governed would serve. Henceforth religion was increasingly relegated to the private sphere. It became the choice of the individual, not the public agreement that held a culture together. To start with, the door was opened to secularity by the violence of the churches themselves.

A second powerful factor was the rise of the natural sciences from the seventeenth century onwards. Using empirical methods such as measuring, testing, forming hypotheses, and retesting results, scientists began to figure out how the natural world works according to its own intrinsic laws. The more they were able to explain, the less room there seemed to be for God to act in a deliberative, interventionist way. From the motion of the planets to the evolution of species on Earth to the splitting of the atom, the world could be explained and its powers harnessed without reference to the Creator's intervention. The story goes that when Napoleon asked the astronomer Pierre Laplace where God factored into his explanation of the movement of heavenly bodies, Laplace replied: "I had no need of that hypothesis." It did not help that the churches placed themselves in conflict with science, as seen in the condemnation of Galileo, the furious debates over Darwin, and other sorry incidents. The natural sciences are the hard core of modernity. Their method of research requires autonomy from religious control. Secularity grew.

Yet a third fissure opened during the nineteenth and twentieth centuries with the vigorous turn toward human autonomy. A host of European thinkers, the so-called Masters of Suspicion, criticized religion for depriving human beings of what is rightfully their due.

❖ Ludwig Feuerbach developed the idea that God is a projection of humanity's best qualities. Rather than humans being created in the image and likeness of God, they have made God in their own image and likeness. Why? Because of self-alienation. Thinking they are unworthy sinners, they project their goodness and other desirable traits onto a divine being. Humanity needs to reclaim its freedom and dissolve religion for the sake of true humanism.

❖ Karl Marx agreed that God is a projection, but argued that this happens because of the suffering that results from social injustice. In their misery people imagine a better life to come after death. They sigh for a future where they will be recompensed for suffering endured now. Religion feeds this hope with the promise of heaven. But this promotes passivity; it cuts the will to resist what oppresses people in this life. Religion is a drug, the opium of the people. Humanity needs to dissolve religion for the sake of social justice.

❖ Sigmund Freud, too, thought that God was a projection, but figured that people projected for psychological reasons. When we are children, we are helpless and dependent on our father for protection. When we become adults, the world still seems threatening. So we project an image of a strong, benevolent father who will protect us against nature, fate, and evil. Religion is motivated by a wish for security. As such it is an infantile illusion. Humanity needs to dissolve religion for the sake of human maturity. Grow up and be responsible for your own life.

Adding to these arguments, the age-old problem of evil took an even sharper edge in this period. In Dostoevsky's novel *The Brothers Karamazov*, the character Ivan spoke for many when, in view of the devastating abuse of innocent children, he rebelliously decided to hand back his entrance ticket to a world which the church taught was wisely governed by God. This instinct received impetus from the ravages of the First and Second World Wars, which led large numbers of people in Europe to discount the goodness of God. The Nazi holocaust of six million Jews, gassed and burned, raised this question in unanswerable form. After Auschwitz, how is it possible to believe in a benevolent God? Subsequent wars and natural disasters have underscored the validity of such a question.

The situation created by these factors comes to a dramatic head in Friedrich Nietzsche's parable of the madman. This crazy character lights a lantern in the middle of the day and runs into the town square asking people, "Where is God?" In the face of their ridicule, he finally smashes the lantern and utters the famous words: "God is dead...and we have killed him." Nothing left to do but go into church and start the funeral. The churches are nothing now but the tomb of God.

The Second Vatican Council made an astute observation. Enumerating various reasons for the development of atheism, it added yet another:

> Yet believers themselves frequently bear some responsibility for this situation. For, taken as a whole, atheism is not a spontaneous development but stems from a variety of causes, including a critical reaction against religious beliefs, and in some places against the Christian religion in particular. Hence believers can have more than a little to do with the birth of atheism. To the extent that they neglect their own training in the faith, or teach erroneous doctrine, or are deficient in their religious, moral or social life, they must be said to conceal rather than reveal the authentic face of God and religion. (*Gaudium et Spes* 19)

The church itself is a factor in the rise of atheism.

In our day these factors and more—political, scientific, philosophical, economic, psychological, moral, and ecclesiastical—have combined to shape a dynamically secular world. With a clear view of this reality the philosopher Charles Taylor wrote an influential book called *A Secular Age* (2007) which led with this question: what is the difference between believing in Christ in the year 1500 and believing in Christ in the year 2000? His answer in a nutshell: choice and pluralism. Five hundred years ago the typical believer lived in an all-encompassing cultural Christian milieu. All neighbors went to the same church; feast days marked the annual calendar; rituals of birth and death were the same throughout the town. The few atheists who might have existed were ostracized and persecuted, perhaps burned at the stake. Today, the typical believer lives in a radically different situation marked by two things: freedom of choice whether to believe or not; and religious pluralism, with a multitude of religions jostling for attention even if one does decide to believe. Thus a person can no longer be a Christian simply out of social convention or inherited custom. Faith now requires a personal decision, the kind of decision that brings about a change of heart and sustains long-term commitment. It is not an easy situation. And so to the second point: in this secular culture, what does it mean to have faith?

THE DYNAMIC OF FAITH

One person who tackled this issue with verve and creativity was the German Jesuit theologian Karl Rahner. Writing through the middle of the twentieth century until his death in 1984, he may well be the best theologian the Catholic Church has had since Thomas Aquinas. Rahner was acutely aware that modern culture had thrown traditional faith into crisis. Educated people questioned what it all meant, this old, rather creaky religion of luxuriant doctrines and rituals, hierarchy and pious customs, and whether any of it was true. So he set himself to contend for the soul of the modern person in secular society.

 Winter. Such is Rahner's metaphor for the spiritual season of our time. The profuse growth of devotions and secondary beliefs, all these leaves and fruits that unfurled in the medieval season when Christianity was dominant in the culture, have fallen away. The trees are bare and the cold wind blows. In such a season, it will not do to spend energy on what is peripheral and unessential, as if it were high summer. To survive, people of faith need to return to the center, to the burning center that alone can nourish and warm the heart in winter. In this situation there is only one big issue, and that is the question of God.

Thinking through what God might mean in a secular climate, Rahner begins not by appealing to doctrine or church authority. This too often results in pouring the pre-settled solutions of former ages into bewildered souls, to ill effect. Rather, he invites people to take a journey of discovery through the experience of their own lives. Turn to oneself. Consider that being a person entails being not a mere object but a subject, someone with interiority, a thinking mind and freedom to choose. See where this goes.

Winter. Karl Rahner's metaphor for the spiritual season of our time.

Of all the aspects of human life that reveal our subjectivity, Rahner opted to focus mainly on curiosity. His doctoral dissertation opens with the words *Man fragt*, which translated means *One asks*, or *A person asks a question*. This is a typical human act, one that can be found at all times in all cultures. From the child's "Why is the sky blue?" to the young adult's "What should I do with my life?" to the mid-lifer's "Do you still love me?" to the dying elder's "Is there any hope?"; from asking directions when lost, to getting advice on how to start a business, to exploring the rain forest, to agonizing over why suffering and death exist in the world, to questioning an official at a press conference, to finding out how to install a new computer program, to asking your beloved to marry you, to figuring out how to deal with your cancer, to wondering about the meaning of life, questions both practical and existential pour forth in an unending torrent. One asks.

Ponder what this ordinary experience reveals about ourselves as human persons. Asking a question presumes that we do not know something. In an interesting way it also implies that we already do know a little or it would be impossible to ask about it to begin with. Most tellingly, asking a question shows that we have a desire to know. It brings to light a certain dynamism in the human spirit that wants to know something more, thereby expanding our connection with our own depths and with the wider world. In asking, we anticipate that there is more to be found out. When an answer crystallizes, the mind grasps it and judges whether or not it satisfies the question that was asked. Even a perfectly good answer does not allow our mind to rest for long, because the answer nestles against a background of related knowledge that triggers our curiosity anew. The answer becomes the basis for a new question.

How long can this go on? Are we born with an assigned number of questions we are allowed to ask? The very idea makes people smile. There is no quota which, once reached, would shut down our desire to know. Imagine how that would cramp the human spirit. It would be like hitting a brick wall, becoming brain dead. Instead of a meager ration of pre-assigned questions, however, human beings are capable of pursuing new questions as long as they live. While analyzing, weighing, judging, and defining concrete objects in the world, our reasoning power keeps on slipping beyond standard definitions to seek new horizons. The number of questions we can ask is limitless.

What makes this basic human phenomenon possible? Only this: the human spirit is structured with an unrestricted openness toward truth. Even in the most mundane inquiry we go beyond the matter at hand toward the next thing, and the next, ultimately reaching toward . . . all truth, which cannot be contained. Our questions, driven by a profound desire to know, are made possible by the very structure of the human spirit which is dynamically oriented toward union with all the truth there is to know.

This same pattern can be traced again starting with the character of love. Here, too, persons experience a never-ending dynamism of desire to give and receive. Every act by which a person loves another deepens the ability to love; every bit of love received opens one to more, in a widening circle of relationship. As an example, Rahner points to the way two people who love each other get married and then have a child, widening their circle with another person to love. Human loving, like questioning, is a dynamism that keeps on transcending beyond everything it grasps. What is the condition for the possibility of freely summing oneself up and declaring to someone, "I love you"? It is the open structure of the human spirit, which is oriented toward a boundless fullness of love.

Once one grasps this pattern of transcending toward ever more truth and love, one can discover this experience present in a thousand forms. Not only do we curiously question and freely love, but we act for our own happiness and that of others, we seek relief in the midst of suffering, we resist injustice, we plan projects, we try to act responsibly, we remain faithful to conscience under pressure, we are amazed at beauty, we feel guilt, we rejoice, we grieve death, we hope in the future. Undergirding all these moments is an immense and driving longing. At root we experience that our human spirit is open and thirsting for something infinitely more than any single moment can deliver. Let us not, for the moment, say what this more is. It is like a horizon that opens up at the edge of the landscape, encircling our lives and beckoning us onward.

In mid-century Europe the atheistic philosopher Jean Paul Sartre made a similar kind of analysis of the human person. But because he thought there is nothing infinite beyond the human person, he figured this dynamic human drive is doomed to endless frustration. Life is absurd. Held for a few brief moments over the void, human beings with all their strivings are the butt of a great cosmic joke.

By contrast, Rahner argues that it is no accident that we experience ourselves so filled with curiosity, so yearning for love, so turned toward hope, regardless. The living God who is infinite Truth, Love, and Life created us this way precisely to be the fulfillment of our questioning, loving, thirsty-for-life selves. Note that Rahner is not trying to "prove" the existence of God in some objective manner. Such proof is not possible. Rather, working within the context of modern culture, he is trying to relocate the question of God. He is moving it from a question about a Supreme Being "out there" to a question about what supports the dynamic orientation of human nature. We must get away for a time, he argues, from the very word G-O-D, which conjures up a too-limiting picture. Strange as it may sound, it would be helpful to use for a time the archaic term *Whither*. This term refers to a point of arrival, a destination, as in the question "Whither goest thou?" The *Whither* of our driving self-transcendence is that ineffable plenitude toward which we are journeying, the goal which summons and bears our thirsty minds and desiring hearts.

To this good plenitude Rahner gives the name "holy mystery." Every epoch, he observes, has different catchwords for God, specific terms that evoke the whole. In this wintry season, mystery will do for us. Mystery here is not meant in the spooky sense of something weird or ghostly. Nor does it have the mundane meaning of a puzzle that has yet to be solved, as in a literary murder mystery. Rather, it signifies an incomprehensible fullness of overflowing Love that is the ground, support, and goal of the world and of each of our little, infinitely yearning lives. This is why it is a mistake to think we can prove the existence of God the same way we prove the existence of new planet or any other particular object of our experience in the world. God is not a being among other beings, but the infinite *Whither* that makes possible

Holy Mystery — best concept for this Season of Winter

the very functioning of our human spirit. The experience of self-transcendence carries every act of knowledge and love beyond itself toward this horizon. Whether we are consciously aware of it or not, whether we are open to this truth or suppress it, our whole spiritual, intellectual, and affectionate existence is borne along by and orientated toward this living Source of life.

Rahner has one more arrow in his quiver for the spiritual seeker in winter. At the heart of Christian faith is the radical belief that the infinitely incomprehensible *Whither* of our existence, the holy mystery of God, does not remain forever remote but draws near in radical proximity to the world. This is accomplished in an act of self-giving by which the Word became flesh and joined us in the struggles of historical life all the way to death. It is also accomplished in the gracious act of self-giving by which the Spirit continues to dwell in and among us to heal, redeem, and liberate. In Christian doctrinal terms these gifts are known as incarnation and grace. Jesus Christ and the Spirit spell out the one sacred mystery of God drawing intimately near to the world in loving self-communication. Herein lies the specific character of the Christian concept of God. Rather than being the most distant being, holy mystery is profoundly and personally engaged with all the realities of the world around us, including each questioning and yearning person, being concerned especially with the desperate and the damned.

Thus one theologian's attempt to meet atheism's challenge and arrive at a sense of God suitable for this wintry season. In the end, Rahner insists, all Christian doctrine really says only one thing, something quite simple and radical, namely, the *Whither* of our existence who is ineffable and beyond imagination has drawn near to the tangle of our lives through Jesus and the gift of grace, even when we do not realize it, in order to be our salvation and support over the abyss.

What then of faith? No longer can faith be considered primarily an intellectual act of belief in a certain set of truths, though it has an intellectual component. Neither can it be simply an array of certain feelings or consolations, though it is not without emotion. Rather, as in the Bible, faith is first of all an existential decision rising up from your personal depths to entrust yourself to

[handwritten marginalia: "This 'ARRow' requires great Faith."]

[handwritten note at bottom: "what is FAith?"]

Whither of your life, the living God. It is a fundamental stance whereby you open yourself to the plenitude of holy mystery who cannot be manipulated but who approaches in compassionate love. It is an act of courage, whereby you risk the meaning of your life on the faithful goodness of the One made known in Jesus Christ, infinitely beyond our comprehension but nearer to us than we are to ourselves. As a result, you see yourself and the whole world with new meaning, and you act and care and suffer with new passion. While the outcome of your own life and that of the world is not yet known, you dare to hope that it is an adventure cared for by overflowing Mercy.

PATTERNS OF GOD'S WAYS WITH THE WORLD

The narrative of God's ways with the world recounted in the Bible gives to the unknown *Whither* a certain character. Subsequent to Rahner's work a number of gifted theologians in widely different situations have been working to bring one aspect or another to light for our day. The results mount a challenge to the simplistic view of God operative in popular culture and in certain quarters of the church.

It is a troubling fact that in contemporary American culture the prevailing view of God is so trivial. Without undue stereotyping, it is fair to say that as referenced in the media, daily language, and even insurance policies, God is an invisible individual of great power who dwells beyond the world but can intervene now and then to bring about changes (a tree falls on your house). Almost always this view envisions God on the model of a monarch ruling the world. Even when this Supreme Being is portrayed with a benevolent attitude, which the best of theology does, "He," for it is always the ruling male who stands for this concept, is essentially remote. Although he loves the world, he is uncontaminated by its messiness. And always this distant lordly lawgiver stands at the summit of hierarchical power, reinforcing structures of authority in society, church, and family.

This simplistic view is known today by the shorthand term "modern theism." Note how it provides a foil for modern atheism. For this is the God who atheism says does not exist. In truth, without any regard for the biblical story of God's gracious self-giving in covenant and salvation, this idea is more a human construct than an expression of the God of revelation. Recently a particularly aggressive crop of attacks against religion has underscored the connection between modern theism and atheism. Richard Dawkins's book *The God Delusion* (2006), for one, sets out the case for atheism based on scientific materialism. In a witty review essay the Irish critic Terry Eagleton perceptively noted that one of the main problems with Dawkins's thesis is that he envisions God "if not exactly with a white beard, then at least as some kind of *chap*, however supersized." Dawkins can then skewer this chap out of existence. In truth, Dawkins has a woefully inadequate knowledge of what Christian theology teaches about God, but he did not spin his superficial view out of thin air. He was drawing on the conventional meaning of God in our culture, and rejecting it. We need to question whether this invisible, mighty chap in the heavens might really not be God at all.

The critique of a naive idea of the divine is particularly important for young adults. Growing up in a secular, pluralistic world, they have not been steeped in a cultural embodiment of the Christian tradition. Hence their question of whether to have faith in God is intertwined with the burning issue of *which* God. Who, if anyone, or what, if anything, is worthy of your life's ultimate trust? Martin Luther had a fine phrase about this, saying, "God is the one on whom you lean your heart," the one on whom your heart depends, inclines, relies, rests. For an individual, if the Rock you lean on is too minuscule to support the range of your life's desires, faith will collapse as you grow into maturity. For a community like the church, if the God they lean on together is inadequate, they will lead a cramped religious life. Because the symbol of God functions, the issue of *which* God to believe in is vital.

Long before modern atheism the fourteenth-century theologian named Meister Eckhart preached a sermon in which he said a puzzling thing: "So therefore let us pray to God that we might be free of God." More recently the German theologian Dorothee Soelle retranslated this to say: "I pray God to rid me of God," and this is the way the saying appears on cards and posters and in the work of spiritual writers today. Why would anyone who is trying to live a life of faith say such a prayer? Why would you want to eliminate God the way you rid your house of termites? Because, Meister Eckhart thought, the narrow, puny notions of G-O-D many people carry around in their imagination are both unworthy of God and damaging to the human spirit. Praying to God to rid us of the popular notions of God characteristic of American culture, one task for religious people today is to seek the God of abounding kindness borne in the fullness of Scripture and the living tradition.

The good news is that in our day a renaissance in theologies of God has been taking place. Among different groups around the world, different kinds of religious experiences have led to new insights that take us beyond the narrow cultural view of modern theism. Consider:

❖ the view we have already looked at, developed by Rahner and others in the winter of post-war Europe's increasingly atheistic society, that God is the unrestricted horizon of our human thirst for truth, love, and life; the ineffable *Whither* who has drawn near in Jesus Christ and the Spirit.

❖ the challenging notion of the suffering God, pioneered by German theology in face of the Nazi holocaust of the Jews. God not only does not will such evil but is compassionately present with the victim. As Elie Wiesel wrote in *Night*: "Where is God? He is hanging there on the gallows," hanging with the youth who wouldn't die quickly enough.

❖ the powerful intuition arising from extreme, unjust poverty in Latin America that God is a God of life who comes to liberate, a God whose mercy opts for the poor and destitute, desiring change in unjust structures, change so there can be bread on the table.

❖ the wisdom born from women's struggle for full human dignity that the ineffable God loves them too, and can be approached with female images of comfort, power, and might, to say nothing of maternal compassion for the world.

❖ the sensibility flowing from African Americans' titanic struggle against slavery and Jim Crow laws that God is Black, being the One who breaks chains.

❖ the realization of Latino/Latina communities that the God of fiesta, flower, and song accompanies them in the suffering and joy of daily life.

❖ the discovery of Christians in Asia who glimpse the generous God of the world's religions, present to all peoples through their various religious ways.

❖ the perception of people engaged in protecting the vulnerable earth that the love of the indwelling Spirit extends beyond the human species to include the whole evolving ecological community of species, being the Giver of life who vivifies all.

Each of these insights into God being explored in detail by different theologies today restate in some way the biblical testimony to the God of love who acts in history to heal and redeem. This is the compassionate God whose reign Jesus preached and embodied; the God praised by saints and sought by mystics; the creative Spirit who is present in and through the natural world; the holy mystery of God who embraces even the dead with a promise of the future. In every instance, a path opens up that leads from daring trust in God encountered in this way toward a meaningful life in winter. No mere projection, such mystical-prophetic understandings of the divine evoke strong patterns of faith amid the roughness of a secular age.

CONCLUSION

It may be winter when luxurious foliage no longer clothes the trees with piety. But the bare branches enable us to see deeper into the woods. There we glimpse the gracious mystery of God, whom we cannot manipulate either conceptually or practically, but who abides as the plenitude of Love embracing the world in its agony and joy. The question facing each one of us is: which do we love better, the little island of our own certitude or the great surrounding ocean of holy mystery? The tiny hut lit by the lamp of our own concerns, or the hill outside overarched by the great dark night brilliant with stars? There is no end of ambiguity either way. But the point to consider is that the purifying fire of atheism, rather than killing faith, can turn faith into an invitation for an adventurous life.

In his play *A Sleep of Prisoners*, Christopher Fry drives this point home with poetic power. Escaping from a burning church, an imprisoned soldier utters a passionate soliloquy which could well be adopted by today's seekers and believers in God:

> Dark and cold we may be, but this is no winter now.
> The frozen misery of centuries breaks, cracks, begins to
>   move.
> The thunder is the thunder of the floes, the thaw, the
>   flood, the upstart Spring.
> Thank God our time is now, when wrong comes up to
>   face us everywhere,
> Never to leave us till we take the longest stride of soul
>   men [and women] ever took.
> Affairs are now soul size. The enterprise . . . is exploration
>   into God.

Adapted from an Ash Wednesday lecture at the College of Mount Saint Vincent, Riverdale, Bronx, NY, 2011.

3

Heaven and Earth Are Filled with Your Glory
Atheism and Ecological Spirituality

The great insight that emerges at the end of the massive study by Michael Buckley SJ, *At the Origins of Modern Atheism,* has to do with the misstep theology took in the seventeenth century when it attempted to respond to Enlightenment attacks on the existence of God. Instead of appealing to its own primary materials, namely, christology with its center in the person and teaching of Jesus the Christ, and religious experience with its focus on personal witness empowered by the Spirit, theology abandoned its distinctive turf. In its place theologians began to call upon both philosophy with its inferential method of reasoning and science with its testing of objective theses in order to defend the existence of God. In this way theology did indeed find common ground on which to dialogue with rising atheism, but at the price of its own unique character: "It is not without some sense of wonder that one records that the theologians bracketed religion in order to defend religion."[1] If this were done only as a first step, the results might not have been so impoverished. But it remained the continuing and complete option of most major thinkers. Consequently, natural theology never intersected with mystical theology, which is to say that philosophical reasoning from the world to God done from the privileged position of the spectator never connected with theological analysis of religious experience. The meeting would have fertilized and extended the usefulness of inferential reasoning, and who knows how the argument with atheism might have turned out.

The challenge for contemporary Western theology being done in a cultural context where atheism is now a given is clear: do not repeat this major mistake. In an essay on atheism and contemplation, Michael Buckley himself gives an example of how particular religious experience can be put into critical dialogue with atheism, facing off the two around the issue of projection.[2] Some popular and theological images of God do indeed bear the mark of projection as atheism charges, being devised by way of extension from believers' psyches. But the ancient path of contemplation, which is becoming one of the great religious movements of our times, draws persons into the purifying darkness of an apophatic moment that breaks all divine images open. As a result of this existentially dark not-knowing, which is actually a religiously profound kind of knowing, persons are moved experientially into the presence of the incomprehensible mystery of God. Reflecting on this experience, mystical theology uses a panoply of intellectual tools to highlight how the descent into darkness, dryness, and the desert foils the tendency to project. It does so through the ineffable experience of receiving what is conceptually beyond human grasp or objectification, the mystery of God who is love. The transforming power of contemplation enables believing persons to be moved by God who is beyond form and beyond control, certainly not like they may have originally imagined. Rather than being a projection, the focus of religious awareness becomes incomprehensible holy mystery "known" in and through the breakdown of projections, itself an event of disclosure.

Theology today needs to appeal to the religious experience; contemplation is one such experience. Agreeing with this position, I would like to focus on one particular type of contemplation growing rapidly in contemporary life, namely, the contemplation of nature. What might this gaze upon the beauty, intricacy, and dynamism of the natural world as revelatory of divine Spirit offer for validating faith in face of the atheistic critique?

The cultural context of this religious type of contemplation is a very peculiar kind of awareness of the earth, shaped by contemporary science in tension with ecological troubles. On the one hand, perception of the vast age, size, and complexity of the universe, awareness of the cosmic processes that have created it and continue to create it, appreciation of the infinitesimal reality of matter at the atomic and quantum levels, realization of the marvelous complexity of biological evolution up to and including the human species, and understanding of the interconnectedness of all life—all of this knowledge gives rise to the sense that the world is a wonder. On the other hand, cognizance of how human practices of pollution, unbridled reproduction, and consumptive use of land and sea are rapidly depleting our planet as a habitat for life engenders a negative contrast experience whereby the treasure of nature is known to be under mortal threat. Wonder at the world in the face of wasting the world: for many religious persons today this experience provides a new entry to an ancient form of contemplation along with a fresh ethical consequence, namely, acts of prophetic witness and repair of the world.

This development in the history of spirituality bears no little irony insofar as it draws its orientation from a scientific community many of whose leading contributors and popularizers publicly reject religious interpretations of the cosmos. Prominent scientists such as Stephen Hawking, Carl Sagan, Edmund O. Wilson, and Stephen Jay Gould, along with many others, have raised contemporary consciousness about the wonder and wasting of the world even as they profess skeptical agnosticism about religious ideas and, indeed, consider such ideas to be illusory and supportive of false consciousness. While such is not the position of all scientists, a small but significant number of whom are newly engaging philosophers and theologians in dialogue, scientific culture has spawned indifference and even hostility to religion. Scientific method works with a necessary practical atheism which does not allow God to be brought in as an explanation for particular natural events. Some practitioners, however, lift this practical method to the metaphysical level and use it to interpret the world as a whole. Clearly such a move goes beyond the warrants of scientific method itself, there being no data from microscope or telescope that can explain the world as a whole. Yet it is a move frequently made, and effectively denies the question of God at the outset.

In this context, the specifically theological appeal to religious experience of the natural world and the consequent moral passion to protect it offers an alternative move, one that allows believing persons to render a credible account of the hope that is in them. The fact that the world is simply there, in splendor and fragility, gives rise to wonder, leading to a religious sense of the living, loving, creative Matrix who grounds it, quickens it, and attracts it toward the future. In such experience the cosmos as a whole and in a special way the earth with its community of life, now under threat, is seen as a sacred place disclosive of the presence of divine mystery. The life-giving Spirit of God encircles, pervades, and energizes the world, empowering its own intrinsic, self-organizing powers that have led to magnificence beyond our imagination, including our own human race. For such a religious vision, the biblical bush still burns and we take off our shoes.

It appears to me that this ecological religious vision of the world among many Christian people is generating a new "natural theology," one quite different from the Enlightenment type based on philosophical inference. The theological procedure is not reasoning from the known to the unknown but critical reflection on the presence and absence of holy mystery being experienced positively in and through the beauty of the world, negatively by contrast with its destruction, and ethically in the summons to resist its destruction. In the spirit of Buckley's insight about the value of religious experience in crafting a theological response to atheism, this essay will explore what might well be called ecological contemplation in both its mystical and prophetic aspects, testing whether this experience may contribute to a reasonable case for belief in the face of atheism.

MYSTICAL INSIGHT

The world is charged with the grandeur of God.
It will flame out, like shining from shook foil.
It gathers to a greatness, like the ooze of oil,
Crushed...[3]

More than a century after Gerard Manley Hopkins penned these ecstatic words, his poetic intuition grows ever stronger in believing persons who encounter the dazzling variety and profound interconnectedness of the world, its denizens, and its systems. At times, some are swept up in an oceanic feeling of oneness with the universe as a whole. Others awaken to the delight of particular creatures, each one with its own intricate, spirit-filled reality. Writing of her goldfish, for example, Annie Dillard describes it in eloquent if poignant detail:

> This Ellery cost me twenty-five cents. He is a deep red-orange, darker than most goldfish. He steers short distances mainly with his slender red lateral fins; they seem to provide an impetus for going backward, up, or down. It took me a few days to discover his ventral fins; they are completely transparent and all but invisible dream fins. He also has a short anal fin, and a tail that is deeply notched and perfectly transparent at the two tapered tips. He can extend his mouth, so it looks like a length of pipe; he can shift the angle of his eyes in his head so he can look before and behind himself, instead of simply out to his side. His belly, what there is of it, is white ventrally, and a patch of this white extends up his sides—the variegated Ellery. When he opens his gill slits he shows a thin crescent of silver where the flap overlapped, as though his brightness were sunburn. For this creature, as I said, I paid twenty-five cents. I have never bought an animal before. It was very simple; I went to a store in Roanoke called "Wet Pets"; I handed the man a quarter, and he handed me a knotted plastic bag with water in which a green plant floated and the goldfish swam. This fish, two bits' worth, has a coiled gut, a spine radiating fine bones, and a brain. Just before I sprinkle his food flakes into his bowl, I rap three times on the bowl's edge; now he is conditioned, and swims to the surface when I rap. And, he has a heart![4]

As Sallie McFague comments on this passage, the juxtaposition of twenty-five cents with the elaborateness, cleverness, and sheer glory of this tiny bit of matter named Ellery is frankly unnerving. For the intricacy of this little creature calls forth wonder, and suddenly its worth is sensed to be priceless.[5]

Such experiences with the extraordinary quality of even the mundane world are to the fore in our ecological times. Michael Buckley has observed, "God has emerged again and again in the history of wisdom as the direction toward which wonder progresses."[6] Hence, wondrous experience of the natural, bodily world including ourselves leads contemplative persons to sense the grandeur of God drawing near and passing by in and through the magnificence of creation. They know, not just with their minds but with a certain kind of experiential feeling, that the utterly transcendent holy God is utterly immanent in the world, present and active in its creatures and dynamic processes. How to explicate this? The biblical concept of glory and the Thomistic category of participation offer theology intellectual tools with which to bring this religious experience to language.

Consulting the Scriptures: Glory

In the Hebrew Scriptures a plethora of metaphors are used to refer to divine presence in the world. These metaphors include the spirit of God, the angel of the Lord, the word of God, the wisdom of God, and the glory of God, among others. Theologically speaking, these figures are not intermediaries between God and the world. Rabbinic interpreters consistently warn against this idea, as if God were so distant that some kind of go-between were needed. Rather, these are biblical circumlocutions that signify the one transcendent God's nearness to the world in such a way that divine transcendence is not compromised. In one sense glory is the metaphor least likely to be personalized, although even it like the others receives a christological interpretation in early Christian reflection: Christ is "the brightness of God's glory" (Heb 1:3). Given that it is less likely to be seized by the anthropological imagination, it has the potential to articulate divine relation to the world in a way that is somewhat congruous with the apophatic character of much contemporary spirituality. This is a wager that needs exploring.

In ordinary speech "glory" is a word that signifies splendor, magnificence, brilliance, luster, rich ornamentation, power, and worth. It connotes something beautiful and desirable. The Hebrew noun for glory, *kabod*, derived from a verb which means "to weigh heavily," weaves these connotations round with a sense of heaviness or deep importance, so that glory signifies a certain weighty radiance. When used in reference to the mystery of God, the *kabod YHWH* or glory of the Lord is a light-filled metaphor meaning the weighty radiance of divine presence in the world, the heavy, plump, fat brightness of God's immanence close at hand to enlighten, warm, and set things right. The more the infinite transcendence of God was stressed in Israel's experience, the more *kabod YHWH* became a technical term in the biblical books for divine presence within the world and its happenings. Though God dwells beyond the heavens and can be compared with nothing created, the approach of divine glory signifies the self-disclosure of God's being, the publicly engaged, unhidden character of the incomprehensible Holy One.

In the wisdom of Scripture, the approach of glory is never directly perceived. Rather, it is revealed in and through the world and its events. Chief among these revelatory bearers is the natural world with its power and beauty: "The heavens are telling the glory of God," exalts the psalmist (19:1). Typically in the Bible the approach of divine glory is depicted by a cloud or the land's fruitfulness or fire or a thunderstorm with its crashing noise, flashing lights, and rushing waters. Indeed the whole natural world is *capax Dei*, capable of revealing the unseen, hidden Creator. As Isaiah's mystical vision of the One who is "holy, holy, holy" perceives, heaven and earth are full of God's glory (6:3).

In the biblical vision, glory is thus a category of divine immanence perceived through the world's participation in divine beauty. The world shares in the weighty radiance of God: the starry heavens sing of it, other natural creatures reveal it in flashes of speed, methods of feeding, and all their intricate, mysterious workings (Job 38–41). Human beings, too, reflect divine splendor, and when they realize this in moments of insight they "give glory" to God. This response entails upwelling sentiments of praise and thanks, as well as efforts to correspond to divine glory through their own loving deeds of righteousness.

But divine glory (divine presence and action) is not confined to the beauty and magnificence of the world. Sin, sorrow, and injustice mar the world's well-being. Therefore, the *kabod YHWH*, never directly perceived, is also manifest in and through historical events of peace-making and liberation. The Exodus narrative makes great play with this symbol, using it to bespeak the God who frees the Israelites from slavery and accompanies them in the glory of cloud, smoke, and fire through the desert, to Mount Sinai, and thence into their own covenanted history.

In this connection, and to an extraordinary degree, the glory of God is a biblical symbol of religious hope. Uttering words of comfort to people suffering the distress of Babylonian exile, Isaiah proclaims that "the glory of the Lord *will* be revealed" (Isa 40:5), and this revelation will occur when they are delivered. Then they will see a resplendent manifestation of divine power in a historical moment of liberation and homecoming, sign of that even greater future day when evil will be overcome and the whole world will be filled with the *kabod YHWH*. In a consistent way biblical yearning for salvation, for victory in the struggle with evil, for lifting the oppression of the poor, for the cessation of violence against the needy, the cry for all that is good is expressed in the hope that God's glory will dwell in the land (Ps 85:9), or will fill the earth (Ps 72:19), or will shine throughout heaven and earth (Ezek 43:2).

Biblically, then, the glory of God does not point to God as a bigger and better Solomon sitting on a throne in isolated splendor. Rather, it signifies divine beauty flashing out in the world and in particular bent over brokenness and anguish, moving to heal, redeem, and liberate. It is a synonym for God's elusive presence and action in the midst of historical trouble. As such, it is a category of relationship and help.

It is interesting to me how resonant the biblical term "glory" is with spirit (*ruah*), wisdom (*sophia*), and active presence (*shekinah*), those grammatically feminine great metaphors of God's indwelling power and concern. Hopkins himself associates the glory of God with *ruah*, the spirit of God, ending his poem about God's grandeur with a hopeful maternal metaphor: "the Holy

Ghost over the bent world broods with warm breast and with ah! bright wings." The book of Wisdom consistently connects God's glory with *sophia,* saying of wisdom that "she is a pure radiance of the glory of the Almighty" (7:25); "she is the brightness that streams from everlasting light" (7:26); and "she is more splendid than the sun, and outshines every constellation of the stars; compared with the light of day she is found to excel, for day gives place to night, but against wisdom evil does not prevail" (7:29–30). In the writings of early rabbinic Judaism glory and the *shekinah* are used as equivalents, the *shekinah* being God's compassionate spirit who accompanies the people, suffering the tragedies of history with them and occasioning hope. Here the typical expression of the *kabod shekinah YHWH,* the glory of God's indwelling spirit, signifies no mere feminine dimension of God but the radiance of God as She-Who-Dwells-Within, divine Spirit in compassionate engagement with the conflictual world as source of vitality in the struggle.

The correlations, mutual amplifications, and at times even the identity between the glory of God and the divine metaphors of *ruah, sophia,* and *shekinah* indicate that we are dealing with the active presence of great beauty that can fittingly be imagined in female metaphors. Thinking with these images is itself a critical move against the dominance of patriarchal metaphors that have come to reify divine being and thus block mystical experience. In the film *Steel Magnolias,* which deals with the life struggles of a group of women in the American South, there is a memorable scene where the women are preparing for a wedding. In the midst of all the beautifying actions being wrought on hair, faces, and clothing, an older woman says delightedly, "What distinguishes us from the animals is our ability to accessorize." You have to hear these words uttered in an inimitable Southern drawl to appreciate their impact! The ability to accessorize might well describe what the glory of God has wrought in the world, so filled with marvels of even a twenty-five cent goldfish, to say nothing of the fragmentary shapes of freedom and justice happening amid destruction and despair. She has adorned the world with beauty, so that her own gracious radiance shines out, even in the darkness.

The New Testament taps deeply into these meanings of glory, now translated by the Greek word *doxa*. It proclaims that the weighty radiance of divine presence is in the world in a new way through the very human flesh of Jesus the Christ, whose ministry makes strikingly manifest how divine glory operates: the blind see, the lame walk, the dead are raised up, the poor have the gospel preached to them (Mt 11:5). It is especially in the light of Easter, as the crucified one is raised to glory by the power of the Spirit, that divine *doxa* pervades the world. Glory rests on the whole community of believers, women as well as men, who are thereby being transformed amid weakness and sin into the image of Christ (2 Cor 3:18). The natural world, too, is involved in this drama of salvation, groaning in the present age but with the hope that it "will obtain the freedom of the glory of the children of God" (Rom 8:21). The orientation toward promise is strong throughout these writings: "Christ in you, the hope of glory" (Col 1:27). Once again, glory is a category of participation in God's redeeming beauty that draws near to share in the brokenness of the world in order to heal and set free.

To sum up the biblical data: the glory of God is a luminous metaphor for the elusive nearness of the ineffable God glimpsed in and through the wondrous process of nature, the history of freedom, and communities where justice and peace prevail. Using the term "the glory of God" signifies that the incomprehensible holy mystery of God indwells the natural and human world as source, sustaining power, and goal of the universe, enlivening and loving it into liberating communion. The category of glory provides language for contemplation's sense of the presence of God, hidden but glimpsed in the natural world.

Consulting Aquinas: Participation

The meaning carried in the biblical notion of the glory of God is cast in a more philosophical idiom by medieval scholasticism, but the two are uncannily consistent with each other. At the heart of Aquinas's vision of God's creative relation to the world is the evocative idea of participation. Through the act of creation the all holy God, whose essence is the very livingness of being itself, gives a share in "to be" (*esse*, or being) to what is other than Godself:

> Whatever is of a certain kind through its essence is the proper cause of what is of such a kind by participation. Thus, fire is the cause of all things that are afire. Now, God alone is actual being through divine essence itself, while other beings are actual beings through participation.[7]

As to ignite is the proper effect of fire, so too giving a share in being is the proper effect of the Mystery of Being. Hence, all that exists participates in its own way in divine being through the very gift of creaturely existence. It is not as if God and creatures stood as uncreated and creating instantiations of "being" which is held in common by both. Rather, the mystery of God is Being itself who freely empowers creatures to be. Nor is the gift of being given only once in the instant when a creature begins to exist, but continuously in a ceaseless act of divine creation. To cite another of Aquinas's fiery analogies, every creature stands in relation to God as the air does to the light of the sun. As the sun is light-giving by its very nature whereas the air is bright and illuminated only so long as it is lit by the sun, so also God alone simply exists (divine essence is *esse*, sheer being) while every creature enjoys existence insofar as it participates in being (creaturely essence receives the gift of being).

The category of participation affects theological understanding of both God and the world. Continuously creating and sustaining, God is in all things not as part of their essence but as the innermost source of being, power, and action. There is, in other words, a constitutive presence of God at the heart of things. Conversely, in its own created being and doing, the world continuously participates in the livingness of the One who simply is. Every excellence it exhibits is a participation in that same quality unimaginably present in the unknowable mystery of God. Take the key example of goodness. Since "it befits divine goodness that other things should be partakers therein," every created good is a good by participation in the One who is good by essence. It follows that "in the whole sphere of creation there is no good that is not a good participatively." In possessing their own specific goodness, creatures share in divine goodness. This is the intelligible basis for speech about the transcendent mystery of God, for in knowing the excellence of the world we may speak analogically about the One in whose being it shares.

One of the strengths of Aquinas's vision is the autonomy he grants to created existence through its participation in divine being. He is so convinced of the transcendent mystery of God and so clear about the unique relation of God to the world that he sees no threat to divinity in allowing creatures the fullest measure of agency according to their nature. In fact, it is a measure of the creative power of God to raise up creatures who participate in divine being to such an extent that they are also creative and sustaining in their own right. A view to the contrary would diminish not only creatures but also their Creator: "to detract from the perfection of creatures is to detract from the perfection of divine power."[8] This is a genuinely noncompetitive view of God and the world. According to its dynamism, to cite Karl Rahner's way of putting it, nearness to God and genuine creaturely autonomy grow in direct rather than inverse proportion. That is, God is not glorified by the diminishment of the creature but by the creature's flourishing. The nature of created participation in divine being is such that it grants creatures their own integrity without reserve, while they in turn become symbols in and thorough which divine mystery may be encountered.

Result: Earth a Sacrament

Contemplative appreciation of the glory of God flaming out in the natural world, undergirded by the theological notion of created participation in being, gives rise to the realization that the world itself is a revelation and a sacrament: revelation, because the invisible grandeur of God can be glimpsed and known experientially in the splendor of the universe, its balance, complexity, creativity, diversity, fruitfulness; and sacrament, because the mystery of divine, self-giving presence is really mediated through the richness of the heavens and the earth. Participating in the glory of God, our whole planet is a beautiful showing forth of divine goodness and generosity. By being simply and thoroughly its magnificent self, it bodies forth the glory of God that empowers it, being as it were an icon. And, in keeping with the biblical theme of glory, this carries with it a note of promise. Pervaded and encircled by the glory of God, nature's beauty, intricacy, wildness, richness, order, and novelty are a sacrament of hidden glory not yet fully revealed.

In the light of mystical insight resulting from contemplative religious experience of nature, the many-faceted ecological crisis suffered by the living planet Earth becomes a matter of intense religious concern, for human beings are rapidly fouling and even destroying the primary sacrament of God's glory, one with its own intrinsic value before God. The critical praxis of justice for the earth, flowing from contemplative attentiveness, becomes in turn an engaged practical form of religious experience in its own right.

PROPHETIC STANCE

If it be the case that, as John of the Cross writes, "contemplation is nothing else than a secret and peaceful and loving inflow of God, which, if not hampered, inflames the soul in the spirit of love,"[9] then the soul so enkindled responds to divine love by trusting correspondence to divine affections for the world. This dynamic, so basic to Jewish and Christian faith, finds a strong contemporary interpretation in the dictum of political and liberation theologies that God is not only to be contemplated but also to be practiced. If the heart of divine mystery is turned in compassion toward the world, then devotion to this God draws persons into the shape of divine communion with all others: "Be merciful, just as your Father is merciful" (Lk 6:36). To deny one's connection with the suffering needs of others is to detach oneself from divine communion.

The praxis of mercy is propelled by this dynamic. So too is committed work on behalf of peace, human rights, economic justice, and the transformation of social structures. For those who engage in this work out of deep contemplative experience, it is far from mere activism or simple good deeds. Rather, solidarity with those who suffer, being there with commitment to their flourishing, is the locus of encounter with the living God. Through what is basically a prophetic stance, one shares in the passion of God for the world.

In the midst of the present ecological crisis, the vision of the natural world as a sacrament of the glory of God motivates contemplative persons to extend this justice model to embrace the whole earth. If the creative glory of God pervades the whole world which is a sacrament of divine fecundity and beauty, then ecological abuse that weakens or destroys the earth's flourishing is contrary to God's intent. The human selfishness, greed, irresponsibility, and ignorance that are newly impoverishing nature need to be challenged both concretely and systematically. The preferential option for the poor must now include the vulnerable, voiceless, nonhuman species and the ravaged natural world itself, all of which are kin to humankind. Loving these neighbors as their very selves, committed religious persons develop moral principles, political structures, and lifestyles that promote other creatures' thriving and halt their exploitation. For the prophetic passion flowing from contemplative insight, action on behalf of justice for the earth participates in the compassionate care of the Creator God who wills the glorious well-being of the whole interdependent community of life. Human beings partner up with the One whom Dante called "the Love that moves the sun and the other stars."[10]

Naming the Abuse

In order to right a wrong, it must first be brought into the open and faced squarely as an evil. Prophetic consciousness infused with the glory of God in the world therefore urges upon the religious and civic communities the realization that the earth, its life-giving systems, and the diversity of creatures it has brought forth are currently undergoing massive assault from human beings on an unprecedented scale. Ever-expanding consumer demands that fuel endlessly swelling growth economies are plundering the planet. These human pressures, coupled with exploding human populations, are destroying the health of planetary ecosystems. Pollution of waters, air, and soil, build-up of toxic and nuclear wastes, destruction of vast stretches of habitat: these are symptomatic of deep abuse. Living species that took millions of years to evolve and that form the life context of humanity's own emergence are disappearing without a trace; we will never see the their like again. Much has already been irretrievably lost, and if human beings do not change their ways, the days are fast coming when, in Catherine Keller's eloquent phrase, the planet will be uninhabitable except by the very rich, the very armed, and the insect (and in the end, maybe just the insect).[11]

Human beings are woven into the planetary fabric of life; there is no human community without the earth, soil, air, water, and other living species. We evolved amid this radiance of abundant life and are interdependent with it for our own flourishing. So wasting the world has dire consequences for the well-being of present and future human generations as well and is, in fact, a practice of intergenerational irresponsibility. Degradation of the earth is also interwoven with social injustices among human beings, for it is poor people and colonialized nations that bear the brunt of exploitation of land, resources, and their own labor for the benefit of the wealthy, industrialized nations. In fact, structures of social domination are chief among the ways that exploitation of the earth is accomplished. Degrading the planetary ecosystems also has significance beyond the human troubles that result. For the world itself is a marvel, the result of millions of years of creative process still under way. Damaging or even destroying it nips its future promise in the bud and begins to wipe out one of the magnificent bright spots of the universe.

We have a duty to know this. Turning our face the other way does not make us innocent. As with any wrongdoing, to remain silent in the face of evil is to be an accessory to the fact. By contrast, naming the evil as an injustice that ruptures divine communion is an act of spiritual practice.

Part of the difficulty in facing this, however, is a certain religious worldview prevalent in Christianity for many centuries according to which the world is merely a backdrop for the drama of human salvation. In this view human beings are individual sinners to whom grace comes as the call to set their minds on the things above, not below. The gracious mystery of God is not interested in things of earth. Supporting this spirituality is a dualistic worldview inherited from ancient Greek philosophy and intensified in Cartesian philosophy. According to this way of thinking matter and spirit are profoundly divided, with the latter assigned a higher value. This basic assumption works its way out in key contrasts: soul over body, reason over emotions, what is active over what is passive, autonomy over interdependence, what is personal over what is natural, and therefore history over nature, the whole system being at root a program of alienated mind pitted against its own matter. Feminist analysis underscores that in each of these pairs, the category related to spirit (the transcendent, heavenly principle) is identified with masculine reality while matter (the lowly, earthly principle) is considered feminine, thus setting up both symbolic as well as practical connections between patriarchal domination of woman and nature.

In this alienated dualism of body and soul, it is virtually unthinkable to assign the earth a serious religious value. By concentrating on the salvation of the immortal soul and denigrating the bodiliness of human nature, dualistic theology also disregards the larger matrix of physical life, the whole world in which human selves are embedded. Consequently, one may ignore the world, trivialize it, flee it, use it, subdue it, rape it, at best one may even responsibly steward it, but to embrace and cherish it as a precious creation is not envisioned as a way of holiness. Removing the sacred value from the earth, seeing it almost as the index of the anti-divine, is a Christian factor contributing to the present assault on the earth, its life-systems, and its diversity of creatures. By contrast, imbued with the contemplative realization of the earth as a sacrament of divine glory, contemporary prophetic consciousness names what has gone awry and seeks a new paradigm that reconfigures the mystery of God, all humans, and the earth in deep interconnection.

Transforming the Abuse

Saving the earth requires hard choices and courageous deeds in the political, social, economic, and cultural arenas. To reflect upon and promote such critical praxis, theology has need of thought patterns that disrupt human dominance and promote the whole community of life. I would suggest that one such configuration consists of the intertwined categories of memory, narrative, and solidarity. As originally developed in the practical foundational theology of Johannes Baptist Metz, these categories function in an emancipatory way in the service of suffering and defeated human beings.[12] It seems to me that they have the capacity to serve the same way with regard to the exploited earth and its creatures.

Memory is a category that serves to rescue lost or threatened identity. Witness the fact that every dominating power tries to wipe out defeated peoples' traditions, while political protest and resistance are fed by the subversive power of remembered sufferings and freedoms. Memory is not understood here as mere nostalgia. Rather, it is a strong visitation from the past that energizes persons. By evoking the sufferings and victories of those who went before, it galvanizes hope that new possibilities can be realized. There is danger in such remembrance for it interrupts the omnipotence of a given situation, breaking the stranglehold of what is currently held to be plausible. The future is opened up in a new way by the surplus of meaning carried in the act of remembering.

Memory is most often communicated by narrative, which preserves the uniqueness of experiences of suffering and victory, preventing them from being reduced to any theory. In the widest sense life itself has the character of a story, and concrete reality is expressed better through narrative than through abstract thought. In oppressive situations, telling certain tales of courage and witness, violence and defeat, has disclosive and transformative power. Robert McAfee Brown has described the method of Holocaust survivor and witness Elie Wiesel:

"You want to know about the kingdom of night? There is no way to describe the kingdom of night. But let me tell

you a story. You want a description of the indescribable?
There is no way to describe the indescribable. But let me
tell you a story."[13]

Within the political experience of unjust suffering, narrated memory is a subversive language with practical effects. Telling dangerous stories does not bring intelligibility to the suffering, as if it
could ever make sense. But evocative telling of tales of tragedy
and triumph gives birth to hope and resistance.

The memory of suffering and freedom creates, strengthens,
and expresses solidarity across times and places. In Christian
political theology solidarity does not refer to a common feeling
with those in our immediate class or neighborhood, or even opti-
mistic sympathy for the less fortunate. Rather, it connotes a partnership of desires and interests with those in need, with those
most in need, perhaps causing us loss. In a vital community one
enters into common reflection and action against the degradation
which so defaces others, and does this with the sense that these
others are part of oneself. The universality of this category is
shown in the fact that it includes not only the living but also
evokes an alliance with the dead, especially with those who have
been overcome and defeated in history. The narrative of the dead
creates solidarity backward through time, which emphasizes the
common character of the destiny of all creatures. It is thus a category of help, support, and togetherness, by means of which the
dead can be affirmed as having a future, the living who are oppressed and acutely threatened can be raised up toward becoming genuinely free, and a more promising future can be created
for those yet to be born. This historical solidarity between the
living and the dead in view of the future breaks the grip of dominating forces and empowers transformative praxis toward a
fulfilling future for *all,* guaranteed only when the value of the
most despised is assured.

Memory, narrative, solidarity: the dynamic of their interaction in the context of a threatened earth can release new energies
for protection and deliverance. Think of the power for transformation if, encountering the glory of God in the sacrament of
the earth, Christian people with their pastors and theologians

remembered the earth with its life-systems and diversity of plants and animals, many going extinct; told the story of its amazing, ancient, creative complexity and ongoing destruction; and did so in solidarity with all earth's creatures, including species long or recently dead. Think of the practical effect of including the living earth and its creatures in every liturgical prayer that is offered for others, every lesson about loving one's neighbor, every ethical discernment about justice and peace. Narrative memory of the earth in solidarity with all the earth's creatures, living and dead, calls present destructive political, economic, and social systems into question and turns those who contemplate toward innovative praxis in the personal and social order, empowering a prophetic edge to the contemplation of God's glory.

CONCLUSION

Decrying early modern theology's neglect of its own resources that permitted atheism to make significant headway, Buckley concludes that such a pattern will inevitably recur if the cognitive claims of religious reason are split off from experience:

> If an antimony is posed between nature or human nature and god, the glory of one in conflict with the glory of the other, this alienation will eventually be resolved in favor of the natural and the human. Any implicit, unspoken enmity between god and creation will issue in atheism.... the origin of atheism in the intellectual culture of the West lies thus with the self-alienation of religion itself.[14]

In light of this insight, this essay has explored aspects of one increasingly widespread religious phenomenon, contemplation of nature as part of an ecological spirituality, to ascertain whether it may offer a resource to counter atheistic criticism. Several conclusions result.

Unlike Heidegger before the God of modern theism, one can certainly dance before the living God whose glory shines thorough the resplendent tapestries of cosmic processes and life on Earth.

Moreover, a powerful sense of the transcendence and immanence of God, the two increasing in direct rather than indirect proportion, arises from this religious encounter with divine glory in the world, thus reinforcing the deep wisdom of the Jewish and Christian traditions that calls for moral responsibility for what is so beloved of God. Here there is no inferential proof that would refute atheistic argument that God does not exist, but rather witness that the Creator Spirit abides with the world and galvanizes human beings to its care and defense. One might even argue that religion can do a better job of fostering the moral inspiration to act ethically in our dealings with nature than can a worldview in which the universe has no ultimate point. This argument would not be conclusive, however. In the end, contemplative experience that heaven and earth are filled with God's glory and the praxis of ecological justice stand with their own integrity, pointing to the meaningfulness of faith in a world ever so in need.

Adapted from Finding God in All Things, *ed. Michael Himes & Stephen Pope (New York: Crossroad, 1996), 84–101.*

Notes

1. Michael Buckley, *At the Origins of Modern Atheism* (New Haven: Yale University Press, 1987), 345.

2. Michael Buckley, "Atheism and Contemplation," *Theological Studies* 40 (1979): 680–99.

3. Gerard Manly Hopkins, "God's Grandeur," *A Hopkins Reader*, ed. John Pick (Garden City, NY: Doubleday, 1966), 47.

4. Annie Dillard, *Pilgrim at Tinker Creek* (New York: Bantam Books, 1975), 124.

5. Sallie McFague, *The Body of God: An Ecological Theology* (Minneapolis: Fortress, 1993), 210.

6. Buckley, *At the Origins of Modern Atheism*, 360.

7. Thomas Aquinas, *Summa Contra Gentiles III*, 66:7.

8. Ibid., 69:15.

9. John of the Cross, *Dark Night of the Soul*, chap. 10, no. 6.

10. Dante, *Divine Comedy: Paradise*, canto 33, line 145.

11. Catherine Keller, "Talk about the Weather: The Greening of Escha-

tology," in *Ecofeminism and the Sacred*, ed. Carol Adams (New York: Continuum, 1993), 36.

12. Johann Baptist Metz, *Faith in History and Society* (New York: Seabury, 1980).

13. Robert McAfee Brown, *Elie Wiesel: Messenger to All Humanity* (Notre Dame, IN: University of Notre Dame Press, 1983), 6–7.

14. Buckley, *At the Origins of Modern Atheism*, 363.

4

Feminism and Sharing the Faith
A Catholic Dilemma

A brief vignette reported in the press last year illustrates the dilemma that I will grapple with this evening. A woman had reached the point in her spiritual journey where she felt called to become a member of the Catholic Church. As she went through the RCIA (Rite of Christian Initiation of Adults) program, however, certain church teachings struck her as being offensive to the dignity of women. Her growing awareness of women's second-class status in the church was buttressed by several small incidents, most likely not even noted by the clergymen involved. In the end, with sadness, she left the RCIA program for the good of her own soul.

This woman haunts me. Her turning toward the Catholic community, with all the personal hope this involved on her part and all the richness being offered on the church's part; and then her turning away again due to a problem that is not a figment of her imagination but a very real bias: these turnings resonate deeply in the psyches of many, especially women. They define a critical dilemma.

On the one hand, at the heart of Christian faith is the good news of salvation coming from God in Jesus through the power of the Spirit. Graced by divine mercy in their own hearts and lives, the community that follows Jesus, which is commonly called the church, has a mission to witness to this treasure, to share it with fellow human beings to the ends of the earth. They are called to participate with the Spirit of God in making salvation effective in all dimensions of life.

On the other hand, despite this good news, the Catholic community in the course of history has developed institutional structures and theologies that are profoundly sexist. The official church today not only promotes the priority of men in theory and practice, but justifies such male dominance with the claim that this is the will of God. Whether made known by natural law or revelation (arguments differ), it is according to God's gracious pleasure that male rule be the norm in the church.

Herewith the Catholic dilemma, illustrated in that one sad story of the woman and the RCIA program. Why would any justice-seeking woman or man want to join a group like this? Why do women stay in a community like this? And how can we continue with integrity to share the gospel with the next generation or with persons in the wider society when our own community's institutional structures and official attitudes are pervaded by sexism and therefore harmful to the well-being of women and men? Such questions, being asked by many in the church today, cannot be taken lightly. They come from a profound experience of disappointment, grief, anger, and, even if passingly, despair.

I propose to wrestle with this dilemma in three points. First, I will describe world feminism in general as the background against which this dilemma arises. Next, I will explore, as the crucible of the dilemma, Christian feminism with its assumptions, critiques, and hopes. Finally, as a way through the dilemma, I will propose three Catholic strengths that may sustain persons in the struggle for a more just church, one converted from sexism toward a community of the discipleship of equals.

GLOBAL FEMINISM

In a generic sense, feminism is a worldview or stance that affirms the dignity of women as fully human persons in their own right; critiques systems of patriarchy for their violation of this dignity; and advocates social and intellectual challenges to bring about freeing relationships among human beings and between human beings and the earth. The engine that drives this stance is women's experience of being marginalized, with all the suffering that entails. The concept of being marginal has become a key category for interpreting women's experience. It identifies women as accessories to men rather than as key players or active subjects of history in their own right. To be in the margin, as African-American theorist bell hooks observes, is to be part of the whole but outside the main body. It is not an unnecessary place but a place of systematic devaluing. Being there signifies being less, being overlooked, not having as much importance, not being able to shape ideas or decide significant matters for the whole community.

The fundamental system that casts women as a group into this marginal position has become known as sexism. In a generic sense, sexism is the belief that persons are superior or inferior to one another on the basis of their sex. It includes attitudes, stereotypes, and social patterns that express or support this belief. Thus it is a prejudice. Like racism, which assigns an inferior dignity to some people on the basis of their skin color or ethnic heritage, sexism views women as essentially less valuable than men on the basis of biological sex. It labors mightily to set up structures and attitudes to keep women in their "proper" social place. In both prejudices, bodily characteristics stand in for the whole human person so that the fundamental dignity of the person is violated.

In civil society women experience the harmful effects of sexism in multiple ways:

❖ For most of recorded history women have been denied political, economic, legal, and educational rights. In no country in the world are these yet equal in practice to the rights of men.

❖ According to the United Nations statistics, while forming more than one-half of the world's population, women work three-fourths of the world's working hours, own one-tenth of the world's wealth and one-hundredth of the world's land, and form two-thirds of the world's illiterate people, the education of girls not being a priority. Over three-fourths of the world's starving people are women with their dependent children.

❖ Subordination on the basis of sex is intertwined with subordination on the basis of race and class. Poor women of color, subordinated to poor men of color who themselves are already socially marginalized, are the oppressed of the oppressed.

❖ To make a dark picture even bleaker, women are bodily and sexually exploited, physically abused, raped, battered, and murdered. The indisputable fact is that men do this to women in a way and to a degree that women do not do it to men. Sexism is rampant on a global scale.

Feminism is the stance that brings these situations to consciousness. It articulates the suffering women endure as a result. It analyzes these situations to reveal the pattern of male dominance that underlies them and makes them possible. It characterizes and resists this pattern as unjust. It embraces alternative worldviews more inclusive of women and the earth. It promotes changes in attitudes, theories, laws, and structures to bring about more wholeness of life. The dynamic of the whole movement is creating a change in consciousness that is irreversible. For those whose eyes have been opened to this worldview, it becomes as unthinkable to return to the endorsement of women's subordination as to return to slavery.

Make no mistake: feminism today is a powerful, worldwide phenomenon. It is part of the surge toward emancipation of oppressed peoples in the modern era. We have seen colonized nations push against imperial rule; people of color demand equality under the law; economically poor people cry out for economic justice; young people search for recognition as persons against inherited authorities; subjugated peoples claim their freedom in revolutions both velvet and bloody. Women too are rising up and claiming their human worth in the face of congealed layers of prejudice. Since women are present although with marginalized status in every social group and nation, the very process of their taking their lives in their own hands and seeking mutual rather than subservient relationships with men signals a radical transformation of human society.

CHRISTIAN FEMINISM

As long ago as 1963, Pope John XXIII took note of women's emerging consciousness in his encyclical *Pacem in Terris*. He named this a distinctive "sign of the times," along with the rise of the working class and the emergence of new nations, writing with foresight:

It is obvious to everyone that women are now taking a part in public life. This is happening more rapidly perhaps in nations with a Christian tradition, and more slowly but broadly among people who have inherited other traditions or cultures. Since women are becoming ever more conscious of their human dignity, they will not tolerate being treated as inanimate objects or mere instruments, but claim, both in domestic and public life, the rights and duties that befit a human person. (41)

The Second Vatican Council picked up this thread in its Constitution on the Church in the Modern World. Teaching that all human persons have equal dignity before God which demands social justice for all, the bishops wrote:

True, all persons are not alike from the point of view of varying physical power and the diversity of intellectual and moral resources. Nevertheless, with respect to the fundamental rights of the person, every type of discrimination, whether social or cultural, whether based on sex, race, color, social condition, language, or religion, is to be overcome and eradicated as contrary to God's intent. (29)

Note how sex leads the list. In clear terms this pastoral constitution is teaching that discrimination based on sex is contrary to God's intent. In theological terms this means it is sinful. It is noteworthy that the examples of discrimination that follow in the next sentence to illuminate all types of discrimination are taken from the experience of women:

For in truth it must still be regretted that fundamental personal rights are not yet being universally honored. Such is the case of a woman who is denied the right and freedom to choose a husband, to embrace a state of life, or to acquire an education or cultural benefits equal to those recognized for men.

In the mind of the Council, these words were aimed at society. But what about the church itself? If a woman in the church is denied the right and freedom to embrace a state of life because of her sex, is this not discrimination which should be overcome and eradicated as contrary to God's intent? Christian feminism argues the logic of this, while the institution's official rhetoric posits an essential difference between church society and civil society to prevent such a conclusion being drawn.

The Second Vatican Council influenced Catholic women enormously. The concept of the church as people of God, the call of the whole church to holiness, the validation of the baptismal dignity of the laity—all of these teachings entail new roles and identity for women. Perhaps it was providential that the Council's teaching arrived in North America in the 1960s just as feminism in civil society was gaining a newly strong foothold. In hindsight it is clear that it was the confluence of these two streams, civil and religious, that created the torrent that is Christian feminism in North America today.

In our day there are multiple forms of Christian feminism. Scholars distinguish liberal, cultural, radical, and socialist feminism. They speak of the first, second, and third wave of feminism according to the time and social location of its practitioners. They identify revolutionary, reformist, and reconstructionist forms of Christian feminist theologies according to their religious goals and relation to secular feminist theories. Differences are enormous and no one presentation can do justice to the richness of the diversity. Nevertheless, for the sake of advancing discussion I will dare to speak of Christian feminism in the singular and put forth the argument that it is based on the deepest truth of the gospel itself. Its assumptions, criticisms, and goals are drawn from the message and spirit of Jesus Christ interpreted through the lens of women's struggle for justice and fullness of life.

ASSUMPTIONS

Christian feminism fundamentally affirms that Christian doctrine regarding the human person applies to women equally as to men. It therefore claims that women are created in the image and likeness of God, redeemed by Christ, sanctified by the Holy Spirit, called to a life of faith and responsibility in this world, destined for glory with God forever, and enjoy all of these blessings in an equal measure with men. To promote women's ownership of this basic Christian anthropology, Christian feminism develops a criterion for what is true, good, and beautiful. Theories, attitudes, laws, and structures that promote the dignity of the female human person are salvific and according to the divine will; theories or structures that deny or violate women's dignity are contrary to God's intent. For Christian feminism, women's flourishing is crucial to the truth of the gospel.

These assumptions, while not very startling at first hearing, signal that at a deep core of their being Christian women are turning away from sexism and turning toward something more fundamental, namely, their inclusion as beloved human beings before God in the mystery of salvation wrought in Christ. I would argue that this existential NO to sexism coupled with a YES to one's own female self as God's beloved creature is an axial event in the history of spirituality. Happening among circles of women on every continent, it is an experience that cannot be denied, nor can the resulting consciousness be reversed. In the face of this religious experience, any institutional authority that argues for the propriety of male dominance loses its moral power.

Critiques

With this vision Christian feminism sees that sexism pervades not only civil society but also the church. For most of ecclesial history women have been subordinated in theory and practice at every turn. Consider how until very recently Christian theology consistently defined women as mentally, morally, and physically inferior to men. Leading male thinkers have characterized women's minds as less rational than those of men, their wills weaker and more open to temptation, their sexuality degraded and its use demeaning. They have spoken of women as the weaker sex, as temptresses, incapable of great virtue unless they deny their own femaleness and become as men. Left to their own devices, of course, women would not have so defined themselves, but the official voice of theology was exclusively male. What is called the "male gaze" looked upon women's differences from men and judged women to be inferior.

Recently efforts have been made to recast this sexist anthropology with a view to overcoming its more blatant inequity, though inequality nevertheless remains. Pope John Paul II's encyclical "On the Dignity of Women," for example, argues strongly that women and men are both created in the image of God as human persons, that both have rational souls. But then drawing on a disputed theory of complementarity, he argues that women have a special nature that defines their dignity and vocation. This nature is one that is oriented to "the order of love":

> In God's eternal plan, woman is the one in whom the order of love in the created world of persons takes first root.... The bridegroom is the one who loves. The bride is loved: It is she who receives love, in order to give love in return.... When we say that the woman is the one who receives love in order to give love in return, this refers not only or above all to the specific spousal relationship of marriage. It means something more universal, based on the fact of her being a woman.... Woman can find herself only by giving love to others. (29, 30)

By nature, then, with their capacity for love, women are pre-ordained to social roles of nurturing and caring for life, while their capacity for thought and active leadership are counted of little worth. This obviously translates into the domestic and private spheres of life being defined as women's proper domain. In the context of patriarchy where public laws, symbols, and structures are shaped by men, such a patriarchal view of "woman's special nature" simply ensures women's continuing secondary social status and dependence upon men. In an ironic twist, it also credits women with being capable of living out Jesus' great commandment of love better than men can, but this seems to go by unnoticed by the promoters of women's special nature.

Women are marginalized not only by theory; church practice likewise effects their exclusion. They may not receive all seven sacraments. Thus they may not preach or preside in the liturgical assembly, or mediate God's grace in officially sacramental ways. The primary effect is to make women dependent on a male clergy for such mediation of God's grace. Such exclusion also bars them from centers of significant ecclesial decision-making, law-making, symbol-making, and other public leadership roles in the institution. Awareness of this subordination has created a crisis over the Eucharist for many women. As Rosemary Radford Ruether expresses it, women come to the table to be nourished by the word of God and the bread of life, only to leave still starved because what has been powerfully ritualized is their own subordination.

Christian feminism argues on the basis of faith in Jesus Christ that even for the church, sexism is contrary to God's intent. Such second-class citizenship disparages the image of God in women, profanes their baptism, distorts the relationship between the sexes, and damages the community that is the church.

Goals

What Christian feminism hopes for is a transformed community more in accord with the reign of God that Jesus preached. Cooperating with the Spirit of life, feminism hopes so to change unjust structures and distorted symbol systems that a new community in church and society becomes possible, a liberating community of all women and men characterized by mutuality with each other, care for the weakest and least powerful among them, and harmony with the earth. This is a vision of the church as a community of the discipleship of equals, that is, a community shaped according to the reign of God, rather than one modeled on imperial Rome or the divine right monarchies of the age of absolutism.

THE DILEMMA INTENSIFIED

Let me point out, lest anyone think we are dealing here with superficial matters, that the deepest questions raised by Christian feminism are of universal import. Who is God? Is God a male ruler who wills male supremacy? Or a triune mystery of love beyond all imagining who wills the genuine equality of women and men in community and who, as a result, can be referred to in female and cosmic imagery? Are women deficient human beings or really created in the image and likeness of God? What is salvation? Is Jesus Christ a savior of all or a tool of patriarchal oppression? Does baptism really recreate women in the image of Christ, or do its effects not quite "take" when the recipient is female? Is the church to be forever sexist, or can it be redeemed from sexism to become a more just community of disciples?

Vatican II taught that the pilgrim church on its way through history is continually in need of reform, called always to increased fidelity to its own mission. Thus, we may look upon Christian feminism as a blessing, not only for women, and not only for women and men together, but for the church itself. In Anne Carr's lovely phrase, in the midst of the history of sexism, feminism comes as an offer of "transforming grace" to the church, an offer to repent and become a living community of justice and peace. In faith and struggle feminist women and men are growing the church into a new moment of the living tradition, one more reflective of God's gracious design for our salvation. However, and terrifyingly, grace may always be refused.

The continuing refusal of the institutional church today to be converted from its ancient sexism makes it, in the eyes of many, an obstacle to faith, that is, a motive not to believe. This is in contrast to the old apologetics where a motive for the credibility of the faith was said to be the church itself. As a result a number of women are leaving the church, some to live out their call to ordained ministry in other Christian bodies; others simply to find a more inclusive community in which to pray and raise their children; still others to seek the divine in worship that honors the feminine. Having taught some of these women, and presently being friends or colleagues with others, I know their stories, resonate with their suffering and search, and greatly respect their decisions. At the same time, my own path and that of others keeps on winding through the Catholic community itself.

There is a need to articulate reasons for this. And so we return to our dilemma. Why remain in the church? How, with integrity, share the faith with others? The force of these questions was brought home to me several years ago when I was giving a lecture on feminist theology on the campus of University of California, Los Angeles. A young woman student in the audience, whom I had noticed listening intently, stood to ask whether I worshiped the goddess. In response I asked whether she thought that praying to divine mystery in female images such as Mother Creator, Holy Wisdom, or feminine Spirit within the contours of following Jesus was tantamount to worshiping the goddess. When she replied "No," I could say in truth that then I did not worship the goddess.

But we were not finished yet, for then she asked "Why not?" Here was a question I had never really considered. To gain time to think (!), I asked if she herself worshiped the goddess. When she answered affirmatively, I asked why. She named respect for the body, connection with the earth and nature's cycles, and sisterhood with other women as her reasons. Saying that these were precious values and that indeed the Christian tradition had not given them significant priority, I asked quietly if her worship of the goddess turned her to work for justice with the poor or motivated her to have compassion on the most abandoned. Her negative answer opened the door to my own attempt at a response: I still followed the Way of Jesus, I offered, because it turns you toward the nearest neighbor in need, without denying the values that she so beautifully affirmed.

And so we conversed, tentatively and respectfully probing one another's stances for the truth that might lie there. I still remember the intense silence in the auditorium as this genuine conversation took place. It was not a matter of one-upmanship but of common search in which all present seemed to be charting their own steps on a vitally important issue. In retrospect I think my intuitive response about care for the oppressed was to some degree inadequate. Not only do many worshipers of the goddess have strong concern for justice but many Christians, in reality, do not, despite the gospels and contemporary Catholic social teaching. Ever since, I have been thinking about how to articulate the values of Christian faith within a feminist consciousness.

CATHOLIC STRENGTHS

As a way to deal with this dilemma, not to resolve it but to struggle with it, I would like to identify in Catholicism today three dynamic strengths that together add up to a rich religious possibility for one's life when interpreted through feminist consciousness. My experience in ecumenical dialogue and with the splendid witness and theological scholarship of so many Protestant and Orthodox Christians has led me to immense admiration for them, so in no way is this intended to suggest that other Christian churches are lacking these or other strengths. Rather, it is the way these factors are combined in the Catholic Church that gives this group its particular character. The three strengths are these: the gospel, the community, and the imagination.

First, the gospel. The community that is the Catholic Church continues to keep alive the liberating, compassionate power of the gospel. We continue to hear from the Scriptures of God's gracious intent to heal, redeem, and liberate all peoples and the cosmos itself. The Jewish Scriptures connect us with divine presence through proclamation of the exodus from slavery to freedom and the making of the covenant; through the prophetic word against injustice that promises release; and through the wisdom word about creation that points to divine ways in the world of nature and everyday life. The Christian Scriptures release the power of the Spirit through the dangerous story of Jesus the Christ: his love of God, his way of relating to people against all social stigmatizing, his challenge to follow, his death and resurrection releasing mercy and hope for all. In other words, if the core of the gospel were missing, there would be no point to remaining in the church or inviting others to share the faith. But I find it is still there. Particularly heartening is the angle of vision opened up on the Scriptures and their traditioning process by feminist interpretation. Thanks to this reading we can see ever more clearly that Jesus-Sophia, in the name of God, gives the world a pattern of hope and meaning by embodying and teaching a loving way of relating to each other. Not domination-submission but the inclusive, mutual connections of sisters and brothers should characterize the community of disciples.

Furthermore, feminist biblical interpretation highlights Jesus' attitude toward women, his outreach toward women in need, his inclusive table community, the influence of women upon him, the witness of his women disciples. These disciples, key among them Mary of Magdala, provide the moving point of continuity in the gospel story. Having accompanied him as disciples around Galilee, they followed him when he set his face toward Jerusalem and were present at all the important events of his last days. They kept faith with him even to the bitter end. It is simply not true to say, as so many do, that all of Jesus' disciples abandoned him during the crucifixion. The circle of women disciples kept vigil by the cross as a sacrament of God's own seemingly absent fidelity. The women disciples, according to the gospels, helped to bury Jesus. Knowing where the tomb was, they were the first to experience Christ risen and receive the apostolic commission to "go and tell." The fire of the Holy Spirit was poured out on women and men alike in the upper room. Accordingly, the participation of women in ministry in the early years of the church was not an aberration but an expression of a new worldview learned from Jesus Christ, both historical and risen.

The egalitarian character of the Jesus movement was eventually co-opted by patriarchy, although it did not go down without a fight. But the revolutionary realization that women are equally made in the image of God, are restored by Christ in the power of the Spirit, and are capable of responsibility commensurate with this blessing surfaces again and again in Christian history. There is thus a critical and transforming tradition stemming from the gospel itself that can add impetus to the conversation of the church today from sexism. The institutional church has already changed its long-held stances regarding the religious correctness of slavery and contempt for the Jews. It is now time for the living tradition to grow away from the subordination of women. The gospel carries this message as a subliminal text even in the midst of sexism.

The second strength I would name is the community. The Catholic people form an ancient and widespread community of all sorts of folks, connected through time and space. The connection with believers throughout the ages as expressed, for example, in the "Litany of the Saints" gives us deep historical roots. In addition to community through time, there is also community through space given the wide geographic spread of Catholicism. The Catholic Church is a major world institution that crosses the lines of the hemispheres, north to south, east to west, linking together populations in western and eastern Europe, North and South America, Asia, Africa, the Pacific islands, and Australia. There are over one billion of us, peoples of various cultures but with a shared faith, sacred memory, and symbol system, struggling to be faithful and make sense of our lives. This vast network becomes wonderfully real when you travel to different countries and participate in the local church.

Being a Catholic means being joined with all these people. I find particular delight in discovering so many women in different countries forming networks of mutual help, moving forward with actions to promote the dignity of women according to the possibilities of their own culture. In North America there are feminist Catholics and Catholic feminists of all stripes, women pastoring parishes, women in peace and justice movements, theologians of multi-cultural, multi-racial, and multi-ethnic traditions. In India there is Virginia Saldanha with her circle of friends heading up the first Women's Desk for the diocese of Bombay. In South Africa there is the artist Dina Cormick creating images of the divine Creator in the likeness of women of color. Wherever I have gone in Latin America I have met women committed to being a voice for the voiceless as they connect the issues of poverty, sexism, and ruination of the earth. Being a Catholic means being joined in a community of faith with all these women, along with so many other women and men working for justice and peace around the world.

Obviously, I have made a distinction here between the church as institution and the church as community. I have also given theological and existential priority to the latter, a move fiercely fought over and then adopted by the Second Vatican Council in the Constitution on the Church when it voted to place the chapter on the People of God before the one on the hierarchy. And yet we also need the institution to link, shepherd, and unite the disparate local churches. In my view the institution need not be sexist in order to fulfill its purpose. Catholic women's experience of community in some places already gives a foretaste of what a renewed church could be.

The third strength to weave into my case for the church is the imagination. The Catholic Church offers a rich heritage of sacraments, sacramentals, prayers, spiritual writings, practices, and guides. Today there is a deep hunger for God and the things of the spirit abroad in our land. Many people are tired of life being so materialistic, superficial, meaningless. Catholicism has what David Tracy calls an analogical imagination that notices the presence of grace in and through the everyday world. With this sense of the presence of grace, the Catholic tradition unlocks the religious dimension of the ordinary. Its diverse spiritual traditions provide a feast for the soul, delineating paths that flow toward the ideal of simplicity and peace. Ambiguity inheres even here, however, as a great deal of classical spirituality denigrates the body with its passions and thus, in an androcentric framework, disrespects women. In accord with the foundational sacramental imagination, however, emergent feminist spiritualities attend to women's ways of being in the world, pouring the search for the transcendent into a path that cherishes the body, sexuality, and the earth. In forging new patterns of wholeness feminist spiritualities draw from deep wells in the Catholic tradition while they comfort, challenge, and empower women to resist the debilitations of religious sexism.

The combination of these three strengths, gospel, community, and spiritual imagination, in their particular pattern in the Catholic community provide, I think, a certain light in the darkness and give some warrants for remaining in the church with its mission of sharing the faith with others. As these strengths operate, they interact with the sufferings that women bear in their membership, along with the sufferings of men sensitive to this injustice, to become a powerhouse of energy to resist sexism in the name of the deepest truths that we profess.

CONCLUSION

During the Vietnam War in reaction to anti-war protests, a bumper sticker appeared that read, "America, love it or leave it." I thought at the time what a stupid sentiment that was. If you really love something, you do not abandon it to its errors but try to make it better. Anguished over that war for moral reasons though I was, the idea of becoming a citizen of a different nation had little appeal. Better to take to the streets and march, to demonstrate, to lobby, to teach, to cast votes, to pressure the government with its deceit and tunnel vision to end the hated violence, for the good of our own country as well as for the Vietnamese people. Similarly today, the struggle for the conversion of the institutional church from sexism locally, nationally, and internationally seems to me worthwhile. Though the errors of the official leadership regarding women are in many instances egregious, and stubbornly so, even a small change for the better can affect a community that is worldwide. This in turn can have profound impact on society, even for generations yet unborn.

I would like to end as I began, with a story, this time one with a hopeful ending. It was recounted to me in a letter from my friend Larry Kaufmann, CSsR, a priest in South Africa. To understand the setting, you should know that Phokeng is a black township, that Father Gerard was its pastor, and that "to supply" is priest-language for saying Mass on Sundays in a place where one is needed. I quote from his letter:

> Let me tell you about some feminist theology in action! I have been going to Phokeng to supply for Gerard while he is away. Two weeks ago I noticed an altar server (male) going up to a young woman in the communion line and speaking to her. She left the line and went back into the pew. The same thing happened a few more times. After Mass I inquired and was told that since Father Gerard's absence, the men of the parish council had decided that women and girls should cover their heads as a mark of respect when receiving communion. No hat, no communion. I vented my anger with those I was talking to, and decided I would have to do something about the situation on my next visit.
>
> Last Sunday I was in the parish again. I noticed all the women wearing hats, berets, or veils (called *doeks*), even Maggie Bopalamo, former detainee in Bophuthatswana, lecturer at a teachers college, a leader in the parish community. After communion and the communion prayer, I

went up to a young woman in the front pew who was wearing a blue hat with white ribbons. I asked if I might borrow it. Then in full vestments I put the hat on my head. Laughter. I adjusted the hat here and there and asked how I looked. More laughter.

Then I opened the Bible and read from Galatians 3:27–28. Because we all drink of the one Spirit, "there is neither Jew nor Greek, neither slave nor free, neither male and female, for all are one in Christ Jesus." Rapt attention. On the basis of this equality, I said, it seems all the men will have to have their heads covered as well. Next week I want to see all the men with hats on if they want to go to communion, and I promised that I, too, would celebrate Mass wearing a hat. The women cheered and shouted "Viva" and clapped and started to dance.

I had found the gap and went right through it, speaking about discrimination against women in the church. More cheers from the women. This empowered me even more and I went on. More dancing. Finally, I said that the reason given why women should cover their heads was to show respect for Christ, but the only respect the gospel demanded was not visible to the eye: it was in the heart of a person who loved God. The women left the pews, went into the aisles dancing. Gradually some of the men joined in as well, and of course, yours truly! It was a wonderful teaching moment.

After some ordinary news and chat, my friend finished his letter by harkening back to the township story, ending with this blessing: "May all women all over the world leave their pews, get into the aisles, and dance their way to freedom and full participation in the church!" With such moments breaking out around the world, the Catholic dilemma of feminism and sharing the faith begins to be lit up by hope.

Adapted from The Warren Lecture, University of Tulsa, Tulsa, OK, 1993.

5

Come Ahead
A Story to Live By

If we were to ask St. Francis Xavier, I expect he would agree that he lived a most surprising life. Consider this: born in Spain, he went to study at the university in Paris where he enjoyed a high-rolling lifestyle—parties, drinking, the usual. But he ended up with a roommate, Ignatius, who challenged this way of life and, despite his resistance, got him interested in Jesus Christ. Some years later, after they founded the Society of Jesus, Ignatius sent him to preach Christ in foreign lands. I'll wager that as a beginning student he never imagined that one day he would leave Europe and travel to India, Malacca, the Molucca Islands, and Japan. He never dreamed that his missionary efforts would attract so many to the Christian faith. He never envisioned that he would die on a desolate, far-off island, still hoping to get into China.

The point is, Francis Xavier is a wonderful instance of a life lived in faith. In a way more dramatic than most, he experienced what nevertheless is common to those who throw in their lot with the God of the Bible, because this God is a God of surprises, always calling us to "go forth," "come ahead," venture into the future promised but unknown.

Some people, of course, live with a focus on the past, on the hurts whose remembrance requires self-pity or even vengeance, or on sweet times that wash them in nostalgia and a desire to return to the way things were. Our own culture tends to fixate us in the present, where we can ignore the suffering of others by busying ourselves with a thousand distractions, entertaining ourselves to death. But faith keeps up a steady drumbeat to move into the

73

future, where the ever-coming God will meet us in new challenging and comforting ways.

To illustrate this, consider two famous ancient stories, one Greek and one Hebrew, that offer contrasting options about how to live.

The Greek story opens at the end of the Trojan War. It features one of the fighters, Odysseus, who spends ten years in the effort to return to his home on the island of Ithaca. There he hopes to rejoin his faithful wife Penelope, his devoted son Telemachus, and his irreplaceable dog Argus. Along the way he endures dramatic hardships—mighty storms! cannibals! a witch who turns half his sailors into swine! shipwreck! His story is spiced with amazing experiences—six-headed monsters! whirlpools! communion with the dead! drugs! lovers! He engages in terrific feats of valor—blinding an enemy! His journey is definitely an adventure. However, in the end, he is driven by the desire to return to what he knows, to the comfort and prestige of the past he remembers.

The Hebrew story starts with an older man and his wife already settled in their home. God addresses Abram, and by implication Sarah, with an unsettling invitation: Leave, go forth to the land I will show you. This invitation is accompanied by a concrete promise: you will have descendants as numerous as the stars in the sky. It carries, too, an even deeper pledge that God will be with them. Centuries later, reflecting on this moment, the New Testament notes with amazement about Abraham: "and he set out, not knowing where he was going" (Heb. 11:8). Through thick and thin he forged ahead, daring to risk everything in trust that God would be faithful, even when things got so bad that he hung on, "hoping against hope," as Paul says (Rom 4:18). The drumbeat of his adventure and that of Sarah was faith in the living God who called them into the future and promised to meet them there.

Dichotomies tend to oversimplify reality, which in truth is complex and ambiguous. No doubt one could find a certain kind of hope in the story of Odysseus, and all kinds of foot-dragging in the biblical ancestors. Yet the stories are not the same, even geographically. One person is looping back to where he began. The others are forging ahead to a new place. It seems to me that the story of Abraham and Sarah, not Odysseus, exemplifies the Christian understanding of what it means to be human. We human beings have a passion to be and become ourselves. This cannot happen if we try to return to the past or stay wedded to the present moment. Only by pressing ahead to the future can we allow the fullness of life to find us.

For the most part the ancient Greeks did not view hope as virtuous but as an evil to be avoided. In the story of Prometheus, after all other evils have fled from Pandora's box, the final one remaining is hope. Adding to humanity's woes, it taunts them with the possibility of something better only to disappoint in the end. This just goes to make their suffering more intense. The Greeks reasoned that if we freed ourselves from hope and simply accepted our fate, then we would no longer feel such pain.

In the Bible, by contrast, the present moment is a growing edge, opening ever further to God's dream for our becoming. It would seem that the living God is not above us but ahead of us, calling with a promise that exceeds expectations. "Leave, go forth," God addresses each of us. Come ahead to the place, the vocation, the relationships, the work, the griefs and joys I will show you. The human instinct is to shrink this promise to our own measure of what seems possible. If we dare to respond, however, we might find ourselves in surprising new territory. Biblical spirituality is awash with this hope.

Ultimately, the future that we all travel toward is death, something made very concrete by the ashes of Lent. Here we Christians live by a new chapter in the Abrahamic story, namely, the death and resurrection of Jesus Christ. At the end of his life Jesus really died on the cross and ended up in the darkness and silence of the tomb. It would seem that his story was over. But the ever-coming God of surprises opens up the future once again. God raises the crucified one to new life in an unimaginable act of faithful love. He is transformed by new life that we fumblingly try to symbolize with bunnies and flowers and eggs, but is perhaps best symbolized by the flame of the Easter candle.

What Abraham was hoping for against all hope arrives in what God has done for the crucified Jesus and, by extension, for all of us whose destiny is to die. The resurrection makes clear God's purpose in creating the world. While death is a part of all life, in the end we and the cosmos are destined not for death and destruction but for transformation into new life. Here we have a whole new vision of what awaits, even if unimaginably so. God intends no empty future where we are annihilated by death, but a future of life transformed through resurrection.

To conclude: Odysseus or Abraham and Sarah? Each enacts a story to live by. Odysseus's tale tells the story of the understandable human desire to return to the familiar past. Abraham and Sarah embody the story where faith in God is an adventure into the unknown. In his death and resurrection, Jesus extends that adventure all the way through the barrier of death into the future where, in the embrace of the living God, we "shall see face to face," and "know even as we are known." For Christians, "come ahead" is the story to live by.

So Francis Xavier believed. And so we hope.

Reflection for students in University Church, Fordham University (2004), as part of a series on inspirations that can be drawn from the life of St. Francis Xavier.

II
GREAT GOD OF HEAVEN AND EARTH

6

Creative Giver of Life

Astronauts who have seen the view of Earth from space with their own eyes speak of its power to change their attitude. Saudi Arabian astronaut Sultan bin Salman al-Saud, member of an international crew, recollected: "The first day we all pointed to our own countries. The third day we were pointing to our continents. By the fifth day, we were all aware of only one Earth." Another astronaut, American Rusty Schweigert who walked on the moon, had this to say: "From the moon, Earth is so small and so fragile, and such a precious little spot in the universe, that you can block it out with your thumb. Then you realize that on that spot, that little blue and white circle, is everything that means anything to you—all of history, music, poetry and art, birth and love and death, tears, joy...And then you are changed forever; your relationship to the world is no longer what it was."[1]

In our day, a new awareness of the magnificence of Earth as a planet that hosts life is growing among people everywhere. It is an ecological consciousness, pervaded by wonder at Earth's living beauty and, simultaneously, by distress at its despoiling. Ecological awareness is a new dialogue partner for theology. It raises challenges and provides opportunities to take yet another step in the age-old journey of seeking understanding of the ineffable mystery of God, Creator of heaven and earth. Toward that end, consider first a view of the world in all its wonder and wasting. This in turn will open the door to insights about the Giver of its life.

A LIVING PLANET

Current scientific consensus holds that the universe originated about 14 billion years ago in a primordial flaring forth rather inelegantly named the Big Bang. From that explosive instant to this day, the universe has continued to expand while hydrogen atoms coalesce to form stars, stars congregate to form galaxies, and galaxies gather in neighborhood groups. In one corner of one galaxy, our own solar system of star and planets formed about five billion years ago, coalescing under gravity's pull from debris left by ancient exploding stars. On one of these planets, Earth, life began about 3.5 billion years ago, emerging from the interaction of minerals and gasses to form communities of single-celled creatures deep in the seas. Life then evolved from single-celled to multiple-celled creatures; from sea to land and air; from plant to animal life; and very recently from primates to human beings, we mammals whose brains are so richly textured that we experience self-reflective consciousness and freedom, or in classical philosophical terms, mind and will.

This contemporary story of the history of the cosmos teaches amazing things.

❖ The universe is unfathomably *old*. We humans have only recently arrived. Carl Sagan memorably used the timetable of a single Earth year to dramatize the cosmic calendar. If the Big Bang occurred on January 1st, then our sun and planets came into existence September 9th; life on Earth originated on September 25th; and the first humans emerged onto the scene on December 31st at 10:30 PM.[2] Placing this timetable into graphic physical motion, the American Museum of Natural History in New York contains a spiraling cosmic walk. Starting at rooftop level with the Big Bang, each normal-sized step one takes down the spiral covers millions of years. At the bottom, you step over all of human history in a line as thin as a human hair.

❖ The observable universe is incomprehensibly *large*. There are over 100 billion galaxies, each comprised of billions of stars, and no one knows how many moons and planets, all of this visible and audible matter being only a fraction of the matter and energy in the universe. Earth is a small planet orbiting a medium-sized star toward the edge of one spiral galaxy.

❖ The universe is profoundly *dynamic*. Out of the Big Bang, the galaxies of stars; out of the stardust, the Earth; out of the molecules of the Earth, single-celled living creatures; out of the evolutionary life and death of these creatures, an advancing tide of life, fragile but unstoppable, up to the riot of millions of species that exist today; and out of one branch of this bush of life, *homo sapiens*, the species in which the Earth becomes conscious of itself. Human thought and love are not something injected into the universe from without, but are the flowering in us of deeply cosmic energies.

❖ The universe is complexly *interconnected*. Everything links with everything else; nothing conceivable is isolated. What makes our blood red? Scientist and theologian Arthur Peacocke explains, "Every atom of iron in our blood would not be there had it not been produced in some galactic explosion billions of years ago and eventually condensed to form the iron in the crust of the earth from which we have emerged."[3] We and all other species are made of stardust. The subsequent story of evolution makes clear that humans share with all other living creatures on our planet a common genetic ancestry. Charles Darwin, who laid out the story of evolution so compellingly, described the result with the metaphor of a great tree of life.[4] Picture a spreading evolutionary tree that links all living creatures into an indivisible whole, spanning the ages. The outer layer of budding twigs and green leaves represents the multitudes of species alive today, topping out in the sun. Below are layers of dead and broken branches that once lived, giving rise to the new life which they now support. What a grand natural system! And the story is not finished yet. Bacteria, pine trees, blueberries, horses, the great gray whales: we are all genetic kin in the great community of life.

This account of our living planet tends to awaken awe. But at the same time we humans are inflicting deadly damage on our planet, ravaging its identity as a dwelling place for life. The way we consume and exploit resources and pollute is dealing a sucker punch to life-supporting systems on land, sea, and air. The litany makes for nightmare headlines: global warming, holes in the ozone layer, rain forests logged and burned, ruined wetlands, collapsed fisheries, poisoned soils. The widespread destruction of ecosystems has as its flip side the extinction of the plant and animal species that thrive in these habitats. By a conservative estimate, in the last quarter of the twentieth century 10 percent of all living species went extinct. The dying off has only become more rapid in the twenty-first century. The behavior of the human species is killing birth itself, shutting down the future of our fellow creatures who took millions of years to evolve. Their perishing sends an early-warning signal about the death of our planet itself. In the blunt language of the World Council of Churches, "The stark sign of our times is a planet in peril at our hands."[5]

The picture darkens as we attend to the deep-seated connection between ecological devastation and social injustice. Poor people suffer disproportionately from environmental damage inflicted in pursuit of corporate profit. Ravaging of people and ravaging of the land on which they depend go hand in hand. Corporate logging of forests in India, to take but one example, not only ruins the habitat for wildlife but deprives poor villagers who live on the forests' periphery of the firewood, fruits and nuts, small animals, and clean drinking water on which they depend for survival. In the United States, major companies export work to factories across the Mexican border (*maquiladoras*) that cheaply employ thousands of young, rural women to make high quality consumer goods for export, while they live in unhealthy squalor in an environment spoiled by toxic waste. Again, the economically well off can choose to live amid acres of green while poor people are housed near factories, refineries, or waste-processing plants that heavily pollute the environment. The bitterness of this situation is exacerbated by racial prejudice, as environmental racism pressures people of color to dwell in these neighborhoods.

Feminist analysis clarifies further how the plight of the poor becomes exemplified in poor women whose own biological abilities to give birth are compromised by toxic environments, and whose nurturing of children is hampered at every turn by lack of clean water, food, and fuel. Women-initiated projects such as the Chipko movement in India, where village women literally hug the forest trees to prevent lumber interests from cutting them down, and the Green Belt movement started by Nobel Peace Prize winner Wangari Maathai in Kenya, whereby women plant millions of trees and receive a small income for nurturing them, show how restoring the earth interweaves intrinsically with the flourishing of poor women and their communities. Poverty and its remedy have an ecological face.

For people of faith, the question of God is profoundly involved in these considerations. Where is God, Creator of heaven and earth, to be found in the great cosmos? What is God doing in an evolutionary world under threat? How might the answers affect our response in faith? As one way into this issue, the ancient but neglected field of pneumatology, study of the Spirit, is poised to make a contribution. On the frontiers of cosmic science and ecological responsibility, it brings creation forward from a long ago event to a matter of religious importance here and now.

THE SPIRIT DWELLING IN ALL THINGS

At the end of his popular book *A Brief History of Time*, physicist Stephen Hawking asks a famous question: "What is it that breathes fire into the equations and makes a universe for them to describe?"[6] In the integrity of his adherence to atheism, he leaves the question open. Biblical faith answers that it is the Spirit who breathes life into the exuberant, diverse, interrelated universe. The mystery of the living God, utterly transcendent, is also the dynamic power at the heart of the world and its evolution. This refers to divine action not just in the beginning at the Big Bang but even now, persistently, as the universe continues to take shape into the future. The Creator Spirit is the unceasing, dynamic flow of loving power that sustains the world, brings forth life, weaves connections between all creatures, and repairs what gets damaged, all the while being profoundly present at the heart of all things.

This has not always been remembered. Classical theology's brilliant achievement was to establish the transcendence of God beyond any second thoughts. But it was less keen on divine immanence, the nearness of the incomprehensible God dwelling intimately in the depths of the world from the beginning, throughout history, unto the end. Just as new cosmology reconfigures the relationship between human beings and the Earth, it also leads to reappropriation of this truth. In no way am I suggesting that theology should ignore transcendence, or collapse the difference between God and the world. But the stunning world opened up by Big Bang cosmology and evolutionary biology points to the value of envisioning and relating to God not at the apex of a pyramid but within and around the emerging, struggling, living, and dying circle of life.

To retrieve this ancient sense of relationship, theology needs a trinitarian framework. In various ways this will express the Christian understanding that the one God known to us through Jesus Christ and the Spirit is threefold, being transcendent, incarnate, and immanent in the world. In the late second century, prior to any developed doctrine, the theologian Tertullian used a suite of nature images to explain this. If God the Father can be likened to the sun, then Christ is the sunbeam coming to Earth, and the Spirit is the suntan, the spot of warmth where the sun actually arrives and has an effect. Similarly, the Trinity can be likened to an upwelling spring of water, the river flowing from it, and the irrigation ditch where the water reaches plants and makes them grow. The triune God can also be compared to the root, the shoot, and the fruit of a tree: a deep unreachable foundation, its sprouting into the world, and its power which produces flower, fragrance, fruit, and seed.[7]

These are all metaphors for the God beyond the world, who as God comes forth in the flesh to be with the world in history, and as God again actually has an effect producing goodness in the world. Note that in this framework the Spirit is always God who arrives in every moment, drawing near and passing by with life-giving power. This divine presence can be understood as having at least three characteristics.

Creative Presence

From the opening scene in the Bible where the Spirit moves over the waters at the beginning of creation, to the last scene where the Spirit invites all who are thirsty for the water of life to "Come," the spirit of God, or *ruah* in Hebrew, also known as breath or wind, is at play everywhere in the natural world. The effect of this presence is to bring everything into being and to empower its life. The book of Wisdom puts this eloquently:

> For you love all things that exist, and detest none of the
>   things that you have made,
> for you would not have made anything if you had hated
>   it. . . .
> How would anything have endured if you had not willed
>   it? . . .
> For your immortal spirit is in all things. (11:24–12:1)

Centuries later the Nicene Creed brings this insight to a different expression when it confesses belief that the Holy Spirit is "the Lord and giver of life," in Latin *Dominus et vivificantem,* the Vivifier.

One mental schema that allows for an intelligible interpretation of this indwelling is known as panentheism, a mash-up from the Greek words meaning all-in-God. Unlike philosophical theism, which infers God to be the uncreated solitary being utterly distant from the created world; and unlike pantheism (all is God), which erases the difference between created and uncreated, thereby collapsing God and the world into each other, panentheism posits a relationship where everything abides *in* the Creator Spirit who in turn encompasses everything. Here the Giver of Life is not only "over all" but also "through all and in all" (Eph 4:6). Conversely, this is the Life-giver "in whom we live and move and have our being" (Acts 17:28). What results is a mutual abiding for which the pregnant female body provides a good metaphor.

Augustine long ago depicted such indwelling in memorable terms:

> I set before the sight of my spirit the whole creation, what-
> soever we can see therein (as sea, earth, air, stars, trees,
> mortal creatures); yea and whatever in it we do not see.
> ...But Thee, O Lord, I imagined on every part environing
> and penetrating it, though in every way infinite: as if
> there were a sea, everywhere and on every side, through
> unmeasured space, one only boundless sea, and it con-
> tained within it some sponge, huge, but bounded; that
> sponge must needs, in all its parts, be filled with that im-
> measurable sea: so conceived I Thy creation, itself finite,
> yet full of Thee, the Infinite; and I said, Behold God, and
> behold what God hath created; and God is good, yea,
> most mightily and incomparably better than all these...[8]

The natural world of Augustine's day was thought to be static, set up by God in the beginning and largely unchanging. The
creative presence of God that he envisioned takes on new contours in an evolutionary universe. Present as sea to sponge, the
Spirit of God is supremely radiant, relational energy, continuously creating in and through the processes of nature which have
their own integrity. Like a great creative Matrix, the Spirit of God
grounds and sustains the cosmos and attracts it toward the future. Throughout the vast sweep of cosmic and biological evolution, the Spirit embraces the material root of life and its endless
new potential, empowering the cosmic process from within. The
universe, in turn, is self-organizing and self-transcending, energized from the spiraling galaxies to the double helix of the DNA
molecule by the Spirit's quickening power.

Cruciform Presence

There is yet more to be said, for the natural world is not only
beautiful in its harmonies. It also presents us with an unrelent-
ingly harsh and bloody picture, filled with suffering and death.
Bodily existence requires eating; hence predation is an inescapable
part of the pattern of biological life. On a grand scale, the history
of life itself is dependent on death; without death there would be
no evolutionary development from generation to generation. The

history of life is a story of suffering and death over millions of millennia. The temptation is to deny the violence and escape into a romantic view of the natural world. But there is another option, namely, to seek the Creator Spirit in the midst of pain.

To do so, theology performs a typical maneuver, taking its eyes off the immediate question to consult the gospel. Christian theology interprets Jesus as the Word and Wisdom of God, the one whose life, death, and resurrection reveal the character of the living God. What do we glimpse through this lens? A merciful love that knows no bounds, a compassion that enters into the depth of human beings' lives of sin, suffering, and terrifying death, to bring new life. An ecological vision gives theology warrant to cross the species line and extend this divine solidarity to all creatures. The Spirit of God dwells in compassionate solidarity with every living being that suffers, from the dinosaurs wiped out by an asteroid to the baby impala eaten by a lioness. Not a sparrow falls to the ground without eliciting a knowing suffering in the heart of God, who constantly works to renew the face of the earth.

Such an idea is not meant to glorify suffering, a trap that must be carefully avoided. But it works out an implication of the vivifying Spirit's relation to an evolutionary, suffering world with an eye to divine compassion. Nature's crying out is met by the Spirit who groans with the labor pains of all creation to bring the new to birth (Rom 8:22–23). Thus is the pattern of cross and resurrection found at work on a cosmic scale.

Futuring Presence

Rather than being a settled place, the universe is ever changing. In the beginning was a homogenous sea of radiation. Rather than remain at a granular level of existence, the universe has taken shape extravagantly over time, emerging into increasingly elaborate forms. Biologists such as Stephen Jay Gould warn against interpreting this story as a necessary, directional, linear march from the Big Bang to the human race. The story of life is more like a branching bush, with humanity itself one recent twig on one branch of the bush. While granting this point, other scientists argue that since the universe as a whole has in fact moved in a certain direction from its cosmic origins, it obviously has propensities toward ever more complexity, beauty, and ordered novelty. Taking the long view we can see that from the beginning the universe is seeded with promise, pregnant with surprise. More has regularly come from less. The cosmic story has been one of restless adventure that produces the genuinely new.

Indwelling the world with creative compassion, the Creator Spirit's presence is future-oriented, luring the world along the paths of creative advance. This realization connects the natural world squarely with the biblical story, where God is a God of surprises who keeps approaching with a call to "come ahead" into the future, promised but unknown. Think of the call to Abraham and Sarah to leave their home and travel to a new land, capped off by the surprising gift of a child to them in their sterile old age (Gen 12–21). Think of the summons to the Hebrew people enslaved in Egypt to pass over the sea into freedom (Ex 1–15). Think of the surprising annunciation to an unknown young woman in a poor village inviting her to bear the Messiah (Lk 1:26–38). Think of Christ's commission to the women disciples at his empty tomb to go and announce that he is risen (Mt 28:1–10; Jn 20:1–18).

Divine presence in human history keeps acting unexpectedly to open up the future. So too with the natural world: the vivifying Spirit is forever at work, generously bringing forth novelty in the world of nature. And the adventure is not yet finished. The natural world is the bearer of divine promise that moves toward the final day when heaven and earth will be transformed by divine blessing: "Behold, I make all things new" (Rev 21:5).

ACTION OF THE CREATOR SPIRIT

The presence of Creator Spirit in the natural world raises in direct fashion the question of divine agency. How does God act in an evolutionary, emergent universe? The scientific picture of the universe indicates that over uncounted millennia, nature actively emerges into new forms at all levels. Even the dawning of life and then of mind can be accounted for without special supernatural intervention. How is one to think of the creative action of God?

One mistaken religious concept places divine intent and action directly into the physical nexus of the universe. The bitterness of the disputes between adherents of intelligent design and the so-called new atheists is due to the fact that they both share this assumption. Fundamentalists posit direct divine action in the evolving world while the materialist scientists find no trace of any such action. I want to say: a plague on both your houses. The fundamental view of how God acts that is held by both parties is inadequate. It is this deficient view of God's action as part of the physical nexus of the universe that gets contemporary discussion into impossible dead-ends.

Disputes within theology over divine agency can be just as fierce as those between science and religion. At least six positions claim a seat at the table. Single action theory understands God to have acted once, in the beginning; since then, God sustains the world while the details of cosmic history are just how it all happens to work out (Gordon Kaufman, Maurice Wiles). Positing much more divine involvement, process thought holds that God provides initial aims to every emerging event, and acts by the power of persuasion to lure the world in a desired direction (Alfred North Whitehead, John B. Cobb, David Griffin). Making an analogy with the agency of embodied human persons, a third position envisions the world as the body of God, with God acting in the world the way the soul acts in the body (Grace Jansen, Sallie McFague). Using information theory, the top-down causality position understands that God acts in the world through the influence of the whole upon the parts (Arthur Peacocke). The "causal joint" theory uses the innate openness of physical processes to predicate that God acts as one of the initial conditions of an event, in-putting the pattern that influences the overall outcome (John Polkinghorne, Nancey Murphy, Robert Russell).

A sixth, more classical position holds to the distinction between primary and secondary causality, or ultimate and created causes. As the unfathomable Source of the world's existence, God bestows natural forces and individual creatures with power to act with their own independence. Divine agency is then effective through the working out of natural causes. These two causes are not two species of the same genus, not two different types of causes united on a common ground of generating effects. They operate on completely different levels (itself an inadequate analogy), one being the ultimate generator of all causes, the other participating in this power to act, as things that are burning participate in the power of fire. This idea continues to be articulated by some Catholic thinkers today. Working in this tradition, Australian Denis Edwards observes,

> Thomas Aquinas (1225–1274) long ago clarified that God's way of acting in the world (what can be called primary causality) is not opposed to the whole network of cause and effect in nature (secondary causality). God's work is achieved in and through creaturely cause and effect. It is not in competition with it. Aquinas never knew Darwin's theory of evolution, but he would have had no difficulty in understanding it as the way that God creates.[9]

While markedly different from each other, these various positions have much in common. They shun an extrinsic model of divine activity as if God had to intervene in the world. They seek to make intelligible the idea that the Creator Spirit, as ground, sustaining power, and goal of the evolving world, acts by *empowering* the process from within. They see divine creativity acting *in*, *with*, and *under* cosmic processes. God makes the world, in other words, by empowering the world to make itself.

Chance and Law

Even granting this, what makes the conversation so dicey for theology is chance. Unlike the science of the Enlightenment period, which envisioned the universe operating in a determined, mechanistic way, today's science has revealed the existence of extensive zones of openness in nature. In these areas what happens next is *intrinsically* unpredictable. This is not because we have not yet developed instruments capable of measuring such systems and thus predicting outcomes. Rather, there is something in nature itself that defies total measurement. The microscopic realm studied by quantum physics is one such zone; large, non-linear, dynamic systems studied by the physics of chaos are another; the biological development of species by natural selection is a third.

Take as an example the non-linear, dynamic system of weather. One day a butterfly flutters its wings in Beijing; the small current of air it sets in motion cascades upward in ever-amplifying intersection with other air currents; one week later, as a result, there is a major storm in New York. There is no simple cause and effect; rather, there is an open, dynamic system that can be tipped this way or that way with the most minute changes. Over time, a certain statistical pattern will emerge as the systems continue to work. But given the sensitivity of the system to initial conditions, in any given instance no sure prediction is possible.

Or take biological evolution. Things run along smoothly until some slight change is introduced: a gene mutates due to bombardment by solar rays, or a hurricane blows a few birds off course to a new island, or the Earth is struck by an asteroid. This disrupts smooth operations to the point almost of breakdown. Then out of this turbulence evolves a more intricate order adapted to the new conditions.

Technically speaking, random events working within lawful regularities over eons of time have crafted the shape of the world that we inhabit today. If there were only law in the universe, the situation would stagnate. If there were only chance, things would become so chaotic that no orderly structures could take shape. But chance working within nature's laws disrupts the usual pattern while being held in check, and over millennia their interplay allows the emergence of genuinely new forms that cannot be reduced to previous components. This chance-within-law pattern over deep time is precisely what one would expect if the evolving universe were not predetermined, but were left free to explore its potential by experimenting with the fullest range of possibilities inherent in matter.

This means that as far as science can fathom, the universe's unfolding has not happened according to a pre-determined blueprint. A startling moment occurred at an annual meeting of the Catholic Theological Society of America when Bill Stoeger, Jesuit astrophysicist from the Vatican Observatory at the University of Arizona, asked: Rewind the clock of the world back to the first moment and let it start ticking again: would things turn out the same way? The scientific consensus is an emphatic "No," given the intrinsic role of chance. There was stunned silence and then an eruption of argument as a roomful of theologians tried to wrap their minds around this idea and relate it to our basic ideas about divine providence.

How does the intrinsic role of chance impact our understanding of divine agency? Theology now discovers that the indwelling Creator Spirit not only grounds nature's regularities, being the source of law, but also empowers the chancy interruptions of regularity that bring about new forms. Boundless love at work in, with, and under the processes of the universe, the Spirit embraces the chanciness of random mutations and chaotic conditions of open systems, being the source not only of order but also of the novelty that causes chaos to happen in the first place. Divine creativity is much more closely allied to disorder than our older theologies ever imagined. In the emergent evolutionary universe, we should not be surprised to find divine creativity hovering very close to turbulence.

The concept of divine power in this ecological theology is obviously different from omnipotence wielded in a monarchical way of giving top-down orders. On many fronts today theology has been working to redefine divine omnipotence as the power of love. Mature love grants autonomy to the beloved and respects this, all the while participating in the joy and pain of the other's destiny. It vigorously cares for, works for, and urges the beloved toward his or her own well-being, but coercion is not in the picture. While worked out primarily in the doctrine of grace, which sees God inviting but never forcing free human response, this idea gains added currency in the framework of an ecology that has discovered the capacity of nature to self-organize and emerge into ever-new, more complex forms. If the empowering source of nature is the Creator Spirit, then divine power is acting here in a self-emptying, infinitely humble, and loving way, a christic way one might say, endowing the universe with the capacity to become itself.

In more classical language, the Giver of life not only creates and conserves all things, holding them in existence over the abyss of nothingness, but is also the dynamic ground of their becoming, empowering from within their self-transcendence into new being. This is not a denial of divine omnipotence, but its redefinition. The Spirit of God moves in the world with compassionate love that grants nature its own creativity and humans their own freedom, all the while companioning them through the terror of history toward a new future.

In view of the openness of the natural world, John Haught suggests, happily in my view, that we should no longer think of God as having a set plan for the evolving universe, but rather a vision.[10] This vision aims at bringing into being a community of love. The Creator Spirit is at the heart of the process, guiding the world in that direction, all the while inviting the world to participate in its own creation through the free working of its own systems. At the quantum level, in non-linear dynamic systems, through natural selection, and by free human agency—the new emerges! Grounded and vivified by such freeing power, the universe evolves in the integrity of its own proper autonomy.

ETHICAL CHALLENGE

An ecological theology of the Creator Spirit in the natural world not only expands our awareness of divine presence. It also reframes understanding of the natural world itself. Instead of being divorced from what is holy, matter bears the mark of the sacred, being imbued with a spiritual radiance. For the Spirit creates what is physical—stars, planets, plants, animals, ecological communities, bodies, senses, sexuality—and moves in these every bit as vigorously as in souls, minds, ideas. Catholic sacramental theology has always taught that simple material things such as bread and wine, water, oil, the sexual union of marriage can be bearers of divine grace. This is so, it now becomes clear, because to begin with the whole physical world itself is the locale of God's gracious indwelling, a primordial sacrament of divine presence.

This leads to the crucial realization that the natural world enjoys its own intrinsic value before God. It is not created simply for human use, nor is it only an instrument to serve our needs. We can no longer reduce divine care to one newly arriving species, *homo sapiens*. Far from being a mere backdrop for our human lives or a stage for our drama, the natural world is a beloved creation valued by God for its own sake.

Hence this creation theology directs the church to hear the divine challenge to practice love and justice in a new key, in terms of responsible, assertive care for the Earth. We owe love and justice not only to humankind but also to "otherkind." In such an ecological ethic, Jesus' great command to love your neighbor as yourself extends to include all members of the Earth community. "Who is my neighbor?" asks Brian Patrick. He answers: "The Samaritan? The outcast? The enemy? Yes, yes, of course. But it is also the whale, the dolphin, and the rain forest. Our neighbor is the entire community of life, the entire universe. We must love it all as our very self."[11] Converting minds and hearts to such an Earth ethic entails at least three responses that will enable us to live as partners with God in continuing creation rather than as destroyers of the world.

❖ The contemplative response. Here we gaze on the Earth with eyes of love rather than with an arrogant, utilitarian stare. We will not save what we do not love, and this response begins by awakening our biophilic desires. As the scientist Louis Agassiz noted: "I spent the summer traveling; I got half-way across my back yard."[12] The wonders of our planet are a source of revelation. Anyone who has ever glimpsed the beauty of God through an experience of delight or awe in the natural world knows this. The contemplative response engages the natural world with religious imagination and heart, allowing it to lift our minds and hearts to God and enfolding it into our religious love.

❖ The ascetic response. Here we restrain our rampant consumerism and self-indulgence in order to protect the Earth. A sensuous, Earth-affirming asceticism leads us to live more simply:

observe the Sabbath as a genuine day of rest; fast from shopping; endure the inconvenience of running an ecologically-sensitive household; and conduct business with an eye to the green bottom line as well as the red or black. We do these things not to make ourselves suffer and not because we're anti-body, but so that we can become alert to how enslaved we are by the marketplace and act to offset its effect on the planet.

❖ The prophetic response. Here we take critical action on behalf of the survival of the planet. The ongoing destruction of the Earth is a deeply sinful desecration. In the tradition of biblical prophecy and the spirit of Jesus, we counter this destruction by acting for the well-being of the ecological world, taking on the opposition of powerful political and economic interests that want to use nature simply as a source of profit. If nature is the new poor, as Sallie McFague insists, then our passion to establish justice for the poor and oppressed must now extend to include suffering human beings AND life systems and other species under threat.[13] "Save the rain forest" becomes a concrete moral application of the commandment, "Thou shalt not kill." The moral goal becomes ensuring vibrant life in community for all.

CONCLUSION

A theology of creation that makes full acknowledgment of the Creator Spirit has two benefits. First, it opens doors to new forms of relationship with the all-holy God present and active throughout the whole world. The Holy One who fires up the blaze of being does not stand over against the world, or rule it as a king from afar, but dwells in vivifying and compassionate relationship with human beings and the whole universe, attracting all into the future. Second, this theology motivates an ethic of care for the Earth. Instead of living as thoughtless or greedy exploiters, we start to live as sisters and brothers, friends and lovers, mothers and fathers, priests and prophets, co-creators and children of this Earth which God so loves.

The creative Giver of life abides in the natural world, forever moving over the void, breathing into the chaos, pouring out, informing, quickening, warming, groaning, interrupting, comforting, setting free, befriending, empowering, challenging, and blessing. Now when we hear that "the love of God has been poured into our hearts by the Holy Spirit given to us" (Rom 5:5), we realize that this love is universal: human, planetary, and cosmic. Then the door will be open to enfold the natural world into the vibrant practice of faith.

Adapted from the Spiritan Lecture, Duquesne University, Pittsburgh, PA, 2008.

Notes

1. Cited in Michael Dowd, *Earthspirit* (Mystic, CT: Twenty-Third Pub., 1991), 95.

2. Carl Sagan, *Dragons of Eden* (New York: Random House, 1977), 13–17.

3. Arthur Peacocke, "Theology and Science Today," in *Cosmos as Creation*, ed. Ted Peters (Nashville: Abingdon Press, 1989), 32.

4. Charles Darwin, *On the Origin of Species*, annotations by James Costa (Cambridge, MA: Harvard University Press, 2009), 130.

5. World Council of Churches, Canberra Assembly, "Giver of Life Sustain Your Creation!" in *Signs of the Spirit*, ed. Michael Kinnamon (Eerdmans: Grand Rapids, MI: 1991), 55.

6. Stephen Hawking, *A Brief History of Time* (New York: Bantam Books, 1988), 174.

7. These images are suggested by Tertullian, *Adversus Praxeas*, 8.

8. Augustine, *Confessions*, VII:7.

9. Denis Edwards, *The God of Evolution* (New York: Paulist Press, 1999), 47.

10. John Haught, *The Promise of Nature* (New York: Paulist Press, 1993).

11. Brian Patrick, cited in Dowd, *Earthspirit*, 40.

12. Cited in Holmes Rolston, *Philosophy Gone Wild: Essays in Environmental Ethics* (Buffalo, NY: Prometheus, 1986), 241.

13. Sallie McFague, *The Body of God: An Ecological Theology* (Minneapolis: Fortress, 1993), 200–202.

7

Creation

Is God's Charity Broad Enough for Bears?

In our day, awareness of the magnificence of Earth as a small planet hospitable to life is growing among peoples everywhere. It is an ecological awareness, ecological from the Greek word *oikos*, meaning household or home. This living planet, with its thin spherical shell of land, water, and breathable air, is home for human beings, our only home in the vast universe. It is also home to a wondrous diversity of species that interrelate to form networks of living ecosystems. Perhaps life exists in some form on other planets (Mars?) or moons (Europa?) of the solar system, or on extrasolar planets in the Milky Way galaxy. Definite knowledge one way or the other lies in the future. At this moment Earth, a jewel of a blue marble floating in a black sea of space, is the only place we know of in the vast universe where life abundant abides.

Thanks to the heritage of Jewish faith, Christians believe in God who creates heaven and earth and everything in them. The Bible and the creeds of the church give pride of place to this belief, starting as they do with the Creator who makes all things, visible and invisible. Is creation only a wondrous event that took place "in the beginning"? Is belief in creation only a backdrop to the more serious business of redemption? Or does the Giver of life keep on singing the natural world into being at every moment of its evolution, with compassion for its suffering and commitment to its wellbeing? In our day of undoubted ecological crisis, we do well to probe the meaning of creation with an eye to expanding nature's religious importance. The goal of such reflection is to invigorate ethical behavior that cares for plants and animals with a passion integral to our love of God. Once we see that the evolving community of life on Earth continues to be the dwelling place of the Spirit and its ruination an unspeakable sin; once we understand that this community is blessedly included in the redeemed future promised in Jesus Christ; then deep affection shown in action on behalf of eco-justice becomes an indivisible part of spirituality.

A provocative story opens up our theme. Once when the noted nineteenth-century naturalist John Muir was hiking in the Yosemite wilderness, he came upon a dead bear. He stopped to reflect on this creature's dignity: an animal with warm blood and a heart that pumped like ours, whose fur was ruffled by the wind, who rejoiced in a sunny day and a bush filled with berries. Later he wrote a bitter entry in his journal, criticizing the religious folk he knew who made no room in their faith for such noble creatures. They think they are the only ones with souls, he complained, the only ones for whom heaven is reserved. To the contrary, he wrote, "God's charity is broad enough for bears."[1]

Is it? Is ours? The question deserves consideration. After introducing the classical theological meaning of creation and reasons for its neglect, this reflection focuses on the natural world's relation to God in the Spirit through Christ, ending with the need to be converted to the earth on which we live in a community of creatures. I offer these probes into a theology of creation not so much in the hope that you will necessarily agree as in the hope that they will stimulate your own thinking about the precious meaning of the world of life.

CREATION: THREE DIMENSIONS

Creation is a religious term that places the natural world in relationship to God as its origin, sustainer, and goal. In popular usage creation is usually taken to refer to an event in the past that began the history of the universe. But in a surprising way it means much more than that. Classical theology speaks of creation in three senses: *creatio originalis, creatio continua, creatio nova,* that is, original creation in the beginning, continuous creation in the present here and now, and new creation at the redeemed end-time.

❖ *Originalis*: At the outset, being created means that all creatures, including plants and animals, receive their life as a gift from the living God and exist in utter reliance on that gift. They owe their existence to God: this is the core of *creatio originalis*. In ultimate terms they do not bring themselves into being nor does their existence explain itself. Their very being here at all relies on the overflowing generosity of the Creator who freely shares life with the world; in the Bible's opening words: "In the beginning God created the heavens and the earth" (Gen 1:1).

Theology has traditionally used the phrase "out of nothing" to stress how divine this act is, and how free. There was no pre-existing material that the Creator used to fashion the world. There were no other gods or no Satan with whom the Creator had to wrestle to bring about the world. And there was no pressure, no necessity, to do this. Nothing and no one was there to bring any coercion to bear. Creation came into being not out of necessity but as an absolutely free and generous act of God's own gracious, loving will, welling up from the unfathomable plenitude of divine being. *Creatio originalis* means that as creatures, plants and animals do not ultimately ground themselves but are rooted in a power beyond themselves. In this light, their existence is a sheer gift. And it is good.

❖ *Continua*: In addition to their origin in God's gracious act, plants and animals continue to be held in life and empowered to act in every moment by the Giver of life. Without this sustaining presence, they would sink back into nothingness. The living God did not retire after the six days of creation, but divine creativity is active here, now, in the next minute, or there would be no world at all. As we read in the book of Wisdom: "The Spirit of the Lord has filled the world (1:7), and "your immortal spirit is in all things" (12:1).

❖ *Nova*: The God of life, source of endless possibilities, continues to draw the world into a future marked by a radical promise, namely, that at the ultimate end of time the Creator of all will not abandon the world but will re-create it anew. On the last day God will transform the world in an unimaginable way into a new creation in communion with divine life. Being created means that living creatures are the bearers of this great and hopeful promise. As we read at the end of the Bible: "Behold, I make all things new" (Rev 21:5).

The fourteenth-century mystic and theologian Julian of Norwich catches the connection between these three dimensions of creation in one of her beautiful visions:

> And in this [Christ] showed me something small, no bigger than a hazelnut, lying in the palm of my hand, as it seemed to me, and it was as round as a ball. I looked at it with the eye of my understanding and thought: What can this be? I was amazed that it could last, for I thought that because of its littleness it would suddenly have fallen into nothing. And I was answered in my understanding: It lasts and always will, because God loves it; and thus everything has being through the love of God.[2]

What a profoundly simple observation, based on the conviction that God is faithful. Creation in the beginning, the fact that it continues to endure, and its promised renewal at the end come from the same source: infinite love.

NEGLECT

The threefold meaning of creation, past, present, and to come, clearly renders the natural world religiously significant in terms of its own relationship to God. Over the centuries, however, especially in the theology of the West as compared to Eastern Orthodox thought, interest narrowed down to focus on human beings almost exclusively. Granted, we are a fascinating lot. But our special identity, our sinfulness, and our need for salvation became all-consuming, to the point where the natural world was virtually ignored. A good deal of recent analysis has tried to figure out why this happened.

One obvious factor is the early Christian encounter with Hellenistic philosophy, which separated spirit from matter and ranked them in value, prizing spirit over matter. Using this dualistic framework, Christian thinkers developed a view that for one to become holy, the body with its passions along with the physical world needed to be tamed if not disregarded, for material things trap the spirit and distract it from the transcendent good of heaven. The spirituality typically associated with this influential thought pattern was shaped by the metaphor of ascent: to be holy a person must flee the material world and rise to the spiritual sphere where the light of divinity dwells. One must turn away from bodiliness and the earth, in other words, in order to have communion with God. This view relegated plants and animals to the realm of the non-important since they lack spirit (souls) and belong solely to earth.

A later factor that promoted the turn away from creation was the medieval distinction between natural and supernatural. The category of the supernatural was introduced to protect the gratuity of grace. Since grace, a participation in God's own life, was a gift that humans neither possessed by nature nor could demand, language about the *super*-natural guaranteed that God was free and uncoerced in giving such a gift: it was not owed to us by nature. While the core of this view is surely true, the distinction itself led thinkers to place all important divine action on the supernatural side and to leach the presence of the divine out of what was simply natural, where, I want to emphasize, God also acts. The law of unintended consequences took over. Instead of being understood as God's free gift, the natural world came to be seen as simply a given. It functioned as prolegomena and background to the more important divine work of supernatural redemption.

A further blow to prizing the natural world occurred with the Reformation. The fight over how Christ saves us from sin, whether by faith alone, the Protestant view, or by faith and good works, the Catholic position (and I am terribly oversimplifying here), led to a focus on the human need for salvation that blinkered our eyes to the rest of creation. With few exceptions, after the sixteenth century one is hard pressed to find a theological treatise on creation in either Catholic or Protestant dogmatics. The theme had a place in the manuals, but it was not a subject of theological development.

The modern era hammered yet another nail in nature's coffin by crafting an imperialistic interpretation of Genesis. In the first creation story, God gives the human couple the mandate to have "dominion" over the rest of life (Gen 1:26). In the post-Enlightenment world, as European nations began to colonize other continents, an aggressive entrepreneurial culture interpreted this mandate to have dominion to mean that humans had the right to have *domination* over nature. Resources were there to be extracted. Plants and animals receded to being mere creatures for human use. Bereft of a robust creation theology due to its long focus on human sin and need for salvation, the church did not have resources to push back against this view. Not to be missed is the way elite peoples also applied this mandate to other human beings: white Europeans had the right to dominate darker, indigenous peoples.

Theological reasons for the eclipse of nature in the life of faith are many and run deep. They shaped the understanding of faith that John Muir so criticized, where the love of God was focused on human beings but had no room for bears. The magnificence of the world as we understand it today, along with its intense ecological distress, challenge us to broaden our focus and reclaim the natural world as religiously meaningful. This is not a matter of either-or, of either human importance or the value of all other life. The ecological crisis makes clear that the human species and the natural world will flourish or collapse together. But given the long eclipse of interest in other species, the mandate now is to bring the buzzing, blooming world of life back into focus. I propose that attending to the largely overlooked meaning of continuous creation goes a fair distance to accomplish this task.

REMEMBERING THE TRIUNE GOD OF LOVE

Recall that besides referring to the beginning and end of things, creation also entails the presence of God at every moment, dwelling within the natural world, sustaining its life, and empowering its evolutionary advance. A search of sources in the Christian tradition reveals that this presence is most often referred to in language about the Spirit: the Spirit of God, the Holy Spirit, the Creator Spirit, the one whom the Nicene Creed calls the "Lord and Giver of life," or in Latin, *vivificantem*, the Vivifier. It becomes clear that neglect of the Spirit is yet another key factor that has contributed to the neglect of the natural world. To do justice to creation, what is needed is a robust pneumatology. Furthermore, continuous creation also needs to engage with christology. This idea is newer on our theological horizon—what has Christ got to do with the plants and animals? But Jesus' preaching recounted in the gospels as well as the meaning of his death and resurrection connect divine compassion to the enormous magnitude of suffering and death entailed in life's evolution, and ground hope.

Let us be clear that once we introduce the Spirit of God and Jesus Christ to the discussion of creation, we are going counter to the prevailing image of the Creator as a single, male authority figure who dwells beyond the world with a transcendence that contrasts with immanence, and whose action in the world has the character of an intervention. Becoming more pronounced at the origin of the modern era, this idea of the Creator was modeled on the image of an absolute monarch ruling his realm. It envisions that the whole world reflects the will of the king who holds sway over his kingdom, directing events. Everything exists according to a prescribed plan, fulfilling its purpose in the way the ruler intends. Reflecting an ancient worldview that knew only a monarchical political system, this metaphor continues to haunt popular language today, affecting even insurance claims about "acts of God."

Difficulties with this picture arise when the theory of evolution makes clear that the world's gorgeous design has not been executed by direct divine agency, from above, but is the result of innumerable, infinitesimal adaptations of creatures to their environment, from below. The problem is made more acute by the fact that the variations (the genetic mutations) on which natural selection works occur by chance. The presence of genuine randomness, the absence of direct design, the enormity of suffering and extinction, and the ambling character of life's emergence over billions of years are hard to reconcile with a unitary, monarchical idea of the Creator. Such an individual is "too small" to go the distance for the natural world, let alone for the vast, incomprehensible richness of the holy Mystery of God. Our idea of the Creator needs expanding toward something always ever greater, namely the trinitarian mystery of the God of love. We turn, then, to an exploration of the Spirit and Christ in relation to creation.

SPIRIT: SINGER OF CONTINUOUS CREATION

A stunning metaphor crafted by the British philosopher Herbert McCabe expresses the creative presence of the Spirit in the world in unforgettable terms: "The Creator makes all things and keeps them in existence from moment to moment—not like a sculptor, who makes a statue and leaves it alone, but like a singer who keeps her song in existence at all times."[3] Theology traditionally speaks about this music in language of the Spirit. Everything enjoys its own existence by the creative power of the Spirit who abides, as Scripture says, "over all and through all and in all" (Eph 4:6). If the presence of the Creator Spirit were withdrawn for even an instant, the world itself would revert to nothing.

To allude to this divine presence, the Bible uses cosmic images of blowing wind, flowing water, and blazing fire. None of these forces has a definite, stable shape; they surround and pervade other things without losing their own character; their presence is known by the changes they bring about. Not that the Spirit of God is impersonal. But compared with anthropomorphic images drawn from human beings who are physically limited in time and place, these natural phenomena seem particularly suited to draw out the surging creative energy which religious language seeks to express.

Take, for example, fire. Prized for its warmth and light but also at times uncontrollably dangerous, fire symbolizes the presence of the divine in most of the world's religions. Lighting lamps or candles and burning incense are typical ritual acts. Biblical references to fire as symbol of the divine are many: recall the burning bush where Moses encountered the call to deliver the Israelites from enslavement (Ex 3:2); recall Pentecost, when tongues of fire descended on 120 of Jesus' disciples gathered in the upper room, women and men alike, "and they were all filled with the Holy Spirit" (Acts 2:4). For human beings, the approach of the fire of the Spirit always signals the coming of grace, liberation, comfort, healing, boldness, something new. As among people so too in nature: the whole of creation is pervaded, lit up, energized, made bold, called forth on its evolutionary journey by the fire of the Spirit. In a lovely poetic oracle, Hildegard of Bingen channels the Giver of life this way:

> I, the highest and fiery power, have kindled every living spark and I have breathed out nothing that can die....I flame above the beauty of the fields; I shine in the waters; in the sun, the moon and the stars, I burn. And by means of the airy wind, I stir everything into quickness with a certain invisible life which sustains all....I, the fiery power, lie hidden in these things and they blaze from me.[4]

The cosmic images of the Bible offer a way for thought and feeling to intuit the omnipresence of the Spirit as life-giving, life-empowering love.

Translating this intuition into more rational discourse, Thomas Aquinas provides a clear conceptual basis for the same subject. Considering God to be the active wellspring of life, the One whose very essence is "to be," he envisions that God creates the world by giving a share in "being" to finite creatures, who in turn *participate* in being in ways appropriate to their own nature. Exploring this relation, Aquinas asks "whether God is in all things." His positive answer draws on fire and light in a way that repays careful reading:

> I answer that, God is in all things; not, indeed, as part of their essence, nor as an accident, but as an agent is present to that upon which it works....Now since God is very being by his own essence, created being must be his proper effect; as to ignite is the proper effect of fire. Now

God causes this effect in things not only when they first begin to be, but as long as they are preserved in being; as light is caused in the air by the sun as long as the air remains illuminated. Therefore as long as a thing has being, God must be present to it, according to its mode of being. But being is innermost in each thing and most fundamentally inherent in all things.... Hence it must be that God is in all things, and innermostly.[5]

Just as fire ignites things and sets them on fire, the Spirit of God ignites the world into being. This obviously happens in the beginning but doesn't stop: just as the sun brightens the air all the day long, the presence of the Spirit sustains creatures with the radiance of being as long as they exist. The symbol of fire and the shining sun bespeak the *innermost* indwelling of the Spirit throughout the universe, including the creatures of the natural world on planet Earth, empowering their life.

Now it becomes clear that the inner secret of ecological communities of plants and animals is the dwelling of the Spirit of God within them. Instead of being distant from what is holy, the evolving world bears the mark of the sacred, being itself imbued with a spiritual radiance. This is not to say it is divine. But unlike dualistic views that disparaged the material world of nature, or the natural-supernatural distinction that divorced it from God's graciousness, the doctrine of continuous creation sees the natural world in its own integrity as pervaded, vivified, and encompassed by the Spirit of God. This means that the natural world is sacramental: it bodies forth and communicates the gracious presence of God. It also means that the natural world is revelatory: it discloses something of divine wisdom, beauty, power, and imagination. If we listen well, we can even hear the plants and animals praising God, as some psalms depict. Augustine once preached to this effect:

Let your mind roam through the whole creation; everywhere the created world will cry out to you: "God made me."...Go round the heavens again and back to the earth, leave out nothing; on all sides everything cries out to you of its Author; nay, the very forms of created things are as it were the voices with which they praise their Creator.[6]

All of this held true before humans appeared on Earth and continues to be true even now, apart from human mediation. Plants and animals are profoundly related to God in their own right. The Creator Spirit is present within the world, sustaining its life, empowering its evolution, calling it forth to a fresh and unexpected future. Conversely, the natural world is the dwelling place of God's Spirit, able to speak in its own voice about the glory of its Maker.

CHRIST AND THE PELICAN CHICK

The natural world of living organisms is not just the beautiful dwelling place of the Creator Spirit, but also a place of agony insofar as life evolves at a terrible cost in pain and death. In Paul's telling observation, all creation is groaning like a woman in childbirth, in hope that it will be set free (Rom 8:18–25). The evolutionary world, some would say, is cruciform; it proceeds along the way of the cross. No new life without the sacrifice of death.

Death is deeply structured into the creative advance of life. Good often comes from this fact. Animals eat one another: in every instance of death by predation, the nutrients in the lifestream of one organism become a resource that nourishes the life of the other. Also, over the long haul, the struggle to escape death brings about rich, complex changes in structure and behavior: the speed and agility of the sea lion is due to the orca's hunt; the cheetah's tooth has carved the legs of the fleet-footed deer, and vice-versa. Furthermore, without death, not only would there be no food for eaters to eat, and no pressure for anatomical improvement, but eventually there would be *no room* for new sorts of creatures to emerge on a finite planet. Death arose as an essential element in a tremendously powerful process that created and continues to create the magnificent community of life on Earth.

And yet! The case of the backup pelican chick, increasingly used in theological discussion, brings this aspect of evolution to a head in riveting, problematic terms. Here is the situation. Female white pelicans ordinarily lay two eggs several days apart. The first chick to hatch eats, grows larger, becomes feisty. When the second hatches, the first tends to act aggressively toward the younger sibling, grabbing most of the food from the parents' pouch and often nudging the smaller bird out of the nest. There, ignored by its parents, the second-hatched chick normally suffers starvation and dies, despite its struggle to rejoin the family. Before this denouement, there is a window of opportunity in which, should some crisis befall the older chick, pelican parents can raise the second offspring and thereby have a successful reproductive season. It may also happen that in an especially good year the parents will feed and raise both chicks. But ordinarily the backup chick has only a 10 percent chance of surviving. It is born as insurance. For the pelicans as a species this has been a successful evolutionary strategy, enabling their kind to survive for thirty million years. As depicted on video and shown on television, however, the ostracized chick's pinched face, small cries, desperate attempts to regain the nest, and collapse from weakness to become food for the gulls is a scene of such distress as to call for an account of this suffering and death in a world that Jewish and Christian religion considers good, the more so as the anguish of this one little creature is continuously repeated on a grand scale.

Let the pelican chick stand for all the creatures on the tree of life who have suffered and died. A theology of continuous creation cannot ignore this unfathomable history of biological suffering and death extending over hundreds of millions of years. Its overwhelming power initially evokes the honest response of being struck dumb in the face of so much agony and loss. We have no words. As with the mystery of suffering among humans, its roots reach deeper than the human mind can fathom.

When theology does speak to this issue, the most fundamental move it can make, in my judgment, is to affirm the presence of God in the midst of the shocking enormity of pain and death. The Creator Spirit who indwells the world empowering its life *abides* amid the agony and loss. God who is love is there, in compassionate solidarity with the creatures shot through with pain and finished by death; there, in the godforsaken moment, as only the Giver of life can be, with the promise of something more.

In daring to think this way, Christian theology draws on a peculiar source of insight all its own, namely, the gospel story of Jesus Christ. After a joy-filled ministry, Jesus of Nazareth, an inspired prophet and compassionate healer, was brought down to a tortured, unjust death of the worst sort: he "was crucified, died, and was buried." Christians believe that in death he did not fall into nothingness but into the embrace of the living God who raised him from the dead, transforming his historical defeat into unimaginable new life in glory. Remembered at every Eucharist and celebrated at the high point of the church's liturgical year at Easter, this paschal mystery is proclaimed as "good news" for human beings, for it pledges that Jesus' destiny will be ours as well. Christ crucified and risen goes ahead of us like a pioneer, awakening hope that the future toward which we are going will be life, not death.

But what about the plants and animals, the pelican chick? Can hope for redemption be broadened to include all creatures that die? There are important reasons to answer "yes," starting with the broad belief that the living God creates and cares for all creatures. But here I would like to stay focused on Christ, and suggest that there is a clue lying in plain sight that allows us to gracefully connect redemption with the pelican chick. That clue is the meaning of "flesh."

Deep Incarnation

Odd as it may seem to others, Christians hold to the radical notion that the one transcendent God who creates and empowers the world freely chooses to save the world not as a kindly onlooker from afar, but by joining this world in the flesh. The prologue of John's gospel states this succinctly, speaking of the advent of Jesus as the coming of God's personal self-expressing Word, full of loving-kindness and faithfulness: "The Word was made flesh and dwelt among us" (Jn 1:14). Note that the gospel does not say that the Word became a human being (Greek *anthropos*), or a man (Greek *aner*), but flesh (Greek *sarx*), a broader reality. *Sarx* or flesh in the New Testament connotes the finite quality of the material world which is fragile, vulnerable, prone to trouble and sin, perishable, the very opposite of divine majesty. Taking the powerful biblical theme of God's dwelling among the people of Israel a step further, John's gospel affirms that in a new and saving event the Word of God *became* flesh, entered personally into the sphere of the material to shed light on all from within.

In truth, the configuration of *sarx* that the Word became was precisely human. However, the story of life on our planet is repositioning our species, connecting *Homo sapiens* historically and biologically to the whole tree of life. Rather than standing alone as a species, we are intrinsically related to other species in the evolutionary network of life on our planet. Consider this example, taken from Darwin's observations:

> What can be more curious than that the hand of a man, formed for grasping, that of a mole for digging, the leg of the horse, the paddle of the porpoise, and the wing of the bat, should all be constructed on the same pattern, and should include the same bones, in the same relative positions?[7]

On the ordinary view of the direct creation of each being, he writes, we can only say that it has pleased the Creator to construct each animal in this way. But if we suppose an ancient progenitor had its limbs arranged this way, he continues, then all descendants inherit the pattern. The bones might be enveloped in a thick membrane to form a paddle to swim, or a thin membrane to form a wing, or they may be lengthened or shortened for some profitable purpose; but there will be no tendency to alter the framework. Indeed, the same names can be given to the bones in widely different animals. What a grand natural system, formed by descent with slow and slight successive modifications!

The Word did indeed became human flesh; but we now know that human connection to nature is so genuine that we cannot properly define our identity without including the great natural world of which we are a part. Danish theologian Niels Gregersen has coined the phrase "deep incarnation," which is starting to be used in theology to signify the radical divine reach through human flesh all the way down into the very tissue of the biological existence itself with its growth and decay.[8]

Born of a woman and the Hebrew gene pool, the Word of God became a creature of Earth. Like all creatures Jesus was an earthling whose blood held iron made in exploding stars and whose genetic code made him kin to the whole community of life that descended from common ancestors in the ancient seas. "Deep incarnation" understands John 1:14 to be saying that the *sarx* which the Word of God became not only connects Jesus to other human beings; it also reaches beyond them to join him to the whole biological world of living creatures and the cosmic dust of which they are composed. As Pope John Paul II realized, the incarnation accomplishes "the taking up into unity with God not only of human nature, but in this human nature of everything that is 'flesh': the whole of humanity, the entire visible and material world. The Incarnation, then, has a cosmic significance..."[9]

Solidarity in Death

With this framework in place, follow what happens when we turn to the cross. In his own agonizing way Jesus of Nazareth shared the fate of all who die, which is every living thing. Christians have always seen in this horrific event a profound outpouring of redeeming grace. The cross discloses the compassionate nature of divine love which in Jesus Christ does not shrink from solidarity with sinful, suffering, dying human beings. It is as if by inhabiting the inside of the isolating shell of death Christ crucified brings divine life into closest contact with disaster, setting up a gleam of light for all others who suffer that darkness. Is the saving solidarity of the crucified God limited to human beings? Or does it extend to the whole community of life of which human beings are a part?

The logic of deep incarnation gives a strong warrant for extending divine love from the cross into the groan of suffering and the silence of death of all creatures. The ineffable compassion of

God embraces all who are perishing in the flesh. They remain connected to the living God despite what is happening; in fact, in the depths of what is happening. The indwelling, empowering Spirit of God, the Spirit of the crucified Christ who companions creatures in their individual lives and long-range evolution, does not abandon them in the moment of trial. The cross gives warrant for locating the compassion of God right at the center of their affliction. One may well ask if this kind of presence of the living God with creatures in their suffering makes any difference. In one sense it does not. Death goes on as before, destroying the individual. Wrestling intensely with this problem, British theologian Christopher Southgate admits as much: "When I consider the starving pelican chick, or the impala hobbled by a mother cheetah so that her cubs can learn to pull a prey animal down, I cannot pretend that God's presence as the 'heart' of the world takes the pain of the experience away; I cannot pretend that the suffering may not destroy the creature's consciousness, before death claims it. That is the power of suffering...." Reflecting further, however, his thought arrives at an awesome insight: "I can only suppose that God's suffering presence is just that, presence, of the most profoundly attentive and loving sort, a solidarity that at some deep level takes away the aloneness of the suffering creature's experience."[10] Understood in this context, the death of Christ becomes an icon of God's solidarity with all creatures in their dying, through endless millennia of evolution, from the extinction of species to every sparrow that falls to the ground. The pelican chick does not die alone.

Deep Resurrection

The gospel story does not end at the tomb. Led by Mary Magdalene, the women disciples who had not abandoned the crucified Jesus found his tomb empty and began the proclamation of the good news. He is risen! For Jesus personally, this means the abiding, redeemed validity of his human historical existence in God's presence forever. The *Alleluias* that break out at Easter, moreover, express the church's joy because Jesus' blessed destiny is meant not for himself alone but for us, for the whole human race. As an early Christian hymn put it poetically: Christ is the "firstborn from the dead" (Col 1:18)—the firstborn, but not the only born.

"Deep incarnation" directs this good news into the whole natural world. As Ambrose of Milan preached in the fifth century, "In Christ's resurrection the earth itself arose."[11] The reasoning runs like this. This person, Jesus of Nazareth, was composed of earthly matter; his body existed in a network of relationships drawn from and extending to the whole physical world. If through death and resurrection this "piece of this world, real to the core,"[12] as Karl Rahner writes, is now forever with God in glory, then this signals the beginning of redemption not just for other human beings but for all flesh, all material beings, every creature that passes through death. The evolving world of life, all of matter in its endless permutations, will not be left behind but will likewise be transfigured by the resurrecting action of the Creator Spirit. The same Colossians hymn that recognizes Christ as "firstborn of the dead" also names him "the firstborn of all creation" (Col 1:15). Christ is the firstborn of all the dead of Darwin's tree of life.

Such would not be the case if Easter marked simply the spiritual survival of Jesus' immortal soul after death. But Christ rose again in his *body*, and lives united with the body forever. As Sandra Schneiders concludes in her insightful discussion of this point, "Glorification is not the eradication of the body; it is the end of subjection to death."[13] While what this entails is unimaginable to us who remain alive within the limits of time and space, the tomb's emptiness signals this cosmic realism. Herein lies the hinge of hope for the final redemption of all living creatures. The coming final transformation of history in *creatio nova* will be the salvation of everything, including the evolving community of life and the whole cosmos itself, brought into communion with the God of life.

Once a year at the Easter Vigil the exuberant hymn *Exsultet* is sung in the light of the new paschal candle. Its opening lines are telling: "Exult, all creation, around God's throne," for Jesus Christ is risen! It continues, "Rejoice, O earth, in shining splendor, radiant in the brightness of your King! Christ has conquered! Glory fills you! Darkness vanishes forever!" Surprising as it may sound to our anthropocentric self-absorption, at the most magnificent liturgy of the year the church is singing to the earth! It, too, needs to hear the good news, because the risen Christ embodies the ultimate hope of all creation. In Jesus Christ, the living God who creates and empowers the evolutionary world also joins the fray, personally drinks the cup of suffering, goes down into the nothingness of death, and emerges victorious. Therefore, the world's affliction even at its worst does not have the last word. Or so we hope.

At this point John Muir's conviction that "God's charity is broad enough for bears" returns with strong new resonance. The love of the triune God includes all creatures. In view of the unfathomable measure of this love it is fair to affirm that the Creator God is with creatures in their magnificent living and flourishing, their suffering and dying, holding each in redemptive love, drawing them into an unimaginable eschatological future in which all will be made new.

CONVERSION TO THE EARTH

Looked at in this faith perspective, the current destruction of life on Earth by human action has the character of deep moral failure. To speak theologically, it is profoundly sinful. By acts of commission and omission we are perpetrating violence against life, deforming its future. In so doing we are pulling contrary to the will of God, whose beloved creation this is. Ethicists have coined new words to name the sin: biocide, ecocide, geocide. Sacrilege and desecration are not too strong a designation. The Catholic bishops of the Philippines name the despoilation an insult to Christ: "the destruction of any part of creation, especially the extinction of species, defaces the image of Christ which is etched in creation."[14] Whatever the language, the moral judgment remains that the ecological damage humans are wreaking on the Earth is profoundly wrong.

In terms of Christian spirituality, the turn from sin to a life marked by grace is known as conversion. In a broad sense conversion is a continuous characteristic of the life of faith, an ever-deepening fidelity in relationship with God. At the same time, as the New Testament term for conversion (Greek *metanoia*) indicates, it can also mean literally a turning, a change of direction, switching away from one path and swiveling toward another. Facing the evils of ecological ruination in a spirit of repentance, the church community needs to be converted to the patterns established by the Spirit in the giving of life itself. Motivated by the love of God, we need a deep spiritual conversion to the earth. This involves several discrete turnings at once.

❖ Intellectually, it entails moving from an anthropocentric view of the world to a wider theocentric one that has room for other species to be included in the circle of what is religiously meaningful. It means letting go of a philosophy shaped by hierarchical dualism that prizes spirit over matter in favor of a philosophy that also intensely values physical and bodily realities as God's good creation. Rather than setting up a contrastive either-or relation between God and the world, this intellectual turning honors the presence of the Giver of life in, with, and under the ecological community of species, and sees the Creator reflected in their flourishing.

❖ Emotionally, being converted to the earth involves a turning from the delusion of the separated human self and the isolated human species to a felt affiliation with other beings who share in our common status as creatures of God. In the beautiful words of Albert Einstein, "Our task must be to free ourselves from this prison by widening our circle of compassion to embrace all living creatures and the whole of nature in its beauty."[15] In the depths of our being we recover a capacity for communion with the natural world, to the point where brother sun and sister moon, brother fire and sister water, brother wolf and little sister bird are more than poetic ways of speaking but felt truths, as with Francis of Assisi.

❖ Ethically, we realize that a moral universe limited to human persons is no longer adequate. Our attention widens beyond humanity alone and re-centers vigorous moral consideration on the whole community of life. Recognizing that we are kin, we start to preserve and protect creation not just because it is useful to us but because it has its own intrinsic value. An excellent lead for action comes from the radical principle articulated by Pope John Paul II: "Respect for life and for the dignity of the human person extends also to the rest of creation, which is called to join humanity in praising God."[16] This calls into play the rich tradition of moral right and wrong, virtue and sin, already so well developed in terms of the dignity of the human person, and invites its challenging application to this new set of lives. Reciprocity rather than rapaciousness begins to mark our relationship with the earth.

Simply put, ecological conversion means falling in love with the earth as an inherently valuable, living community in which we participate, and bending every effort to be creatively faithful to its well-being, in tune with God who loves it unconditionally. Being converted to an ecological vocation entails more than an ascetic or moral mandate. It is a call to deeper relationship with God the Creator of heaven and earth, an invitation that transforms us toward greatheartedeness, in resonance with the Love who made and empowers it all.

A NEW PARADIGM: COMMUNITY OF CREATION

A key and formidable obstacle to this kind of change of heart, both personally and institutionally, is the overriding notion that due to our innate superiority human beings have the right to master the natural world, which in turn is created to serve human purposes. Gleaned from a particular interpretation of the dominion text in Genesis (1:26), the predominant idea in recent centuries has been that of rule and control. We picture ourselves at the apex of the pyramid of living creatures with rights over otherkind. This self-understanding has seeped into the depths of the Christian approach to nature, accounting for the tenacious human-centeredness that attends most theologies.

Careful reading of that Genesis text in its own context makes clear that dominion can be interpreted beneficently as a call to responsible stewardship. Unable to be present throughout an extensive territory, a king would appoint an official to oversee the region in his name. Such an official would be said to have "dominion" over that part of the kingdom, charged with carrying out the wishes of the ruler he stands in for. In this light, the Genesis mandate to have dominion clearly does not give human beings permission to *dominate* the natural world. God has just created all living things, blessed them and their fertility, and pronounced them all good. Having dominion in the royal sense means that humans are to be God's representatives, carrying out the divine will that other creatures should flourish.

Among ecological theologians, however, there is serious doubt whether dominion on its own, even if its original meaning is recaptured, is sufficient to change human sensibility and our consequent behavior in our day. We are sinners, after all, and being in charge offers an ever-present temptation to self-aggrandizement. The strong hubris entailed in the history of dominion needs to be remedied by a different paradigm of the human place in the world, religiously speaking. Such an alternative presents itself in the biblical vision of the community of creation. Widespread in the words of the prophets, the psalms, and the wisdom writings, this understanding positions humans in the first instance not above but within the living world which has its own relationship to God. Within such a paradigm the role of dominion can find its rightful but limited place.

In the paradigm of the community of creation the center is God rather than human beings. The central insight is simple but radical: we are all creatures of God. Since all share in having been created, humans and other species have more in common than what separates them. In complex interactions each gives and receives, being significant for one another in different ways in a community grounded in absolute, universal reliance on the living God for the very breath of life. In this view, where humans are first of all fellow-creatures, caring dominion becomes a role within the larger sphere of community relationships, which are mutual rather than one-way.

It is fascinating to see how this ancient religious wisdom coheres with contemporary ecological knowledge. A key scientific insight holds that all life on this planet forms one community. Historically, all life results from the same evolutionary biological process; genetically, living beings share elements of the same basic code; functionally, species interact without ceasing. In this life community, human beings need other species profoundly, in some ways more than other species need them.

Take, for example, trees. To stay alive trees take in carbon dioxide, synthesize it in the presence of sunlight, and give off oxygen as a result. Thanks to this process, Earth's atmosphere is rich in oxygen. Human beings breathe in this oxygen and exhale carbon dioxide as a waste product. Which species is more needy of the other? In a thought experiment, remove humans from the Earth. Trees would survive in fine fashion, as they did before humans emerged and started to cut them down. Now imagine trees removed from the planet. Humans would have an increasingly hard time surviving, with growing amounts of carbon dioxide in the atmosphere and less oxygen to breathe. The point is, human beings are not simply rulers of the life-world but dependent upon it at the most fundamental level.

The biblical vision of the community of creation offers a similar view of interdependence for religious reasons. In its origin, history, and goal, the whole living world with all its members is ultimately grounded in the creative, redeeming God of love. When parsed to its most basic element, the community of creation is founded on the belief that all beings on Earth, humans included, are in fact *creatures*, sustained in life by the only Creator of all that is. Hence, for all their uniqueness, human beings have more in common with other creatures than what separates them. We all participate in an interdependent world fundamentally oriented to God. This is a kinship group of hugely diverse members whose mutual relationships are rich and complex. Within this guild of life the distinctive capacities of human beings are part of the picture and can be exercised without lifting our species out of creation, as though we were demi-gods set over it.

Situating the marvel of the human species with its singular abilities within the community of creation centered on the living God opens a new avenue for religious self-understanding and sound practice. While embracing the best of stewardship theology and its moral practice, this model's different imaginative framework unleashes intellectual, emotional, and ethical responses that express kinship at a fundamental level. The relationship envisioned here does not encourage communion by the ploy of blurring the lines between species, as if *Homo sapiens* were not a singularity. Rather, it allows each species to stand in its own difference, but encompassed by a wider whole that affects the interaction of all.

No biblical book presents the community of creation more firmly and eloquently than the book of Job. Its theological vision offers a strong antidote to the human arrogance that has flowed in the modern era from the view of dominion as domination. As the ancient folk tale unfolds, Job is suffering loss on every front: possessions, offspring, personal health. Mouthing the standard conviction of their culture, his three friends argue he must have sinned greatly to deserve such punishment. In a debate that grows increasingly acrimonious, Job maintains his innocence. Flinging anguished accusations against divine justice, he brings a lawsuit, challenging God to appear in court to defend the way the world is ordered.

> Then the Lord answered Job out of the whirlwind.
> (Job 38:1)

The answer is unexpected. In gorgeous poetic language over the course of four chapters (38–41), the text paints a picture of God's activity in creation, emphasizing that the human role in the life of other species is next to nothing. The voice from the whirlwind sets the theme with a daunting question: "Where were you when I laid the foundation of the Earth?" (38:4). This query repeats over and over again, putting Job and with him all human beings in their proper place vis-à-vis the Creator and other created beings. Where were you when the Earth was measured out, when the stars began to sing together, when the sea was placed within boundaries and its proud waves given limits? Have you commanded the light to rise at dawn? the snow and rain to fall even where no one lives? the thunder and lightning to play? Orion and the other constellations to run their courses across the sky?

Once the physical world is laid out, the questions from the whirlwind turn to the behavior of animals who for the most part are wild and free, living out their lives without serving human purpose. Who provides prey for the lion, hunting food for her young who lie waiting in their den? Who gives prey to the raven, whose young ones are crying out with hunger? Do you know when the mountain goats crouch and give birth, their young then growing strong and roaming away? Have you given the wild ass its freedom? Is the wild ox willing to serve you, to be tied up at night and plough your fields by day? Look how the ostrich flies, laughing at riders on horseback. Do you give the majestic war horse its might? Is it by your wisdom that the hawk soars or by your command that the eagle mounts up, spying its prey from afar?

As centuries of profound commentary on this book have made clear, the divinely sketched panorama of the created world does not resolve the presenting problem of the suffering of an innocent person. Instead, it places Job's pain in the context of God's nearness in cosmic creation...and he is filled with wonder. Stunned by encounter with the immensity, beauty, and intricate order of things, his stance is reoriented: "I had heard of you by the hearing of the ear, but now my eye sees you" (42:5). Shifting perspective, he now knows a different God, bigger than the tit-for-tat ruler both he and his friends had envisioned. "He is taken out of himself and given a broader vision of the universe and God's ways with it. What brings home to him the incalculable wisdom and power of God is the *otherness* of the cosmos, precisely that it is not a human world."[17] This expands Job's horizon to the point where he deeply grasps that God's love does not act according to rules of retribution, rules insisted upon by a penal view of history, but like all true love operates freely in a world of grace that completely enfolds and permeates him, even in pain. With new clarity of vision, his story moves toward healing and peace.[18]

The biggest difference between Genesis and the creation narrative unspooled from the whirlwind in Job is the absence of the mandate to have dominion. Instead of being placed at the apex of creation, Job is led to see divine activity in the independent working of the natural world over which he has no mastery, not only technologically but also theologically: "Where were you...?" The whirlwind's vision of creation's grandeur makes a religious point, namely, that the human place in the scheme of things is not first of all one of supremacy. We are not the center of everything. It is not all about us. Granted, as Sallie McFague compassionately admits, "We have lived for so long with this picture of ourselves, as subjects inhabiting a world that is our object and resource, that it is difficult to imagine it might not be true."[19] However, the repeated questions from the whirlwind urge a different view. With a humility essential to being properly human, we take our place as creatures among other beloved creatures in whom the living God is independently interested.

CONCLUSION

There is a text in the book of Job that has been guiding the explorations of this lecture:

> Ask the beasts and they will teach you;
> the birds of the air, and they will tell you;
> ask the plants of the earth and they will teach you;
> and the fish of the sea will declare to you:
> has not the hand of the Lord done this?
> In his hand is the life of every living thing,
>   and the breath of every human being. (Job 12:7–10)

If you interrogate the flora and fauna of land, air, and sea, the text suggests, their response will lead your mind and heart to the living God, generous source and sustaining power of their life, as well as of the life of human beings.

Theology, which seeks to understand faith more deeply in order to live more vibrantly, has work to do here. For a long time, we have seldom asked the beasts anything. Doing so now, I have been proposing, brings at least three answers. Speaking scientifically, they say, "we are the result of the process of evolution, which is still going on." Speaking theologically, they say, "we are created by God, who sustains and accompanies our lives, and this is still going on." Speaking ecologically, they say, "we are being ruined, and this is still going on; please stop."

A flourishing humanity on a thriving Earth in an evolving universe, all together filled with the glory of God: such is the global vision of creation we are called to in this critical age of Earth's distress. The immediate aim is to establish and protect healthy ecosystems where all creatures, including poor human beings, can thrive. The long-term goal is a socially just and environmentally sustainable society in which the needs of all people are met and species in the natural environment can prosper, onward to an evolutionary future that will still surprise. Ignoring the urgent call to be converted to the earth keeps people of faith and our churches, synagogues, mosques, and temples locked into irrelevance while a terrible drama of life and death is being played out in the real world. By contrast, living the ecological vocation in the power of the Spirit sets us off on a great adventure of mind and heart that expands the repertoire of our love—even for bears.

Adapted from the Mary Milligan RSHM Lecture in Spirituality, Loyola Marymount University, Los Angeles, CA, 2014; published as "Creation: Is God's Charity Broad Enough for Bears?" (Marymount Institute Press and Tsehai Pub., 2014).

Notes

1. John Muir, "Thoughts on Finding a Dead Yosemite Bear," in *The Wilderness World of John Muir*, ed. Edwin Way Teale (New York: Houghton Mifflin, 2001), 317.

2. Julian of Norwich, *Showings* (New York: Paulist Press, 1978), 183.

3. Herbert McCabe, *God, Christ and Us*, ed. Brian Davies (New York: Continuum, 2003), 103.

4. Hildegard of Bingen, *Mystical Writings* (New York: Crossroad, 1990), 91–93.

5. Thomas Aquinas, *Summa Theologiae* I.8.1.

6. Augustine, *On the Psalms, Ancient Christian Writers*, Vol. 29 (New York: Newman Press, 1960), 272.

7. Darwin, Charles, *On the Origin of Species*, annotations by James Costa (Cambridge, MA: Harvard University Press, 2009), 434.

8. Niels Gregersen, "The Cross of Christ in an Evolutionary World," *Dialog: A Journal of Theology* 40 (2001): 192–207.

9. John Paul II, *Lord and Giver of Life*, par. 50.

10. Christopher Southgate, *The Groaning of Creation* (Louisville, KY: Westminster John Knox, 2008), 52.

11. Ambrose of Milan, *PL* 16:1354.

12. Karl Rahner, "Dogmatic Questions on Easter," *Theological Investigations* IV (New York: Seabury Press, 1974), 129.

13. Sandra Schneiders, *Resurrection: Did It Really Happen and Why Does That Matter?* (Los Angeles: Marymount Institute Press, 2013), 44.

14. Catholic Bishops of the Philippines, "What Is Happening to Our Beautiful Land? A Pastoral Letter on Ecology," in *And God Saw That It Was Good: Catholic Theology and the Environment*, ed. Drew Christiansen and Walter Grazer (Washington, DC: U.S. Catholic Conference, 1996), 316.

15. Albert Einstein, cited in Michael Dowd, *Earthspirit: A Handbook for Nurturing an Ecological Christianity* (Mystic, CT: Twenty-Third Publications, 1991), 81.

16. John Paul II, *Peace with God the Creator, Peace with All of Creation*, par. 16.

17. Richard Bauckham, *Bible and Ecology: Rediscovering the Community of Creation* (Waco, TX: Baylor University Press, 2010), 45.

18. This is the compelling interpretation of Gustavo Gutiérrez, *On Job: God-Talk and the Suffering of the Innocent* (Maryknoll, NY: Orbis Books, 1987), 82–92.

19. Sallie McFague, *Blessed Are the Consumers: Climate Change and the Practice of Restraint* (Minneapolis: Fortress Press, 2013), 23.

8

A Theological Case for Naming God She

❖ What is going on when women biblical scholars today point out that the Hebrew word for divine mercy, *rechem,* comes from the root word for a woman's uterus, so that when Scripture calls upon God for mercy, it is actually asking God to forgive with the kind of love a mother has for the child of her womb? The prophet Isaiah intensifies the connection with his oracle:

> *Can a woman forget her sucking child,*
> *that she should have no compassion on the child of her womb?*
> *Yet even if these may forget, I will not forget you.* (Isa 49:15)

In Phyllis Trible's memorable phrase, we witness here the journey of a metaphor from the wombs of women to the compassion of God.[1] What happens when we make this an explicit part of our understanding of divine mercy rather than leave it tucked away in the text?

❖ What is going on when women draw attention to long-neglected biblical texts about Holy Wisdom, *Sophia* in Greek, a female figure of power and might? Not only does she mother the world into birth, but, being all powerful, she also saves the world and makes people holy. In a retelling of Israel's history in the book of Wisdom, "She" leads the people out from slavery in Egypt, bringing them across the waters of the sea and leading them through the wilderness with fire and cloud (Wis 10:15–19). The biblical book of Proverbs opens with her crying out at the city gates, excoriating those who will not listen to her words of instruction, but promising that "whoever finds me finds life"

(Prov 8:35)—words adapted to signal the saving significance of Jesus in John's gospel (Jn 10:10). Most tellingly, against her evil does not prevail (Wis 7:30). Far from being a mere aspect, this female figure represents the fullness of divine mystery.

❖ What is going on when women New Testament scholars today remind us that in Luke's gospel, right after Jesus tells the parable of the good shepherd who leaves ninety-nine sheep to look for the one that got lost, he goes on to preach a parable with a female protagonist, a woman searching for her lost silver coin? Both parables depict the work of God the Redeemer, one in the imagery of male work, one in that of female work.[2] But for all the churches and statues of the Good Shepherd, where are the churches dedicated to God the Good Homemaker? Why has this seeker of a treasured coin that is very important to her not become a familiar image of the divine?

❖ What is going on when women scholars of medieval religious history shed light on women mystics and their articulation of their experience of God in female metaphors? To cite but Julian of Norwich and her daring view of God's courtesy:

> *As truly as God is our Father, so truly is God our Mother ... I understand three ways of contemplating motherhood in God. The first is the foundation of our nature's creation; the second is Christ's taking of our nature, where the motherhood of grace begins; the third is the motherhood at work in the Spirit. And by the same grace, everything is penetrated, in length and in breadth, in height and in depth without end; and it is all one love.*[3]

Why are we so forgetful of this blessed motherhood? What would result if the church began to use this language equivalently with that of divine fatherhood?

❖ What is going on when, in the tradition of Wisdom and Julian, Linda Reichenbecher, a young woman studying for ministry at the Presbyterian Seminary in Louisville, Kentucky in 1993, composes this meditation:

I stared at my doctor who had treated my burns, and in her eyes saw intelligence and care, and knew that I had looked upon the face of God.

I stared at the soft, worn hands of my grandmother, and in them saw the thousands of potatoes peeled to nourish her family, and knew that I had looked upon the face of God....

I stared at my small child's excited face at the beach, and in her saw new wonder at the world, and knew that I had looked upon the face of God.

I stared at the mother robin angrily diving at me as I came too close, and in her I saw fierce protection, and knew that I had looked upon the face of God.

I stared at the darkness of the night, and in it saw the constant companionship of my faith, and knew that I had looked upon the face of God.

❖ What is going today on when two Jewish women, Naomi Janowitz and Maggie Wenig, compose a Sabbath prayer for their community that prays in part:

Blessed is She who spoke and the world became. Blessed is She.
Blessed is She who in the beginning, gave birth.
Blessed is She who says and performs.
Blessed is She who declares and fulfills....
Blessed is She who lives forever, and exists eternally.
Blessed is She who redeems and saves. Blessed is Her Name.[4]

What would be the spiritual and political results if every sabbath saw religious communities of Jews and Christians praising Her Name?

❖ What is going on when Mary Kathleen Schmitt, an Episcopal priest, works for years with her whole parish to create inclusive language prayers for Sunday liturgy in a three-year cycle? One prayer for Christmas Day addresses God this way:

Maker of this earth our home,
You sweep the heavens with your starry skirt of night

and polish the eastern sky to bring light to the new day.
Come to us in the birth of the infant Christ,
that we may discover the fullness of your redemption through-
    out the universe;
O Mother and Child of Peace bound by the Spirit of Love,
One-in-Three forever. Amen.[5]

What is going on in these and a multitude of other examples, I suggest, is that the question of the right way to speak about God in contemporary theology is coming to the fore with great vigor. This situation is not entirely new. In the late fourth century bishop Gregory of Nyssa recorded how his contemporaries, high and low, seriously engaged the question of how to speak about God. Their issue, in a culture awash with Greek philosophical notions, was whether Jesus Christ was truly divine or simply a creature subordinate to God the Father. The question engaged not only theologians and bishops but just about everybody. "Even the baker," wrote Gregory, "does not cease from discussing this. For if you ask the price of bread he will tell you that the Father is greater and the Son subject to him."

In our day interest in how to speak about God is alive and well again thanks to a sizable company of bakers, namely, women who throughout history have borne responsibility for lighting the cooking fires and feeding the world. The women's movement in civil society and the church has spotlighted the centuries-long exclusion of women from public discourse and their resulting absence from the formation of cultural and theological symbols. This exclusion has had a decided effect on how we do—and do not—speak about God. While theology has consistently acknowledged that God is Spirit, and thus beyond gender identification, the church's daily vocabulary for preaching, worship, catechesis, and evangelization broadcasts a different message: God is male, or at least more like a man than a woman, and "he" is more fittingly addressed as male than as female.

Today, women and men in a variety of settings are questioning an exclusive reliance on male images for God. In prayer and study they are rediscovering female imagery for God long hidden in Scripture and tradition. Feminist artists, poets, composers, and theologians are fashioning new metaphors and idioms for God out of women's embodied experience. Language about God is expanding, even to the point of addressing divine mystery as "she." In this article I would like to make a theological case for the legitimacy of such language and argue that its development is of the highest religious significance.

First Step

The starting point for this case is careful attentiveness to a spiritual experience taking place among women. For centuries male theologians defined women as inferior to men, more bodily than spiritual, more emotional than rational, more passive than capable of agency. As with any oppressive notion, once this takes hold it begins to be taken for granted. Over time women internalize the image that the system feeds them, and instinctively think of themselves as less than worthy. The exclusively male image of God, a powerful element in this system, promotes this "mood." Consequently it reinforces, even legitimizes, patriarchal social structures in family, society, and church. Language about the father in heaven who rules over the world justifies and even necessitates an order where men rule, thanks to their greater similarity to the Source of all being and power.

As the women's movement has developed in the religions, something akin to a spiritual uprising is taking place. Women are experiencing themselves as blessed before God. They are being converted from trivializing themselves to honoring themselves as genuinely beloved. Such rebirth brings in its wake a positive judgment about women's ways of being in the world. Female bodiliness, feelings, ways of knowing, love of connectedness, friendships, and a host of other historically developed characteristics are being revalued as good rather than deficient or evil. Given the ingrained negative assessment of women's nature by centuries of patriarchal theology, women's experience of themselves in this way is a powerful religious event, the coming into maturity of suppressed selves.

Because the experience of self is profoundly intertwined with the experience of God, this profound conversion to the goodness

of what is female brings in its wake a new sense of God as beneficent toward women and an ally of women's flourishing. Great images of the divine, Martin Buber observed, come into being not
simply as a projection of the imagination but are awakened from
the deep abyss of human existence in real encounter with divine
power and glory. Images with the capacity to evoke the divine are
given in encounters that, at the same time, bring persons to birth
as persons, as Thous, in reciprocal relation with the Eternal Thou.
If this be true, I suggest that far from being a superficial development, language about holy mystery in female symbols is emerging
gracefully, powerfully, and necessarily from women's encounter
with the divine in the depths of their own blessed selves.

One artist has captured this experience almost perfectly. In a
dramatic play about the metaphysical dilemma of being black,
being female, and being alive, Ntozake Shange follows the adventures of seven women in a racist and sexist society. After roil-
ing adventures of prejudice, hurt, and survival, one character
rises from despair to cry out, "I found god in myself and I loved
her, I loved her fiercely."[6] It is this finding and fierce loving of the
female self in relation to God and God in relation to self that is a
major root of women's assuming the power of naming toward
God. In turn, female images of God function to affirm the excellence of being women sexually, psychologically, intellectually,
politically, socially, and religiously.

Second Step

The first step in the case for naming God using female imagery
has attended to the conversion experience of vast numbers of
women around the world. The theological case gains strength
from a second step, consulting the basic resources of Scripture.
Numerous biblical texts offer potent female images of the living
God: God as a woman in labor, giving birth, midwifing, nursing,
and carrying a child; God as an angry mother bear robbed of her
cubs; God knitting, baking, washing up, searching for a treasured
coin; God as holy Sophia, woman Wisdom, creating, ordering,
and saving the world. The figure of Wisdom provides one of the
earliest interpretive frameworks for New Testament christology,

Jesus even being called the Wisdom of God who announces her message and does her deeds. In a special place is the symbol of the Spirit, God's moving presence and activity in the world, often presented in female metaphors. When Scripture is read with an eye for the subject, such images provide a treasure trove of new yet ancient ways to speak about God.

For some literal-minded believers, however, the Christian community is not free to expand its language about God. They argue that since Jesus himself spoke to and about God as father, or *abba* in Aramaic, this mandates that the church do likewise. Indeed, Jesus did address the God of Israel in whom he believed as father, but the argument to limit our language to this one name sets its sights too narrowly. Jesus' language about God, far from being exclusively paternal, is diverse and colorful, as can be seen in the imaginative parables he created about the reign of God. In addition to a forgiving father, he depicts God as a woman searching for her lost coin, a shepherd looking for his lost sheep, a bakerwoman kneading dough, a traveling businessman, a farmer, the wind that blows where it wills, the birth experience that delivers persons into new life, an employer offending workers by his generosity. Jesus used these and many other human and cosmic images—in addition to the good and loving things that fathers do—as metaphors for the divine mystery.

In the light of Jesus' own usage, the difficulty with restricting our language about God to "father" alone is readily apparent. Jesus' speech, which was originally pluriform, subtle, and subversive, gets pressed into an exclusive, literal, and patriarchal mold. This does not do justice to Jesus' own language nor to his understanding of God. Furthermore, it fails to examine the deleterious effect that relying almost exclusively on the father symbol has had in Christian history. Diverse images of God, including female ones, are not only plausible. They are necessary, and they are biblically justifiable.

It should be noted that retrieving biblical female symbols of God requires another critical move. Since even these symbols are embedded within a text, a culture, and a tradition shaped by sexism, they cannot be merely lifted and plunked down whole like the prophet Habakkuk. They must first pass through the fire of feminist interpretation and be used by a community struggling to be a community of the discipleship of equals. Otherwise they will remain supplementary, subordinate, and stereotyped symbols within a traditionally dualistic male-female framework.

Third Step

Turning to classical theology is a third step in this argument. Very clearly and deliberately, the Fourth Lateran Council in 1215 articulated the limits of language about God with its teaching that whatever similarity is said to exist between Creator and creature, the dissimilarity is always greater. While limited by its androcentric view of the world, subsequent theology worked with this teaching in a salutary way that furthers our case. It deals wisely with God's incomprehensibility; the play of analogy in speech about God; and the consequent need for a plurality of ways to address God.

A. The reality of God is a mystery beyond all imagining, being literally incomprehensible. We can never wrap our minds completely around the ineffable God and capture divinity in the net of our concepts. The history of theology is replete with this truth: recall Augustine's insight that if we have understood, then what we have understood is not God; Anselm's argument that God is that than which nothing greater can be conceived; Hildegard's vision of God's glory as Living Light that blinded her sight; Aquinas's working rule that we can know that God is and what God is not, but not what God is; Luther's stress on the hiddenness of God's glory in the suffering of the cross; Simone Weil's conviction that there is nothing that resembles what she can conceive of when she says the word God; Karl Rahner's image that we are a little island of knowledge surrounded by a deep ocean.

It is a matter of the livingness of God.

B. Consequently, no expression for God can be taken at face value as if it delivered a totally clear and distinct idea of God. Whether explained by a theory of analogy, metaphor, or symbol, all human words about the divine bump up against limits. As the apostle Paul knew, at present we know only in part, "for now we see in a mirror, dimly" (1 Cor 13:12). We are always naming *toward* God, who always goes beyond. The reason for this is that God is not a being among other beings in this world. Our words about God indeed begin in our understanding of finite goodness and beauty in this world. Then they have to stretch to refer to the infinite. They make us mindful of the One who is the source and goal of all creation, but they are not able to define or control or encompass the Mystery. As Aquinas notes, "All affirmations we can make about God are not such that our minds may rest in them, nor of such sort that we may suppose God does not transcend them."

The dissimilarity is always greater.

C. This being so, there must be many names for God. If human beings were capable of expressing the fullness of God in one straight-as-an-arrow name, the proliferation of names, images, and concepts observable throughout the history of religions and in the Bible itself would make no sense. But since no one name alone is absolute or adequate, a positive revelry, a symphony of symbols for the divine is needed to nourish the mind and spirit.

Speech about God is a rare kind of human endeavor. We are not talking about some objective being within the world, even a supreme one. There is always the danger of forgetting the humble nature of such speech and absolutizing particular expressions. An expanded treasury of metaphors, including female imagery, introduces a greater sense of the mystery of God who is beyond all telling.

Fourth Step

A fourth step in the case for female symbols of God is taken when we consider the existential and practical effects of God language in the church. A faith community's imagery of God is its lodestar. The way a faith community speaks about God indicates what it considers the highest good, the profoundest truth, the most appealing beauty. The idea of God in turn molds the community's corporate identity and behavior as well as the self-understanding of its individual members. The symbol of God functions. It is neither abstract in content nor neutral in effect, but carries and shapes the community's bedrock conviction.

This being so, the fact that the Christian community ordinarily speaks about God in the image of a patriarchal ruling man is a problematic practice. The difficulty does not lie in the fact that male metaphors are used. Men as well as women are created in the image of God and their excellence can serve as points of reference for the divine. Good fathers, good husbands, good men leaders are a blessing in this world. The problem arises when these images are used exclusively. Then, without anything to offset their limitation, they get magnified and taken literally.

But in truth, God is not a man. In truth, the dominance of elite men over those who by sex, race, or class are not part of this privileged group is not compatible with the following of Jesus, who warned his disciples against lording it over others as the Gentiles do. Given the lodestar quality of a community's idea of God, such language results in a church bent out of shape by the relations of patriarchy. Broadening the treasury of metaphor allows the church to discover the sacred in places where tradition had long stopped looking to find it, namely, in what is associated with women. What is at stake in this matter is not only the truth about God but the identity and mission of the whole Christian faith community itself.

A Way Forward

One remedy used by a number of contemporary scholars and liturgists is to forswear personal pronouns and to speak of God simply as "God." This has produced some positive results but is, in the end, unsatisfactory. The persistent use of the term "God" clouds over the personal or transpersonal character of divine mystery. It hampers not only the sense of divine presence but also the insights that might accrue were female symbols of God allowed to guide thought. In a serious way this usage papers over an assumption that needs explicit scrutiny, namely, that women's reality is fundamentally inadequate to represent God.

I would argue to the contrary that women, created in the image and likeness of God, bear excellences that reflect the being of their Creator. If the experience of God in our day is summoning up female symbols; if Scripture and tradition are open to this development; and if there are negative effects from not using inclusive language and positive effects from doing so, how shall we proceed? For Christian theology, speaking about God involves reflection on the one triune God made known in creation, incarnation, and grace. Female symbols act as a corrective not only for sexist distortions of God-talk in general, but for trinitarian symbols in particular. To wit: the Spirit, being faceless, with no proper name, is virtually forgotten in the West; the Christ is distorted through assimilation to the framework of male dominance; and God's maternal relation to the world is eclipsed through concentration on the paternal metaphor. As Moses said to the people of Israel, so women say to the church: "You forgot the God who gave you birth" (Deut 32:18).

Incorporating female patterns of speech puts all of these notions back into play. We speak about the vivifying Spirit, forever drawing near and passing by. She is the giver of life who pervades the cosmos, creating like a mother bird hovering over the primordial chaos (Gen 1:2). She shelters those in difficulty under the protective shadow of her wings (Ps 17:8), and she bears up the enslaved on her great wings toward freedom (Ex 19:4). Other images deepen understanding of the Spirit's work. Like a woman she knits new life together in the womb (Ps 139:13); like a midwife she works deftly with those in pain to bring about new creation (Ps 22:9–10); like a washerwoman she scrubs away at bloody stains till the people be like new (Ps 51:7).

We can also speak about Jesus-Sophia, Wisdom made flesh in a particular history. Not only does the use of this female symbol remove the male emphasis in christology that so quickly turns to male dominance, but it evokes Sophia's gracious goodness, her life-giving creativity, and her passion for justice, all key elements in understanding the person, ministry, death, and resurrection of Jesus Christ.

We can also speak about God as the origin without an origin, the Mother Creator of all that is seen and unseen. Since it is women whose bodies bear, nourish, and deliver new persons into life and who, as society has been traditionally structured, most often carry out the responsibility of raising children into maturity, language about God's maternity is easily assimilated. In her, as once literally in our own mothers, we live and move and have our being, as some of our poets now say (see Acts 17:28).

What comes forth in these and other such symbols is the exuberant, life-giving dignity and power of women, applied with humility to the divine persons. The eternal Love that is the triune mystery opens to encompass the whole broken world, awakening in those who are responsive the experience of her compassion and freedom. Such symbols are but modest starting points for more inclusive God-talk. As the history of theology shows, there is no "timeless" speech about God. Rather, even revealed symbols of God are cultural constructs, entwined with the changing situation of the faith community that uses them. Honoring the language of two thousand years of Christian life, we are called to do for our generation what our ancestors in the faith did for theirs, and speak "God" in a meaningful way.

Aquinas dealt with the legitimacy of such historical development in an interesting way. He noted that since Scripture does not use the word "person" to refer to God, some had objected that we should not use the term either. But, Aquinas argued, "person" can be used with confidence of God since the perfections the word signifies, namely being, intelligence, and love, are in fact frequently attributed to God in the Bible. Furthermore, if our speech were limited to the very terms of Scripture, we could speak about God only in the original languages of Hebrew and Greek. Third, Aquinas defended the use of extra-biblical language on the grounds of historical need: "The urgency of confuting heretics made it necessary to find new words to express the ancient faith about God." Finally, he exhorted his readers to value these new expressions: "Nor is such a kind of novelty to be shunned; since it is by no means profane, for it does not lead us astray from the sense of Scripture."

Aquinas's arguments provide a useful framework for evaluating new patterns of speaking about God. In light of the longevity and pervasiveness of sexism in culture and religion, it is imperative to find more adequate ways of expressing the ancient good news. The present ferment about imaging, naming, and

conceptualizing God in female symbols is a contemporary manifestation of the fact that, as in every epoch before us, we as a faith
community are involved in an open-ended history of faith seeking understanding that is not yet finished.

No language will ever adequately encompass the unquench-
able mystery toward which we direct our words of praise, lament,
thanksgiving, and petition. But the living God and the vitality of
the faith community require that a more inclusive way of speaking
be developed that bears the ancient wisdom with a new justice.

I rest my case.

Adapted from Commonweal CXX *(February 29, 1993): 9–14; and from the
Boardman Lecture, University of Pennsylvania, Philadelphia, PA, 2000.*

Notes

1. Phyllis Trible, *God and the Rhetoric of Sexuality* (Philadelphia: Fortress Press, 1978), 31–59.
2. Turid Karlsen Seim, "The Gospel of Luke," in *Searching the Scriptures*, Vol. 2: *A Feminist Commentary*, ed. Elisabeth Schüssler Fiorenza
(New York: Crossroad, 1994), 729–31.
3. Julian of Norwich, *Showings*, trans. Edmund Colledge and James
Walsh (New York: Paulist Press, 1978), 296–97.
4. Naomi Janowitz and Maggie Wenig, "Sabbath Prayer," in *Womanspirit Rising: A Feminist Reader in Religion*, ed. Carol Christ and Judith
Plaskow (San Francisco: Harper & Row, 1979), 176.
5. Mary Kathleen Speegle Schmitt, *Seasons of the Feminine Divine:
Christian Feminist Prayers for the Liturgical Cycle* (Cycle B) (New York:
Crossroad, 1993), 52; notice that in this Christmas prayer Mother refers to
God, not Mary the mother of Jesus.
6. Ntozake Shange, for *colored girls who have considered suicide / when
the rainbow is enuf* (New York: Macmillan, 1976), 63.

9

The God of Life
in Feminist Liberation Theology
To Honor Gustavo Gutiérrez

Among the many vital, long-lasting contributions Latin American liberation theology has made to the church's understanding is the insight that the Holy Mystery in whom believers place their trust is the God of life. God creates life, loves life, empowers its ongoing vitality. This means that in situations where unjust death cuts people down either quickly by violence or slowly by grinding poverty, either by the direct action of persons or through unjust structures, the living God is not neutral. Rather, with a burning heart the Lover of life enters the list against the dealers of death. The Israelites learned this during the miserable time when they were held as an enslaved workforce in Egypt. The God of their ancestors did not act in a manner typical of the gods by taking the side of the powerful pharaoh, himself considered to be a god. Rather, placing divine power and love at the service of those on "the underside of history," the God of life inspired Moses to lead them out into a new chapter of their lives, sealed by covenant. This God makes a "preferential option for the poor," the unforgettable phrase that signals at one and the same time the divine will for liberation of these "non-persons" and the conversion of those who crush them.

IDOLATRY

In exploring this insight, liberation theologians, led by the pioneering work of Gustavo Gutiérrez, have made creative use of the ancient motif of idolatry.[1] Engaging in idolatry means worshiping something less than divine. It entails trusting in a graven image that cannot give life. In the situation analyzed by Latin American liberation theology, such a towering false god is wealth. Starting with the *conquistadores* and continuing for five centuries through successive ruling systems up to multinational corporations today, greedy desire for wealth has divinized money and its trappings, that is, turned them into an absolute. Desire for the comforts it brings and the scramble for power necessary to make and keep it create unjust havoc in the human community. Like all false gods, money requires the sacrifice of victims. Whether poor people are offered up indirectly through the economic systems necessary to produce profit, or directly through the violence necessary to sustain these conditions, their lives are the required sacrifice.

In its analysis of traditional preaching and catechesis, liberation theology has uncovered how the church put a superficial Christian veneer over the face of this idol. By presenting God as omnipotent King and Lord who rules over the world through his appointed delegates, ecclesial authorities implied that the current situation was in accord with God's will. Rather than resistance to injustice, what was required of believers was obedience to civil and ecclesial authorities as the price of future joy. What results is more death. Thus theology's criticism that the monarchical idea of God perverts the truth of the God of life in the service of moneyed interests. "By deforming God we protect our own egotism," Juan Luis Segundo contends with startling insight. "Our falsified and inauthentic ways of dealing with our fellow human beings are allied to our falsification of the idea of God. Our unjust society and our perverted idea of God are in close and terrible alliance."[2] In light of revelation, by contrast, liberation theology articulates the radical realization that in situations of injustice, the God of life who creates the world out of love does not stand idly by. This holy God glories when the beloved creation flourishes rather than when it is violated. Consequently, liberation is the signature deed of divine saving action in history.

Liberation theology's ground-breaking analysis of the God of life did not, at least in its initial phases, take account of the specific situation of women, deeply affected not only by degrading poverty but also by sexist beliefs and structures that reduce them to insignificance in church and society. In a fascinating parallel development, however, feminist theology (from the Latin *femina*, meaning woman) worked out another analysis of idolatry that focused on the configuration of deity in the image of a ruling man. If indeed "our falsified and inauthentic ways of dealing with our fellow human beings are allied to our falsification of the idea of God," then the subordination and dehumanization of women is in terrible alliance with the representation of deity drenched in exclusively patriarchal images and concepts.

MARGINALIZATION VS. HUMAN DIGNITY

Simone de Beauvoir coined the memorable phrase "the second sex," meaning the inferior sex, to describe the status of women in relation to men, the first sex.[3] The term points to the fact that despite women's dignity as human persons and the rich range of their gifts, their worth has consistently been marginalized, if not demeaned, in theories, laws, symbols, and practices throughout most of history. Male dominance and female subordination are always characteristic of communities in which men design and administer the public sphere, and such has been the case for millennia. The bias against women is intensely exacerbated by prejudices of race and class, placing poor women of color on the lowest rung of the social ladder.

Society. During the celebrations that marked the year 2000, the United Nations drew up a list of eight millennium goals that governments and volunteer organizations pledged to try to achieve by 2015. Five of the goals, such as cutting extreme poverty and hunger in half and reversing the spread of diseases like HIV/AIDS, affect the whole community of men, women, and children alike. Three of these goals, however, deal specifically with females: to see that girls as well as boys receive a complete primary education; to reduce by three-quarters the death of women in childbirth; and to empower women economically in order to promote equality between women and men. The fact that these goals need to be articulated at all reveals how lacking these social goods are in the lives of millions of girls and women. Factoring in race and class makes clear the complexity of forces against which women struggle for fullness of life. This is not to make women into a class of victims nor to deny women's agency, both sinful and graced, which is abundant. But it is to underscore statistics that make clear the inequity women face in society because of their gender. In no country on earth are women and men yet equal.

Church. In the Catholic Church a similar situation exists. An early Christian hymn declares that the waters of baptism make people into a community of brothers and sisters bonded in mutual love: "There is no more Jew or Greek, slave or free, male and female, but you are all one in Christ Jesus" (Gal 3:28). Despite this theology rooted in the ministry of Jesus and the life-giving power of the Spirit released by his death and resurrection, and despite the irreplaceable participation of women in the founding and spread of the early Christian movement, women were increasingly marginalized once the community became established and adopted the mores of the Roman empire. Barred from governing, women have for centuries had no voice in articulating the church's doctrine, moral teaching, and law. Banned from pulpit and altar, their wisdom has not been permitted to interpret the word of the gospel nor their spirituality to lead the church assembled in prayer. The sheer fact of the omission of women from the public sphere led to the assumption that men have a privileged place before God. In this milieu theology developed grossly misogynist views about women's very nature.

"Woman, you are set free." The women's movement in civil society in the 1960s and 1970s galvanized women to analyze the causes of their subordinate situation and to strategize for change. This spilled over into women's religious lives, leading to something akin to a spiritual uprising. Gathering in Latin American ecclesial base communities and mothers' clubs; or in Asian neighborhood associations and mutual aid societies; or in North American prayer groups, book clubs, and political action committees; or in African community centers and health education partnerships; or in European retreat centers and ministerial support groups; or in Australian reform alliances, Christian women started to come to grips with their subordination in church and society and critiqued it in light of the gospel. Silent and invisible for centuries, they began to stand up straight like

the woman in Luke's gospel, bent over for eighteen years, whom Jesus declared to be free (Lk 13:12). Speaking critically, they examined the sin of sexism and exposed its abuses. In a more positive vein they probed the meaning of Christian faith, uncovering its rich emancipatory possibilities for themselves, their daughters, and the whole Christian community.[4] In the light of this work, it became clear that the liberating goal of feminist, womanist, *mujerista* or Latina, Asian American, and third-world women's theology is not reached by simply integrating women into a society and church where patriarchal structures and androcentric theory still prevail as a norm. This "add women and stir" recipe just results in further problems as women are pressured to disregard their own gifts and try to fit into a male-defined world. Rather, the whole structure of church and society needs to be transformed to make space for a new community of mutual partnership. The goal is a new justice.

It is in this context of struggle for justice against embedded patterns of subordination that women glimpse the idol that justifies their exclusion.

IDOLATRY REVISITED

Drawn from Scripture, the wisdom of the Christian tradition has always held that the God of life who is source, sustaining power, and goal of the world cannot be confined to any one set of images but transcends them all. One would think that in a church that believed this there would be a diversity of representations of God drawn from all the perfections of the created universe. But such has not been the case. Reflecting the characteristics of those who exercise public authority in the church, the dominant image of God has been that of a ruling man. Consequently, verbal depictions of God in liturgy, preaching, and catechesis along with visual representations in art have forged a strong link in the popular mind between divinity and maleness.

Take, for example, the ceiling of the Sistine chapel in Rome, which has indelibly influenced the imagination of the West. From one end of the chapel to the other these well-known paintings depict God as an old, white, well-fed man, the epitome of those who held power in Michelangelo's society. In one famous panel this deity reaches out his divine finger to create a young white man in his own image. Note that race and class as well as sex enter into this picture. Why could God not be depicted as young, or black, or female, or all three together? But the traditional image is tenacious. As Celie says in *The Color Purple*, it is a struggle "to chase that old white man out of my head," but you have to do it before you can see anything at all.[5] When it became public knowledge that the grandparents of Mikhail Gorbachev, then the head of the Soviet Union, had him baptized when he was a baby, an American reporter asked him whether he believed in God. He replied, "Oh, I don't believe in him." Even atheists take it for granted that God is male.

The symbol of God functions. It is never neutral in its effects, but expresses and molds a community's bedrock convictions and actions. Women's groundbreaking work on this subject has made it piercingly clear that the practice of naming God exclusively in the image of powerful men has created an idol, one moreover that needs its sacrificial victims.

Idol. Because it offers no alternatives, speaking about God exclusively in masculine images sets up a literal equivalence in the mind. Such picturing leads people to forget the ineffable mystery of divine plenitude that can never be grasped in concept or name. Instead, these images reduce the living God to the fantasy of an infinitely ruling man. That such a powerful masculine figure might not really be God at all is never seriously considered. More solid than stone, more resistant to iconoclasm than bronze, is the ruling male substratum of the idea of God cast in theological language and engraved in public and private prayer. It is a disastrous theological error.

Sacrificial victims. The exclusive use of patriarchal language for God has baleful effects on both women and men. This is because representations of deity reinforce psychological moods and social structures. "One God, one Pope, one Emperor": from the time of Constantine onwards these dominant male images have functioned to justify patriarchy in church and society. In the name of the King of Kings and Lord of Lords who rules the world, men have assumed the duty to command and control, exercising authority on earth as it is in heaven. Mary Daly's succinct, inimitable phrase captures the rationale: "If God is male, then the male is God."[6] In addition to the political effect, such language also has deleterious spiritual effects. By giving rise to the unwarranted idea that maleness has more in common with divinity than femaleness does, exclusively male images imply that women are somehow less like unto God. Such language thus robs women of the dignity that would accrue if the gracious reality of God were addressed in their own womanly image and likeness. As Carol Christ astutely observed, a woman may see herself as created in the image of God only by abstracting herself from her concrete bodiliness. But she can never have the experience that is freely available to every man and boy in her culture of having her full sexual identity affirmed as being in the image and likeness of God.[7] Thus is set up a largely unconscious dynamic which alienates women from their own spiritual power at the same time that it reinforces dependency upon male authorities to act as intermediaries for them with God.

THE GOD OF LIFE REVISITED

Prophets and religious thinkers, including liberation theologians, have long insisted on the need to break down false idols and escape out of their clasp toward the living God. In the imagination of their spirit, their prayer, and their practical activities, women have been making this turn. By the grace of God they are having religious experiences that assure them they are of inestimable worth in the eyes of God, thus contradicting what has been said about them for centuries and what they may well have internalized. The resulting surge of proper self-love leads to conversion, to turning away from assessments that trivialize their personhood toward a profound affirmation of their humanity in all its diversity. As a result of these experiences, women so engaged report strong discomfort with the dominant images of God as a ruling father, lord, or king. This is more than simply a matter of words or images; rather, the relationships entailed in these names are a problem. As hallowed by tradition and currently used, these images are hierarchal constructions built up from the unequal status of women and men. Furthermore, they function to maintain this arrangement. Once women no longer relate to men as patriarchal fathers, lords, and kings in society, these sacred images become religiously inadequate. Instead of evoking the reality of God, they block it.

Latina theologian María Pilar Aquino describes the shift that takes place: once women realized that their ancient oppression could be lifted, and moreover that God is on their side, this realization challenged the traditional view of God ruling in the male interest.[8] The patriarchal lord who requires their obedience begins to be replaced by a God whose essence is love, who freely conceives and creates, whose peculiar mode of being is compassion and mercy for both women and men.

From their own situation in life women have sought new ways of understanding the divine that would bring mutuality into the relationship. They have found God as lover according to the pattern of the biblical Song of Songs, where both woman and man take initiative in seeking each other and, once found, praise each other's beauty. They discovered God as a life-giving Spirit present within themselves and in everything that fosters life. Rather than a sovereign God who takes care of every problem, like a father or a big brother caring for a helpless little girl who in turn pleases him most by being quiet and dutiful, they encountered a love that liberates them into their own freedom. In this relationship they began to trust their own spiritual power as a function of being female in all its fullness. Astrid Lobo, a scientist and active lay leader in the Catholic Church in India, put it clearly when she noted that no longer did she see God as a rescuer, but more as a power and strength within her, who calls upon her to use her own resources. God is the creative force, befriender, friend, and companion who cherishes women in their gladness and pain, gratitude and anger, and ability to change the world.

By envisioning the ineffable mystery of God in such non-authoritarian ways, women come upon a further question. Should femaleness be an obstacle to naming the divine? Or can women's reality function as a sacramental sign of God's presence and action? If God created women in the divine image and likeness, can we not return the favor and employ metaphors taken from women's lives to point to the living God? Consider these biblical examples.

❖ *Maternity.* In biblical Hebrew the root of the word for God's mercy (*rechem*) is a cognate of the word for a woman's womb (*rhm*). Every time we appeal to the mercy of God, we are asking God to have "womb-love" on our wayward mistakes, the way a mother takes pity on the child she bore. The basic metaphor here casts the absolute mystery of God in the image of a mother who passionately loves the child to whom she gave life. While not often alluded to, a number of biblical passages use maternal imagery of God to comforting and powerful effect.

Sallie McFague's work on this metaphor makes an unexpected connection between mothering and economic justice. Across cultures, races, and historic periods, mothers ordinarily do three things. They give the gift of life to others and, when it appears, exclaim with delight, "It is good that you exist." In addition, maternal love nurtures what it has brought into existence, mainly by feeding the young and also by training them to acquire personal and social behaviors. Finally, mothers passionately want their young to grow and flourish; they rise up to fight against anything that would do them harm.

In its own way good paternal love does all of these things too. Parental love is the most powerful and intimate experience we have of giving a love whose return is not calculated, and good fathers as well as good mothers are an inestimable blessing. But the irreplaceable role of women's own bodies in giving birth and their close connection with breast-nursing and child-rearing lend a special resonance to the maternal idea.

Working with maternal images of God in Scripture and tradition, McFague notes how divine maternal love acts with the same triad of characteristics. Like a mother God gives life to the world, then nurtures and guides it, and continuously desires the growth and flourishing of all. The practice of mothers everywhere shows that far from being a passive relationship, this kind of love entails looking out for everyone in the household. If there is little food, a mother sees that it is fairly distributed. If one child is sick or has a special need, she tries to provide what is needed. "The mother-God as creator, then, is also involved in 'economics,' the management of the household of the universe, to ensure the just distribution of good to *all*."[9] God's preferential option for the poor can be seen in the expression of a mother's strong instinct to care for the child most in need. Social justice is an expression of this maternal metaphor. And as mothers rise up to defend their young, so too the maternal love of God is active to defend, seek justice, and heal the suffering whenever people do violence to one another, aggrandize themselves at the expense of the poor, or ruin the ecological well-being of the Earth. Like the mother bear in the prophet Hosea, God the mother rears up to protect her cubs, even tearing the attackers' hearts out from their chest (Hos 13:8). The wrath of God has a place in this maternal metaphor.

❖ *Wisdom.* In relating to God, people need more than parental models, which, if used exclusively, can place them in the role of children rather than responsible adults. In addition to the idea of God as life-giving and nourishing mother, women's quest has discovered other metaphor clusters. One of the most important centers on the figure of Wisdom.

Long-neglected texts in the biblical wisdom writings feature Sophia, Holy Wisdom, a divine figure of power and might. She shouts in the marketplace and at the city gates in a most unladylike manner, calling people to grow up, stop hurting each other, and walk in her path of justice. Playing in the world at creation, leading the Hebrew slaves over the deep waters of the Red Sea, sending her spirit as a blessing throughout the earth, spreading a banquet in which all are invited to partake, prevailing against evil, she is Israel's God in female imagery. Indeed, her promise, "Whoever finds me finds life" (Prov 8:35), could be made by no one else.

❖ *Coin seeker.* In a pair of parallel parables, Luke depicts Jesus using earthy examples to illuminate the passion of God the Redeemer who seeks for the lost (Lk 15:1–10). In one, a shepherd leaves his ninety-nine sheep to go looking for the one that got lost. In the other, a woman turns her house upside down looking for one of her ten silver coins that went missing. Both call upon their neighbors to rejoice when they find the sheep, the coin. Neither tells more about God's care for the sinner than the other. "Holy Divinity has lost her money and it is us!" preached Augustine. But unlike the good shepherd, this vigorous seeker of money that is very important to her has not become a familiar image of the divine. She has even been disparaged. Once in my hearing a cardinal preaching on this text accused this woman of being "mercenary." Contrast this judgment with that of a woman in an ecclesial base community in southern Mexico who shared that this behavior is exactly what a poor woman would do who needed those *pesos* to buy tortillas for her children's breakfast.

The use of these and other female symbols signals the rediscovery of the face of the living God beyond the limited imagination of patriarchy. Revealing that exclusively male imagery for the divine is indeed partial, female images reveal the God of life by lassoing the idol off its pedestal. God is not literally a king or a father or a lord, but a mystery of Love ever so much greater. This is not to say that male metaphors cannot be used to signify the divine. Men, too, are created, redeemed, and sanctified by the gracious love of God and excellences taken from their lives can function in as adequate and inadequate a way as do female ones. But given the grip of the male-dominant tradition, the broader range of imagery has the effect of breaking the stranglehold of patriarchal discourse and its deleterious effects. Naming toward God with female metaphors releases divine mystery from its age-old idolatrous cage so that God can be truly God: not a superior elderly man but incomprehensible source, sustaining strength, and goal of the world, holy Wisdom, indwelling Spirit, the ground of being, the beyond in our midst, the absolute future, being itself, mother and father, matrix, lover, friend, infinite love, the holy mystery that surrounds and supports the world.

Such naming of divine mystery blesses rather than demeans human persons who are women. Critical for the integrity of the church's prayerful faith in God, it also has the advantage of opening up rich new veins of social justice that counteract prevailing sexism. As the history of religions makes clear, changing God-language alone cannot bring about this transformation. Female deities and the subordination of women have and still do coexist. But in the context of the social movement for women's equality and human dignity which now reaches global proportions there is a unique potential for affecting change at a deep and lasting level. If God is "she" as well as "he," and in fact literally neither, a new possibility can be envisioned of a community that honors difference while inviting women and men to share life in equal measure.

The prophetic, critical action that flows from thus dethroning the idol is the praxis of justice preferentially oriented toward those subordinated on the basis of gender, the more so as this is entwined with the oppression of race and class. As transformative action it seeks to make whole whatever silences, degrades, or violates the human dignity of women. Gustavo Gutiérrez brilliantly rephrased Irenaeus's beautiful adage "The glory of God is the human being fully alive" to give it powerful specificity: "The glory of God is the poor person fully alive." Using the lens of gender analysis women theologians specify yet again to say, "The glory of God is the woman fully alive," all women in their diversity created and loved by God. The glory of God cannot be separated from the reign of God, from the divine will that all should flourish. Consequently, women draw hope that the last word on their lives will be uttered not by a pharaoh who sees them as the second sex or marginalized objects or subordinate auxiliaries, but by the liberating God of life whose preferential option affirms them precisely as women.

CONCLUSION

As in any passage through the wilderness, the journey toward more just and liberating images of God is not without its dangers. Some conservative thinkers fear that Christians will lose their true heritage, which is indelibly intertwined with the name of God as Father, Son, and Holy Spirit. As a theologian I share this concern; my own conviction, committed as I am to the Christian faith, holds the trinitarian formula dear. But this formula was never intended to be the only way that Christians name God. So long as the female words or images can be connected with the patterns of acting and loving of the God of Israel, revealed in the life, ministry, death and resurrection of Mother Jesus (as Julian of Norwich calls Christ), or Jesus-Sophia (as I would have it), so long as they point us toward the God who creates and redeems the world and whose Spirit fills the whole earth, this danger can be satisfactorily countered.[10]

Far from being silly or faddish, the approach to the God of life that feminist liberation theology has pioneered goes forward with the conviction that *only* if God is named in this more complete way, *only* if the full reality of women of all races and classes enters into our symbol of the divine, *only* then will the idolatrous fixation on the patriarchal image of God be broken and sacrificial victims no longer be needed. Naming the God of life in this way is a basic element in the conversion of religious and civic communities toward a healing kind of justice for our time.

Adapted from Libertad y Esperanza: a Gustavo Gutiérrez por sus 80 años, *ed. Consuelo de Prado and Pedro Heghes (Lima, Peru: Centro de Estudios y Publicaciones—Instituto Bartolomé de las Casas, 2008), 313–29.*

Notes

1. Gustavo Gutiérrez, *The God of Life* (Maryknoll, NY: Orbis, 1991).

2. Juan Luis Segundo, *Our Idea of God* (Maryknoll, NY: Orbis, 1974), 8.

3. Simone de Beauvoir, *The Second Sex* (New York: Alfred A. Knopf, 1952).

4. A compendium of essays from around the world appears in *The Power of Naming: A* Concilium *Reader in Feminist Liberation Theology,* ed. Elisabeth Schüssler Fiorenza (Maryknoll, NY: Orbis Books, 1996); see also Susan Frank Parsons, ed., *The Cambridge Companion to Feminist Theology* (Cambridge University Press, 2002); and Janet Martin Soskice and Diana Lipton, eds., *Oxford Readings in Feminism: Feminism & Theology* (Oxford University Press, 2003).

5. Alice Walker, *The Color Purple* (New York: Harcourt Brace, 1982), 24.

6. Mary Daly, *The Church and the Second Sex* (New York: Harper & Row, 1975), 38.

7. Carol Christ, "Why Women Need the Goddess," in *Womanspirit Rising,* ed. Judith Plaskow and Carol Christ, eds. (New York: Harper & Row, 1979), 273–87.

8. María Pilar Aquino, *Our Cry for Life: Feminist Theology from Latin America* (Maryknoll, NY: Orbis Books, 1993), 130–40.

9. Sallie McFague, *Models of God* (Minneapolis: Fortress Press, 1987), 97–123.

10. Julian of Norwich, *Showings* (New York: Paulist Press, 1978), 298; Elizabeth Johnson, *She Who Is: The Mystery of God in Feminist Theological Discourse* (New York: Crossroad, 1992).

10

Sacred Ground at the Bedside

The Hospice Caregiver and Divine Compassion

When exploring the role of the hospice caregiver, a story in the biblical book of Exodus comes to mind. The scene is the desert, where a crucial encounter takes place between a man minding a flock of animals and the God of his ancestors Abraham, Isaac, and Jacob. Prior to this story we saw scenes of the Hebrew people being held under the whip of slavery in Egypt. Now Moses, the shepherd, sees a burning bush that is not consumed despite the fact that it is blazing with fire. The voice of divine mystery calls to him from the bush: "Remove the sandals from your feet, for the place on which you are standing is holy ground." Moses does so, and the sacred voice resounds with a stunning disclosure:

> I have seen the misery of my people who are in Egypt; I have heard their cry because of their taskmasters; I know well what they are suffering. Therefore I have come down to deliver them out of that land and bring them into a good land flowing with milk and honey.... So come, I will send you to Pharaoh to bring my people, the Israelites, out of Egypt.

Quite taken aback and fearful, Moses objects. He is not up to this job; he stutters; send somebody else. But the Holy One ends the encounter by saying simply, "I will be with you." The rest, as they say, is history (Ex 3:1–12).

In this encounter, a certain patch of ground becomes holy because the burning love of the all-holy mystery of God is present there. The verbs used in the divine address from the flaming bush are highly instructive in the way they reveal the character of this God. Rather than being distant and far removed from the turmoil of the earth, the Holy One is involved with those who are sore distressed: *I have seen, I have heard, I know well what they are suffering.* The verb *know*, in this instance, means a knowing in the heart, a felt experience. It is the same verb used earlier in the Bible to indicate sexual intercourse: "Adam knew his wife Eve, and she conceived and bore Cain" (Gen 4:1). To know in this way is intimately personal. God's own heart feels experientially what the people are going through. Moved by love, the Holy One takes action to deliver them—*I have come down*—and does so in a typical way by calling on a human being to carry out divine compassion in the world: *Come, I will send you.*

The bedside of the hospice patient is sacred ground for the same reason that the ground around the burning bush is sacred: because someone is suffering, because God is present there, and because the caregiver is called to embody divine compassion in accompanying the dying person through the time of transition, out of the place of pain. In effect, the voice of God says to the caregiver: Come, I will send you to bring my presence, warmth, and help to those suffering persons in and through your own human heart and expert care.

The term compassion comes from joining the Latin words *cum* meaning *with*, and *pati* meaning *to suffer*. It means to "suffer with" someone; to have a certain fellow feeling that allows you to gain an interior connection to someone else's pain; to enter into a relationship with the suffering person in such a way that he or she feels respected and comforted; simply to stand with someone, recognizing that despite the pain or disfigurement he or she is a person of worth, beauty, and strength. Through their own compassionate hearts, those who do hospice care have the profound calling of being the ones through whom God's care is in reality poured out over dying persons.

It is instructive to trace how often in the Bible the compassion of God is imagined in female metaphors. Of course, God is neither male nor female but Creator of both in the divine image and likeness. Since both male and female persons image God, the excellence of both can provide metaphors for speaking about God. It is a sad thing that in the course of history a certain prejudice against the goodness of women tilted traditional Christian language in favor of exclusively male images of God. It was thought that a woman's life, her body and emotions, were not worthy to image God. In our day, however, the upsurge in awareness of women's dignity around the world is reclaiming the worth of being female even before God, and thus female images of God are once again coming into play.

Using female metaphors to speak of God does not mean that God is literally female, just as using male images does not indicate a literal maleness in God. No images are adequate, for the holy mystery of God goes far beyond human ability to comprehend. In accord with biblical usage, we use metaphors to say that the way God acts and feels and relates is something like this. With regard to suffering, women's experiences of caring and loving provide beautiful language for divine compassion. Some examples:

When Scripture says that God has compassion on suffering people, the underlying metaphor signals that God is loving them as a mother loves the child of her womb. Channeling the divine voice, the prophet Isaiah writes, "I cry out like a woman in child-birth; I gasp and pant" (Isa 42:14). Showing infinite mercy, God is in labor to bring forth new life, being more of a mother than any mother. In the New Testament, Jesus, who himself showed such compassion, uses a form of this maternal metaphor, telling Nicodemus that a person must be born again of water and the Spirit in order to enter the kingdom of God (Jn 3:5). Here the Spirit of God is like a mother birthing new life into withered spirits.

Another powerful female image of God's compassion is the *shechinah*, or the great Spirit of God who dwells in the world. Mobile and free, she doesn't remain static but accompanies people wherever they go. No place is too hostile. She walks with them through the desert once they have escaped from slavery and, centuries later, she goes with them into exile again, never abandoning them through all the byways of rough times. As the rabbis wrote: "Come and see how beloved are the Israelites of God, for wheresoever they journeyed in their captivity the *shechinah* journeyed with them." God's indwelling Spirit was with them and her accompaniment gave rise to hope and encouragement in the darkness, a sense the Holy One would see them through. When the people are brought low, then the *shechinah* lies in the dust with them, anguished by human suffering. Even when a criminal is hanged, God feels compassion. As the rabbis write, "When a human being suffers what does the *shechinah* say? My head is too heavy for Me; My arm is too heavy for Me. And if God is so grieved over the blood of the wicked that is shed, how much more so over the blood of the righteous." In this saying, the biblical understanding that the Spirit of God moves throughout the world to bring life and blessing receives a special edge in situations of conflict and trouble. God's presence, imaged in female form, embraces those who suffer, becoming a source of peace, vitality, and consolation in the struggle. The point is that rather driving God away, terrible trouble brings divine compassion ever closer.

The burning compassion of God becomes embodied in the many women and some men who are hospice caregivers. The patients are in need; they face the darkness of death and need to feel that they are not abandoned but are enfolded in care. The dying who are people of faith also need to feel deeply the nearness of God's caring presence. Being carried by God's love, they can trust that their dying opens to a future even when it seems empirically there is no future. Whether or not patients have faith, each one has the dignity of a human person and needs respectful care as their death draws near. Such relationships can be of mutual benefit. Patients on the edge of life can respond in deeply human ways with gratitude, humor, and relief. Merely by being there they give caregivers the privilege of serving them.

Hospice caregivers are replete with riches to give. Their medical expertise relieves pain and soothes jangled bodies. Even more, their own human compassion is the medium that reaches patients at the deepest level of personal need. At the same time, caregivers also have a full range of human emotions that must be respected, including the need to get away and to protect themselves from drowning in too much sorrow. The temptation here, as for other health-care professionals, is to reduce patients to objects, referring to them as a bed number or a room number and forgetting that they are fellow human beings. Hospice principles set up a different ideal, asking caregivers to relate to patients on a more person-to-person level. In this relationship both can grow and be more fully and maturely themselves in different ways, provided they honor their own and each other's human dignity.

The bedside is sacred ground. Caregivers see the misery of people at the end of life; they hear their cries; they know well what dying persons are suffering. They come to deliver patients from pain, but even more profoundly to share in their suffering in a compassionate relationship that sustains human dignity and sees them and their families through to the end. In this, they are midwifing persons throughout the "birth" process into the hands of God. And when the task seems too overwhelming, they, like Moses, receive the promise from an ever-faithful God: "I will be with you." Hospice work is a profession that is also a vocation. Caregivers make effective the love of God, bending over pain and distress at a most critical moment of human life. In doing so, they embody in a beautiful and real sense the mystery of divine compassion.

Adapted from Connecticut Medicine *61 (December 1997): 787–88.*

III
JESUS THE LIVING ONE

11

Jesus Research and Christian Faith

Since the birth of modern biblical scholarship in the nineteenth century, scholars have been honing methods to use in exploring concrete details of the life of Jesus of Nazareth, along with the way his memory was shaped and passed on by the early communities of disciples. Tools taken from fields of historical, literary, cultural, religious, and geographic research have helped to place gospel texts in their wider contexts. In recent years yet another renaissance in Jesus studies is occurring thanks to even newer methods drawn from the social sciences, augmented by greater knowledge of first-century Judaism and the Greco-Roman world due to discoveries of ancient scrolls and archaeological excavations. This work has yielded a wealth of insight into the story of Jesus and the origins of Christianity in the specific circumstances of first-century Palestine.

The knowledge that results from this research inevitably gives rise to existential, religious questions within the Christian community of faith. Those who personally experience its impact ask how it might shape their own discipleship and relationship with the mystery of the living God mediated through Jesus Christ. Insofar as this knowledge impinges on the corporate, public identity of the church, we ask about its meaning for the community's global faith and practice.

Theology, as distinct from biblical scholarship, grapples with these questions. At the start of the second millennium, the medieval theologian Anselm defined theology as *fides quaerens intellectum*, or faith seeking understanding. This is a lively, open-ended definition that implies that the meaning of faith keeps needing interpretation for different groups of believers in historically changing times and places. To the extent that this work succeeds, the Christian tradition remains a living tradition rather than an ossified one. This lecture is an act of theology in the sense just described. It grapples with the significance that research into Jesus in his own time and place may have for what Christians believe and do today.

Let us be clear at the outset that we are dealing with an issue that is relatively new for faith. The church has lived for most of its two thousand years without what is called the quest for the historical Jesus. Indeed, the very notion of history that undergirds this quest, namely history itself as the record of "what really happened," emerged only during the latter part of the Enlightenment in eighteenth- and nineteenth-century Europe. Consequently, this is a fresh conversation in the living tradition. Insofar as many of the insights about Jesus generated by biblical scholarship are genuinely new to people who have lived with the gospel texts as Sacred Scripture, this new data poses challenges to traditional patterns of thought. Insofar as large swaths of contemporary people operate with a type of thinking marked by a more critical rather than an older legendary understanding of history, this research also offers opportunities to answer basic questions about the meaning of Christian faith in a new way.

THREE DISPUTED OPTIONS

In my judgment, contemporary Jesus research is a blessing for the church. Not everyone would agree. The question of whether and to what extent Jesus research even should impact the life of faith is highly controversial. At least three positions have emerged.

One trajectory, traceable from Reimarus in the eighteenth century through David Friedrich Strauss in the nineteenth, to some, though certainly not all, members of the Jesus Seminar in our day, takes delight in using Jesus research to puncture what it considers the over-inflated balloon of christological doctrine. Given the difference between what the gospel texts portray and what "really" happened, the gospels are mere pious fabrications, goes the early argument, or outright deceptions concocted by the disciples. The probability that Jesus ever said most of what the gospels attribute to him is minimal, goes the recent argument, making his teaching unreliable. Faith that holds he is the incarnate Word of God has no grounding in the historical record. The best we can do is think of him as a failed prophet or a misguided revolutionary. Thus are critical historical methods used to debunk the faith response that Christians offer toward Jesus as the Christ who mediates divine mercy and love. In this option, Jesus research triumphs at the expense of faith.

In resistance to this onslaught, an opposite trajectory has developed. Traceable with different nuances from Martin Kähler in the nineteenth century to Luke Timothy Johnson and Joseph Ratzinger in our day, this position basically holds that the "real" Jesus is not the person who lived in history *per se* but the historic biblical Christ of the gospel texts. There one encounters the living figure of the risen Christ and is challenged existentially to place one's trust in him. While some historical knowledge may be legitimate and even necessary—for example, the facts that Jesus actually existed and was crucified under Pontius Pilate—the ever-shifting sands of historical research and its results are not terribly relevant for faith. Rather, the witness of the biblical text itself provides a "storm-free region" for the saving act of faith, made in view of the risen Christ's continuous and powerful presence in the church here and now. In this option faith triumphs by diminishing, if not outright dismissing, the impact of critical inquiry into the pre-Easter Jesus.

A third trajectory, shared over the years by biblical scholars for whom faith matters and by theologians for whom history matters, opts for a both-and approach. This third option finds the skeptical "history alone" idea deficient insofar as it does not respect the interpretive power and dynamism of faith in peoples' lives. But this third stance also finds the devout "faith alone" position lacking insofar as it does not respect the importance of critical thinking in the lives of contemporary Christian people. Correlating history and faith, this third position allows a kind of mutual light to be shed back and forth between historical reasoning and trust in God through Jesus Christ. Here it is not thought in some simplistic way that history "grounds" faith or gives rise to faith, which is always a gracious gift from God. But when received in a faith context, historical research can indeed strengthen as well as challenge faith, for divine presence and action in the world are not so intangible as to leave no discernible historical traces.

The First Vatican Council—yes, the First—addressed the potential conflict between the insights of human reason and the truths of faith in a helpful way. Drawing on ancient Catholic tradition, it argued in the decree *Dei Filius* that there can never be any real discrepancy between faith and reason because the same God is the source of both. God both reveals the truths of faith and gifts the human mind with the power of reason to figure out how the world works. If a contradiction between the two does arise, it is due either to the doctrines of faith not having been rightly understood or to what in fact are opinions of reason being taken for final verdicts. Furthermore, not only are faith and reason not at odds but they can be of mutual help. Faith enlightens reason as to the true purpose of human life in the world. When reason seeks to understand this truth carefully, devoutly, and calmly (*"sedulo, pie, et sobrie"*), it can arrive at insights that are most fruitful. By making analogies with things already known and crafting new connections between faith and human life, reason can serve a positive purpose in promoting understanding of the mystery of God who, however, always remains beyond human understanding (*Dei Filius* #43, 44).

This nineteenth-century council spoke of reason as an abstract, logical power and focused on philosophical and scientific types of reason. But its insight holds equal validity, I think, for other kinds of reason including historical thinking that construes ideas about the past. In this spirit the third "both-and" position regarding Jesus research and Christian faith holds that faith and historical reason are capable of being partners rather than enemies. This is the conviction that shapes this lecture. I hope to affirm the significance of historical research into the life and times of Jesus for the intelligibility and liberating practice of the faith of persons in the contemporary world where historical consciousness is part of the air we breathe and where the hunger and thirst for justice impels our conscience.

Let me be clear that I am assuming rather than defending Christian faith in Jesus Christ, although the precise meaning of incarnation, to say nothing of resurrection, has been a matter of fierce theological debate in recent years. Setting out from this home base, I propose this thesis: Jesus research affects faith mainly by changing our imagination. To put this another way: if God became a human being, it is not unimportant what kind of human being God became. Being Christian means casting one's lot with Jesus, taking cues from his preaching and praxis as to the pattern of one's own life, drawing hope from his destiny, in a word, being a branch on the christic vine. Consequently, recasting the image of the one who is at the center of belief and practice has far-reaching results.

After developing this thesis a bit further, this lecture will explore its ramifications in four areas: the person of Jesus, his saving work, the church that follows him, and the mystery of the living God revealed in and through the event of his life and destiny.

CHANGING IMAGINATION

The image of Jesus is crucially important in the life of Christian faith. Since no one any longer meets Jesus of Nazareth in the flesh, he is encountered through a memory image that mediates his living presence through the power of the Spirit. Down through the centuries this image has been built up in various ways from Scripture, doctrine, liturgy, piety, moral practice, and available human experience. It functions at the very center of Christian life. Existentially, it is the means by which believers come to know and relate to Jesus Christ, whether as children or adults. Corporately, it shapes the church's creeds, ethics, doctrines and theology, liturgical celebration and preaching, spirituality and practices of piety, catechesis and public values. Theologically, set within a narrative framework, the memory of the life, death, and resurrection of Jesus Christ ensures that the content of *Jesus* in the confession that "Jesus is the Christ" is not reduced to a cipher or a projection but remains a gracious, challenging gift from God.

Subtract the memory of Jesus from the church and the whole life of faith implodes.

In a dramatic way, especially for churches that have traditionally lived by a high doctrinal christology supported by a literal reading of the gospels, Jesus research is changing this memory image. It is painting new pictures of how Jesus interacted with his world and providing new categories by which he can be understood. Scholarly books now portray Jesus as a marginal Jew; a prophet of Israel's restoration; a Spirit-filled leader, compassionate healer, subversive sage, and founder of a revitalization movement within Judaism; a Mediterranean Jewish peasant; an eschatological prophet proclaiming the dawning of the reign of God and paying the price with his life. These and other profiles are changing the traditional Christian imagination regarding the dynamic of Jesus' life and destiny.

Granted, they are not all the same, and real contradictions exist between various scholarly methods, use of sources, and readings of the evidence. Still, taken singly or together, these depictions encapsulate an awareness of the figure at the origin of Christianity different from that of the doctrinal Christ of traditional piety. This is not to say that these images are opposed to doctrine, but they do give rise to a different appreciation. Obviously the images emerging from contemporary studies do not exhaust the reality of the actual Jesus who lived. But I would argue that given the critical tools being utilized, this changed imagination approximates aspects of the first disciples' memory of Jesus more closely than the church's memory image has done for many generations.

This changed imagination is affecting understanding in at least four significant areas which we will now explore, albeit too briefly to do justice to the full range of the impact of Jesus research.

THE PERSON OF JESUS CHRIST

Classical doctrine, hammered out in Hellenistic terms by early church councils, affirms that Jesus' identity as the one Christ, Son, Lord involves a double relationality. He is "one in being with the Father as to his divinity" and "one in being with us as to his humanity" (Council of Chalcedon, 451). Truly divine and truly human: much subsequent theology has used philosophical categories to shed light on the meaning of this two-natures doctrine, attempting to explain how the incarnation of the Word of God results in a genuine human being. Despite these efforts, the genuine humanity of Jesus has rather regularly been neglected or allowed to slip from view. Ironically, this is particularly the case with highly orthodox christology. Its benchmark of truth is the confession that "Jesus is truly God," while equal importance is not attached to the equally doctrinal belief that "Jesus is truly human," that is, a real, genuine, limited human being with his own experience, like us in all things except sin.

Indeed, a major pattern of christology has been plagued by a mysterious undercurrent whereby Christ's divine nature tends to swallow up his human nature, thus undermining the fullness of the confession that doctrine seeks to protect. Why this should be the case has been the subject of some interesting speculation. Intellectual dualism that prizes spirit over matter, body over soul, and thus pure divinity over enfleshed humanity is one contributing factor. A competitive model of God's relation to the world whereby the infinitely powerful One overwhelms the puny integrity of the creature is another. A political power structure that privileges an elite group over the grubby masses, absorbing Christ into the glorified image of the ruling Emperor, is yet another. It may also be the case that we are so little at home in our own skins that the idea of God's truly entering into our earthy condition becomes seriously unimaginable.

Precisely here, Jesus research refreshes the imagination of the church about the genuine humanity of the eschatological prophet from Nazareth. Fed by historical research, a clearer grasp of Jesus' humanity now provides christology with a new yet ancient starting point. Instead of beginning in heaven and tracing a descending pattern as the Word becomes flesh (christology from above, modeled on John's gospel), leading edges of contemporary christology begin on earth with Jesus of Nazareth and trace an ascending pattern from his life through death to resurrection into glory (christology from below, modeled on the synoptic gospels). As aspects of this paradigm shift to an ascending pattern are explored, the full humanity of Jesus becomes harder and harder to ignore.

And here is a key point. Jesus research affects the imagination of faith about the true humanity of the Word made flesh not by generalizing but by *particularizing*. Jesus of Nazareth is not a generic human being but a specific one. His human nature is not an abstraction but an expression of a concrete human life shaped by a real history in the world. He is situated in time and place, namely, first-century Palestine. Like everyone else he descends from a line of ancestors, in his case the people of Israel. He is Jewish, both culturally and religiously, and his worldview is fed by streams of that religious tradition. His human identity is shaped by his relationships to a quite specific family in a politically oppressed society. He is no stranger to the passions of red-blooded humanity but experiences the vagaries of the flesh in his own circumstances. Despite his many gifts he is limited in knowledge and needs to grow in self-awareness and discernment of his vocation. His career is not pre-programmed but the result of free decisions, not always easily made, about his ministry and its focus.

Even a few such details change the imagination and feed the rediscovery of the truly historical human dimension of christological belief. Now it becomes harder to maintain a "Superman" model of Jesus' life, one where he is a mild-mannered worker in wood and stone on the outside, with secret, souped-up powers on the divine inside, as if his mind and will were not utterly affected by his finite, social location in history.

However, while it may be easy to admit that Jesus was human insofar as his body was real flesh that could experience pleasure and pain, and while it may even be admissible that he thought and spoke in Jewish categories, resistance to the impact of Jesus research often draws a line in the sand over Jesus' own self-consciousness. Such resistance finds it difficult to allow that the one confessed as Lord and Christ actually experienced nescience and exercised genuine human free will. One of the earliest theologians to grapple with this issue was Karl Rahner, whose 1961 essay continues to shed a helpful light. Far from being an actor reciting lines already written, or a puppet whose strings were pulled by a heavenly power, Jesus' self-knowledge and decision-making had a "truly human" character. How is this thinkable?[1]

In his typical turn to the subject, Rahner proposes that we start by observing the way in which we know ourselves. Taking a page from transcendental philosophy, he figures that human self-consciousness is structured around two related poles. At one pole, the subjective one, we enjoy a wordless, pre-thematic, intuitive grasp of who we are. Here we "know" our self by being fundamentally present to our self as the person we are. This deep self-presence guides how we typically conduct daily life, react to emergencies, make major life decisions. Obviously, this sense of who we are can never be totally expressed in words. Rather, it is a continuous, subliminal self-knowledge that grounds and pervades all we do as human subjects. At the other pole, the objective one, we "know" who we are by means of words and facts. Our name, age, and vital statistics, family lineage, likes and dislikes, conscious preferences all are forms of self-knowledge that we can articulate out loud and communicate to others. Knowledge of ourselves at this objective pole is a matter of definition. Since this knowledge can never spell out who we are in the depths of our person at the subjective pole and is always subject to further development, there is always a sense in which we both know and don't know ourselves at the same time.

Throughout our historical lives various experiences provide the occasion to translate our intuitive self-awareness at the subjective pole into self-defining words and concepts at the objective pole. Reflective people do this more than others, but all do it to some degree. Success and failure, experiences of love or rejection, temptations we wrestle with, choices we make, skills we develop, and so forth all help us to spell ourselves out in a more concrete way as life goes on. This is a life-long process, with new experiences enabling us to get a more secure handle on our identity as time goes by, so that people enjoy a more articulated knowledge of themselves at the age of forty than when they were twenty. Since there is no limit to learning about ourselves, the process of self-interpretation can continue all the way up to the moment of death.

What is true for human beings in general is also the case with Jesus of Nazareth. He experienced a living history of interpreting himself to himself as a result of his life experience: "and Jesus grew in wisdom and age and grace before God and human beings" (Lk 2:52). At the subjective pole of self-knowledge he grasps himself non-verbally as the person he is, namely, the Word made flesh. This self-consciousness, however, is not explicit but pre-conceptual, intuitive. One could argue that it is the source that propels his own adult assumption of teaching authority, his profound relation with the mystery of God whom he called 'abba, and his compassionate connection to the dispossessed. But this self-knowledge is not a clear and distinct definition. The carpenter from Nazareth does not wake up in the morning reciting the prologue of John's gospel or the formula of the Nicene Creed. Rather, it takes his whole lifetime with all its experiences for him to grasp himself in concrete terms. It takes the events of his ministry, of those who love or reject him, of those who ask "Are you the Christ?" all the way up to and including the moment of his agonized death when he felt abandoned even by the God whom he had passionately served. It is this very limitation of knowing that allows for Jesus to make genuinely free human decisions, for such entail a certain darkness about future outcomes.

To ask the question bluntly: did Jesus know he was God? Rahner concludes: yes and no. Yes at the subjective pole of self-awareness where we intuitively grasp who we are. No at the objective pole of self-awareness where we define ourselves in concrete terms. To put the question another way: did this first-century Jewish man think he was Yahweh? Of course not. The very parameters of the faith in which he worshiped forbade such a self-definition. In later years Christians would have to develop the very concept of God into trinitarian terms in order to make this identification.

Allowing for psychological development and a genuine situated freedom in Jesus of Nazareth is an acid test of how radically "one in being with us as to his humanity" we are prepared to allow him to be. The subjective/objective structure of human self-consciousness operating in history is simply one theological construct that permits us to think how this could work. If one holds to a position that considers Jesus a "mere man," even if an extraordinary Jewish one, then the impact of Jesus research on Christian imagination is not so dramatic. But if one holds deeply to the classical confession of faith, this scholarship brings to birth a renewed appreciation of just how radical the incarnation really is.

The biblical scholar Raymond Brown concluded his own research into the gospels' evidence of how much Jesus knew or didn't know by quoting the ultra-orthodox fifth century doctor of the church Cyril of Alexandria, who wrote: "We have admired his goodness in that for love of us he has not refused to descend to such a low position as to bear all that belongs to our nature, included in which is ignorance."[2] The Word of God with us and for us under the conditions of genuine human existence, which is inevitably particular and limited—how much further could Love go?

THE GOOD NEWS OF SALVATION

Changing the memory image of the historical humanity of Jesus is also broadening ways of understanding the redeeming impact of his life and destiny. "For us human beings and for our salvation": thus does the Nicene Creed sum up faith in the overflowing, beneficent results that flow to needy humankind thanks to Jesus Christ. How can this be understood?

In the decades after Jesus' death and resurrection, biblical scholars point out, early Christians ransacked their religious heritage and their surrounding culture to find ways of expressing the meaning of what they had experienced in his death and resurrection. The New Testament is rich with their imaginative expressions. They appealed to business metaphors of buying, redeeming, or ransoming something for a price. They employed medical metaphors of healing and being made whole again. They called into play legal metaphors of justification, someone on trial being declared not guilty; political metaphors of being liberated, delivered, set free; and military metaphors of victory over the powers of evil. Experience of animal sacrifice in the temple provided them with the cultic metaphor of sacrificial atonement. Experience of a

peaceful end to personal and corporate animosity gave them relational metaphors of reconciliation, breaking down walls that divide, and being brought near. Paul uses the family metaphor of
being adopted children to describe their new relationship to God,
while John envisions the even more profound relationship of being
verily born of God.

Unlike conciliar declarations that delineated the inner constitution of Jesus Christ in terms of one person in two natures, language about his saving work was never subject to ecclesial
dispute and definition. In the course of time, however, especially
in Western Christianity, one metaphor came to predominate,
namely, that of sacrificial atonement. This was largely due to the
influence of Anselm's treatise *Cur Deus Homo* written in the tenth
century. Reflecting the feudal context in which he wrote where
the feudal lord's word was the sole source of law and order, Anselm interpreted sin as an act that deeply offends the honor of
the Lord of the universe. Continuing the parallel, he reasoned
that in order to restore order, satisfaction had to be paid. But
human beings, being finite, can never make sufficient satisfaction because the nature of the Person offended is infinite. So God
became a human being to accomplish this end. How is it done?
As a human being Jesus owes God loving obedience at every
moment, so if he simply lived a perfect life, that would not accomplish anything. Because he is sinless, however, there is one
thing that by rights he should not suffer, namely death, which is
a punishment for sin. So Jesus Christ freely dies on the cross,
giving God something that is truly un-owed. He thereby earns
infinite satisfaction which, because he does not need it himself, he
distributes to us sinners.

Anselm intended this inquiry as a demonstration of the mercy
of God who did for humankind what we could not do for ourselves. Thanks to Jesus' sacrificial death, the debt of the rest of humanity is paid: we are freed from sin and restored to right
relationship with God. But this satisfaction theory soon took on
darker colors in the hands of lesser thinkers and the growing juridical power of the medieval church. Despite Aquinas's efforts to
tone down the *necessity* of a bloody, sacrificial death, the metaphor
promoted a heavily sinful view of the world and forgetfulness of

the free grace already liberally poured out in Christ. Despite Scotus's criticism of the image of God as a mighty Lord concerned mainly with his own honor, preachers promoted the notion of God as an offended, even angry father who needs to be placated by the blood of his precious son.

The metaphor's narrative focus on the cross, moreover, led to the idea that death was the very purpose of Jesus' life. He came to die. The script was already written before he stepped onto the world stage. This not only robs Jesus of his human freedom, but it sacralizes suffering more than joy as an avenue to God. It tends to glorify violent death as having some kind of value. Liberation theologies note how, as a result, the cross can be used wrongly to inculcate passivity in the face of unjust suffering rather than inspiring action to resist, because one is supposed to imitate the Suffering Servant who died obediently and opened not his mouth.[3] Referencing the experience of domestic abuse, particularly the abuse of children, feminist theologies critique this model's notion of a father who allows or even needs the death of a child, no matter what benefit might result for others. Our salvation is no excuse for cosmic child abuse.[4]

The difficulties that have accrued around the sacrificial atonement metaphor of salvation, exacerbated by its almost exclusive use for centuries, do not negate the importance of the cross or the power of redemptive suffering. Rather, new theological interpretation is called for that will head off debilitating complications while doing justice to the centrality of Jesus' death "for us." By setting the cross in its historical context, Jesus research contributes to this needed solution. It offers a new imagination with which to appreciate the Messiah's saving work.

1. The view of salvation fed by Jesus research links the cross with the ministry that preceded it and the resurrection that followed it in an organic way, rather than let the cross stand alone as the saving act of atonement.

Restoring people to wholeness in their relationship with God and each other begins in the public ministry itself. Jesus' preaching of the coming reign of God, by turns joyful and challenging, coupled with his healings, exorcisms, inclusive table fellowship, and partisanship for marginalized people, already offers a foretaste of the world in which God reigns, a world without tears. In his company diverse people—including sinners, the sick, women, men, the young, the established, seekers, poor of all kinds—experience new community with God. In those days, separation of religion and state was not something anyone had yet conceived of. The enthusiasm stirred up by the people around Jesus was seen as politically dangerous in a time of mass movements against Roman occupation; a messiah would be an enemy of the emperor. In addition, driving home his vision with prophetic passion, Jesus performed a symbolic action against the temple in Jerusalem during the feast of Passover, overturning the tables and freeing the animals meant for sacrifice. Thereby he earned the animosity of the entrenched priestly class who would prove to be formidable enemies.

In historical perspective, Jesus' death on the cross is a consequence of his prophetic ministry. Historically it was not foreordained. If he had changed course, taken seriously the warning not to go up to Jerusalem, the crucifixion probably would not have happened. But he opted for fidelity to his vocation, preaching the reign of God and enacting God's compassion to the poor. As his movement proved a thorn in the side of the powers that be, they removed him. Repressive regimes do this all the time. He was put to death in the prime of life, his movement in tatters, his promises mocked, to all intents and purposes even abandoned by the God whose merciful drawing near he had so passionately proclaimed.

Such darkness puts into high relief the power of the resurrection, restoring it to the pivotal role it enjoys in early Christian preaching and the New Testament itself. The resurrection of Jesus into glory is not a natural outcome to his life story but an irruption of divine power that creates an irreplaceable turning point. God raised him up. Herein lies the saving power of this event: death does not have the last word. The crucified one is not annihilated but brought to new life in the embrace of God, who remains faithful in surprising ways. Thereby the judgment of earthly judges is reversed and Jesus' own person, intrinsically linked with his preaching and praxis, is vindicated. This event unleashes a new Spirit into history, the Spirit of life. Through the presence of Jesus, the crucified one who is now the Living One, a future is offered to all others who have come to grief.

2. In this organically unified view of life-death-resurrection, Jesus research gives rise to an interpretation of the death of Jesus as the destiny of the prophet sent from God.

As an event shaped by the forces of history, his death did not happen with ironclad necessity but was the result of contingent circumstances and free human decisions. Promoting the coming reign of God in word and deed, Jesus and his movement ran afoul of the interests of ruling powers in his corner of the world. Knowing his life was in danger, he continued nevertheless to preach and act in accord with the burning passion of his life, which was God's drawing near as salvation for all, especially the poor and marginalized people, in hope that his ministry would succeed. Our own era presents living examples of this dynamic in the persons of Oscar Romero, Ignacio Ellacuría, Martin Luther King, the four North American churchwomen Ita Ford, Maura Clark, Dorothy Kazel, and Jean Donovan, and others who have given outstanding witness to the point of their death. They are not seeking death but a transformation of people's hearts with so-cial ramifications in the name of God. In an antagonistic world, they are crushed. Then others who are affected begin to feel the power of their remembered lives and interpret their deaths, in continuity with their lives, as redemptive suffering for others.

So too, and uniquely so in view of the resurrection, with Jesus of Nazareth. Subsequent to the traumatic events of the end of his life, the women and men who followed him sought to interpret what had happened as somehow connected with God's merciful plan to save. They developed the language of this having hap-pened "for us," and retrojected their new understanding back into their oral retelling of events of the ministry. They came to see that Jesus' love which caused him to risk all and end up in un-holy suffering mediated the gracious compassion of God over human misery. But as the events actually unrolled in history, there was no prior necessity for this bloody outcome.

To put it simply, Jesus, far from being a masochist, did not come to die but to live and to help others live in the joy of divine love. God the Creator and Lover of the human race, the covenanting God of Israel, Jesus' own *abba*, did not need Jesus' death as an act of atonement but wanted him to flourish in his ministry of the coming reign of God. Human sin thwarted this divine desire yet did not defeat it. The unjust, tormented death of this marginalized Jewish victim of state punishment becomes, for faith, the opening for a new, surprising, healing, and liberating presence of God in the world.

3. Flowing from this interpretation of the cross as the historical death of the prophet sent from God, an interpretation rooted in Jesus' ministry and completed in the resurrection, the view of salvation fed by Jesus research shifts theological emphasis from the cross as a sole, violent act of atonement for sin before an offended God to the cross as an act of suffering solidarity that brings divine saving power into intimate contact with human misery, pain, and hopelessness.

Part of the difficulty with the atonement/satisfaction metaphor, especially as it has played out in a juridical context, lies in the way it valorizes suffering. Rather than being something to be resisted or remedied in light of God's will for human well-being, suffering is seen as a good in itself or even a condition necessary for God's honor. It is true that in the course of human life a measure of suffering can teach us wisdom and help to mature character. Its presence can also call forth responses of enormous charity and care for the weak and vulnerable, thereby developing the virtue of those not personally suffering. While suffering is a genuine mystery whose meaning can never be fully elucidated, all of the world's religious traditions seek to connect this experience with the ultimate power of the universe in some way, helping people to cope and promising release. However, the particular angle taken by the juridical atonement construal of Jesus' death makes suffering in itself a good. Not only has this led to masochistic tendencies in piety, which are far removed from genuine asceticism, but as this has played out in the public sphere it has promoted acceptance of suffering resulting from injustice rather than energizing resistance.

In the light of what Schillebeeckx calls the "excess" of suffering in our world, in the light of the unjust, bloody deaths of mil-

lions of people in violent wars and the continued unjust suffering
of multitudes of people due to poverty, oppression, and violence,
the cross cannot be used to valorize continued misery. Jesus research gives rise to a theology of salvation that argues that the
depth of suffering Jesus experienced on the cross, the wretched
suffering as such, is not *in itself* salvific. Indeed, speaking from
the historical point of view, numerous theologians today do not
hesitate to call his execution a tragedy, a disaster, a fiasco, an un-
mitigated failure. Rather than being an act willed by a loving
God, it is a strikingly clear index of sin in the world, a wrongful
act committed by human beings. What may be considered salvific
in such a situation is not the suffering endured but only the love
poured out. The saving kernel in the midst of such negativity is
not the pain and death as such but the mutually faithful love of
Jesus and his God, not immediately evident.

Such a view brackets any idea of God as a sadistic father,
Jesus as a passive, sacrificial victim, his death as a payment for
our benefit, and human misery as willed by God as penalty for
sin. To the contrary, Jesus' suffering, a fate resulting from his free,
loving fidelity to his prophetic ministry and his God, is precisely
the way our gracious God has chosen to enter into solidarity with
all those who suffer and are lost in this broken world. Divine participation in Jesus' suffering coupled with the outpouring of the
Spirit of life in his resurrection gives assurance of new life in,
through, and beyond sin, misery, guilt, and death. Rather than
endorsing apathetic indifference, this interpretation impels Christians to enter the list of those who struggle against injustice for
the well-being of those who suffer, for this is where God is to be
found, trying to bring about joy in the beloved creation even here,
even now.

To sum up this point: the view of salvation fed by Jesus research allows the rich tapestry of metaphors found throughout the
New Testament to be brought back into play. Being liberated,
healed, ransomed and set free, justified, forgiven, reconciled,
adopted or born as God's very own children, all augment the
sense of being brought to safety with God thanks to Jesus Christ.
No one image and its accompanying theology can exhaust the experience and meaning of salvation through Jesus Christ. Taken to-

gether they correct distortions that arise when one alone is overemphasized. The whole New Testament promotes the growth of a plurality of theologies of salvation fit for today's different times and places.

THE CHURCH: FOLLOWING JESUS CHRIST

Christians form the community of disciples graced by the Spirit who follow Jesus. As such, they take their cue for right action, belief, and relationship from their memory image of him. Originally the community in Palestine was comprised of Jewish disciples, male and female, who in the light of the resurrection increasingly interpreted Jesus as the expected Messiah, the Christ. Far from giving them any reason to leave their Jewish religion, this encouraged their continued religious observance while they preached the good news of the fulfillment of God's ancient promise to their fellow Jews. They engaged in some distinctive acts such as baptism and gathering in each other's homes for the breaking of the bread while continuing their pattern of Jewish prayer and temple worship. Over time, the success of their preaching to the Gentiles widened their membership demographically, creating fierce tensions about observance of Torah. As the number of Gentile Christians grew, the number of Jewish Christians declined, but it was decades before the latter group split, or were put out, from the synagogue.

As was the case with Jesus' historical life, there was no blueprint for early Christians to follow in those earliest decades. What is clear is that the words and deeds of Jesus as recounted in the gospels did not set up patriarchal structures among his disciples. Recall his warning against lording it over others like the Gentiles, his calls to loving service, his washing feet. Recall, too, the women disciples who followed him in Galilee and stood by the cross, among them Mary Magdalene to whom the risen Christ entrusted the proclamation of his resurrection. The New Testament gives further evidence of the active leadership of women in the founding of the church. But once the fledgling church became established under protection of the Roman emperor, it took on the shape of the patriarchal empire itself.

Did Jesus found the church? Not in the sense of setting up the hierarchical Vatican offices of pope and bishops as we have them today. Yes, in the sense that he gathered a group of women and men disciples to follow him and imbued them with a certain style of life and prayer in view of the coming reign of God. In changing circumstances after his death and resurrection they faced new issues, nor could the particularities of Jesus' own life be duplicated. Empowered by the Spirit they had to improvise, discerning how the truth of his message and presence could best be embodied in new times and places. They followed Jesus not by slavish imitation but by creative application of his values, imprinting his presence in new situations as best they could.

Ever since, through a terribly messy history, the core dynamic has been the same. The future of what Jesus started is being lived out. In the dramatic words of Edward Schillebeeckx, "The living community is the only real reliquary of Jesus."[5] Down through the centuries we keep alive the dangerous memory of Jesus. We encounter his presence in word and sacrament. Inspired by the Spirit we follow in his footsteps, creatively engaged in ministries of healing, liberation, and compassionate justice that mediate fragments of salvation into the world here and now. The better the church does this, the more the presence of Christ can vibrantly affect the world:

> By following Jesus, taking our bearings from him and allowing ourselves to be inspired by his Spirit, by sharing in his Abba experience and his selfless support for the "least of these," and thus entrusting our own destiny to God, we allow the history of Jesus, the Living One, to continue in history as a piece of living christology, the work of the Spirit in the world.[6]

The church as a piece of living christology: herein lies the link with Jesus research, for new understandings of Jesus' own historical story lead to critique of some of the church's practices and inspire new directions. As a piece of living christology, the church is awakened and challenged by Jesus research to a new faithfulness.

THE LIVING GOD

Since Christians believe Jesus to be the Word, Wisdom, and revelation of God, truly divine, then what scholarship turns up about
the specificity of this particular first-century Jewish human being
has great import for understanding the character and intent of the
living God. Under the rubric of a high and confessionally orthodox christology, recovering the history of Jesus becomes a route to
recovering aspects of divine mystery generally submerged by the
classical doctrine of God. That doctrine, drawn largely from philosophical principles apart from revelation, conceives of God as an
absolute, self-subsistent being with attributes of infinite perfection
such as omnipotence, immutability, and impassibility, and so constituted as to have no real relation to the world or its history. Reversing direction, theology today seeks to think the reality of God
from the history of Jesus Christ. If Jesus belongs to the definition
of God, what does the concrete shape of the history of this human
being reveal about the incomprehensible divine mystery? So
strongly is this work being done that many claim nothing short of
a "revolution" is occurring in the concept of God.[7]

The being of God as triune self-relation, truly related to the
world, able in freedom to self-empty, able in love to suffer with
beloved creation, powerfully compassionate over the pain of the
world, willing to be its liberator from evil: such insights are now
on the table. Leander Keck states the logic simply: "whom God
vindicates discloses the character of God."[8] In raising Jesus from
the dead, God vindicates a prophet who proclaims the compassionate rule of the living God come to overturn evil and set the
world free from powers that enslave. God vindicates a preacher
and teacher who liberates people from a constricting view of this
God, understanding that divine mystery draws near to seek the
lost. God vindicates a lively, Spirit-filled human being who in
gracious acts of inclusive table community, forgiveness, and healing lives out his own message in the concrete. In this way of
thinking, Jesus not only teaches parables about God. He becomes
concretely the parable God is telling in this historical world.

These narratives fuse into a symbol of the character of God.
In the framework of belief in Jesus' divinity, Jesus research tracks

how early Christians extrapolated from the words and actions of Jesus to the conception of God's own being as fundamentally and essentially Love (1 Jn 4:8). God is the lover of the earth and human beings who desires the well-being of all. That places God in total opposition to whatever degrades or destroys the beloved creatures. It makes God particularly partisan toward those who are powerless and suffering. Far from being allied with forces or structures that oppress, God's liberating love opposes them and seeks their transformation so that the downtrodden might be released into fullness of life, the singular pre-condition for all human beings to dwell in a new community of mutual regard. It follows that to know and love God, then, is to hunger and thirst for justice, to ally oneself compassionately with the cause of God in solidarity with those who suffer in this world. Understanding God as the ever-coming, liberating God of life is a profound result of theology's reception of Jesus research.

CONCLUSION

Some might object that too much scholarly probing into the life and times of Jesus of Nazareth robs his story of mystery and therefore of its capability of serving faith. In truth, the opposite is occurring. Not only can research never exhaust the reality of a person, any person, whose depths remain unreachable, but historical study succeeds in placing Jesus so carefully in first-century Palestine that he becomes helpfully strange to contemporary persons. The inveterate tendency to domesticate him, making him like unto ourselves, is upended when his own historical concreteness is asserted. Completing his study of the first hundred years or so of Jesus research, Albert Schweitzer used the startling image of a swinging pendulum to describe this result. Research had loosed the bands by which Jesus had been riveted to "the stony rocks of ecclesiastical doctrine," and rejoiced to see his figure begin to live and move again. The historical Jesus advanced to meet the modern world. "But he does not stay; He passes by our time and returns to His own." To its dismay, theology could not keep him in its own era but had to let him go. "He returned to His own time, not owing to the application of any historical ingenuity, but by the same inevitable necessity by which the liberated pendulum returns to its original position."[9] Jesus of Nazareth's historical particularity stands as a block to the perennial temptation to co-opt him for our own purposes, whether ecclesiastical, tribal, or personal.

At the same time that scholarly research protects the non-negotiable reality of Jesus in his own time and place, it also feeds the quest for greater understanding today. By giving us clues that Jesus of Nazareth was one kind of person and not another; taught specific things about God and human life and not something else; lived a certain life and died one kind of death and not another; called people to one kind of response and not another, Jesus research is providing new imaginative fodder for Christian life and practice. Neither history that is skeptical of faith nor faith that exists in an a-historical vacuum will suffice to satisfy questions asked in the spirit of our age. But history and faith in mutual relationship can open fruitful new paths.

The work of interpreting the meaning of Jesus Christ will not end as long as there is a Christian community left in the world. Schweitzer concluded his own massive work with a famous statement about the spiritual power flowing from the actual Jesus of history to our time; with this I also conclude:

> He comes to us as one unknown, without a name, as of old, by the lake-side, he came to those who knew him not. He speaks to us the same word: "Follow thou me!" and sets us to the tasks that he has to fulfill for our time. He invites. And to those who respond, whether they be wise or simple, he will reveal himself in the toils, the sufferings, the joys they shall pass through in his fellowship; and, as an ineffable mystery, they shall learn in their own experience who he is.[10]

Adapted from a lecture at the Cardinal Suenens Colloquium, Jerusalem, sponsored by John Carroll University, 2000; published in Jesus: A Colloquium in the Holy Land, *ed. Doris Donnelly (New York: Continuum, 2001), 146–66.*

Notes

1. Karl Rahner, "Dogmatic Reflections on the Knowledge and Self-Consciousness of Christ," *Theological Investigations* V (New York: Seabury/ Crossroad, 1975), 193–215.

2. *PG* 75, 369; Raymond Brown, *Jesus God and Man* (Milwaukee: Bruce, 1967), 102.

3. Carlos Bravo, "Jesus of Nazareth, Christ and Liberator," in *Mysterium Liberationis: Fundamental Concepts of Liberation Theology*, ed. Ignacio Ellacuría and Jon Sobrino (Maryknoll, NY: Orbis Books, 1993), 420–39.

4. Joanne Carlson Brown and Rebecca Parker, "For God So Loved the World?" in *Violence against Women and Children: A Christian Theological Sourcebook*, ed. Carol Adams and Marie Fortune (New York: Continuum, 1995), 36–59.

5. Edward Schillebeeckx, *Christ: The Experience of Jesus as Lord* (New York: Seabury, 1980), 641.

6. Ibid.

7. The claim to revolution is made by Jürgen Moltmann, Hans Küng, Walter Kasper, Jon Sobrino, Leander Keck, among others. See Elizabeth Johnson, "Christology's Impact on the Doctrine of God," *The Heythrop Journal* 26 (1985): 143–63.

8. Leander Keck, *A Future for the Historical Jesus* (Minneapolis: Fortress Press, 1981), 234.

9. Albert Schweitzer, *The Quest of the Historical Jesus* (New York: Macmillan, 1968), 399.

10. Ibid., 403, paraphrased: Schweitzer thinks with a more monarchical understanding of God than I do; consequently he used a command-and-obey model, rather than an invite-and-respond model, to describe the relationship between Jesus and the believer.

12

"Christ died for us"

Text: Romans 5:1–8

> Therefore, since we are justified by faith, we have peace
> with God through our Lord Jesus Christ. Through him we
> have obtained access to this grace in which we stand, and
> we rejoice in our hope of sharing the glory of God. More
> than that, we rejoice in our sufferings, knowing that suf-
> fering produces endurance, and endurance produces char-
> acter, and character produces hope, and this hope does not
> disappoint us, because the love of God has been poured
> into our hearts through the Holy Spirit who has been given
> to us. While we were yet helpless, at the right time, Christ
> died for the ungodly. Why, one will hardly die for a right-
> eous person, though perhaps for a good person one will
> dare even to die. But God shows his love for us in that
> while we were yet sinners, Christ died for us.

Christ died for us. Indeed, "God showed his love for us in that
while we were yet sinners, Christ died for us . . . ," bringing us, as
our text tells us, a treasury of blessings: we are justified, at peace
with God, full of hope and rejoicing, our hearts full of love. During
this Lenten season we are keeping vigil with this death, seeking
deeper, reconciled relation with the living God. At this Vespers, let
us reflect further on the meaning of this text: Christ died for us.

The very heart of Christian faith confesses the surprising belief that this violent, tortured, bloody death is a pathway to life.
For God did not abandon Jesus to annihilation but held him in a
faithful embrace and raised him to new, unimaginable life in the

Spirit. This becomes the pledge, indeed the first shining forth of the future promised to us as well, and to the whole world.

But still, there is that death—unjust, abandoned, ending with an agonized cry. It haunts our memory. Once during an interview with a Catholic journal I said that personally I hated Good Friday. I couldn't stand the violence and the pain, the destruction of a good person. In fact, in recent years during the reading of the gospel at the liturgy of that day, when the congregation participates by calling out "Crucify him! Crucify him!" I find myself calling out "Don't do it!" The journal printed this musing, and subsequent "Letters to the Editor" were lively, as you might imagine. A few even accused me of losing the faith. But others caught the dilemma. How in our day do we cherish and value the good done for us on the cross without allying ourselves with forces of unjust power and the use of violence?

The problem is exacerbated by the medieval doctrine of the atonement, which holds that Jesus' death is somehow necessary to satisfy God's honor, horribly offended by our sin. Jesus Christ, who is sinless, does not owe God any such debt. Out of love for us he freely undergoes death, thereby taking on his own shoulders the punishment we deserve and earning a surplus of satisfaction that goes to make up for our sins. Anselm, the theologian who gave this version of the cross intellectual rigor, meant this as a signal of God's mercy. But in the hands of lesser preachers, it soon became the notion that our sins have angered God and so "he"—and I use "he" deliberately—demands that recompense be made through a bloody death. This view has had a long run in Christian preaching and teaching.

Today it is a view that has run into major difficulties. Liberation theology offers the criticism that this view of the cross puts such a premium on suffering as a way of satisfying God that it creates passivity in believers who are told to be like the Suffering Servant, obedient unto death without opening one's mouth; this is a victim mentality that cuts the nerve of the struggle for justice. Biblical theology points out that the medieval version of atonement offers a horrendous, even sadistic, image of God who needs blood and death in order to show mercy—quite contrary to the God pictured in the parables of Jesus. A number of women theologians argue that even if it results in good news for us (we are saved), the violent method, set within a father-son narrative, models an abusive parent-child relationship. Why should a human father refrain from beating his child if even God did not spare his own Son? Note that this is not what the atonement theory intends, but it is the way the symbol functions when seen from the vantage point of those who have in fact been abused.

If indeed Jesus did not have to die to placate a God wrathful over our offenses, what do we mean when we say, in faith, that "Christ died for us"? Indeed, that "God showed his love for us in that while we were yet sinners, Christ died for us..."?

One way to begin is to reconnect Jesus' death to his life that led up to it and his resurrection that followed. Then we can interpret the cross in its own historical context as a not-completely-unexpected outcome of his prophetic ministry that he undertook in politically turbulent times. The resurrection is an act of new creation in which God shows everlasting faithfulness, vindicating the crucified Jesus as a pledge of the future that awaits all those defeated in death.

Proclaiming the reign of God and enacting this liberating message in his healings and table fellowship, bringing joy to all sorts of marginalized people, Jesus challenged religious authority and the way it interpreted his own Jewish tradition. Given the Roman occupation, this was not without political consequences. All who are engaged in a dangerous ministry have to face the price they might pay. Freely, but not without struggle, Jesus chose to be faithful to his God who was the passion of his life. He remained committed to those he loved and served, and to his vocation, despite very real threats. His hopes for success were not fulfilled. In historical terms, his death was a failure, an event of the power of evil overcoming good.

Christian faith dares to believe that this evil does not checkmate God's compassionate and loving power. Rather, God's victory over this particular initiative of evil in history shows itself in the resurrection of Jesus from the dead. What a revelation! Far from siding with the powerful judges, God is in solidarity with the victim, opening up a new future despite defeat. Now we understand that we are saved by the death of Jesus thanks to the life that leads up to it, the way he clings faithfully to God in his abandonment, and the way God keeps faith with him despite the worst that humans can do. The whole event unleashes a new Spirit into history, the Spirit of living hope. Through the proclamation of the crucified Jesus, the Living One, a future is offered to all those who have come to grief, even though suffering remains intractable. The salvation of the world becomes a new and strong possibility.

Scripture becomes very helpful here. Different New Testament authors interpreted the cross with a variety of metaphors taken not only from temple sacrifice but from business, law, medicine, political peace-making, and family life (through the cross we are adopted as heirs of God; through the cross we are born again as God's own children). Each of these images shifts the paradigm radically away from Jesus as a passive victim who died to satisfy a divine demand and toward the cross as a primary instance of suffering born of love that gives life. In the interest of a deeper grasp of this point, let us explore the last-mentioned idea that we are born of God, a maternal metaphor prevalent in the gospel and letters of John.

If you have ever given birth yourself, or witnessed birth-giving live or on film, you will recall what a profound experience of death-to-life this is. The woman is seized with contractions she is powerless to resist. Her only choice is whether to cooperate freely or not. The pain becomes so intense that it blocks out all thought. She gasps, sweats, cries out, pushes, sheds blood from deep within herself. In the end, she delivers into the world a new life, a precious person who is her very own child. One of the most eloquent writers about the connection between woman's experience of childbirth and the saving work of Jesus is the fourteenth-century theologian and mystic Julian of Norwich. Listen to her words and see if they don't interpret the violence of the cross in a new way.

> We know that all our mothers bear us for pain and death, oh yes.... But our true Mother Jesus, he alone bears us for joy and for endless life, blessed may he be. So he carried us within himself in love and travail, until the fullness of time when he delivered us, suffering the cruelest pains. And at the last, he died. And when he had finished, and had borne us so for bliss, still all this could not satisfy his wonderful love.

What else could a mother do? Julian writes,

> The mother can give her child to suck of her milk, but our precious Mother Jesus can feed us with his body, and does so most courteously and most tenderly with the blessed sacrament, which is the food of true life.

This connection between the cross and the Eucharist, between the maternal power of giving life and then nourishing it, is a profound insight, present in the writings of the early fathers of the church and expressed by many mystics. Julian knew well that the office of motherhood does not end with our infancy. She writes:

> As the child grows in age and stature, the mother acts differently but she does not change her love. And when the child is even older, she allows it to be chastised to correct its faults, so as to make the child able to receive virtue and grace. This work, too, with everything which is lovely and good, our Mother Jesus performs in those whom he loves.

As adults, of course, we fall and sin and become wretched. But even then, especially then, Christ's maternal love does not abandon us. Writes Julian:

> The mother can lay her child tenderly on her breast, but our tender Mother Jesus can lead us easily into his blessed breast through his sweet open side [pierced by the lance], and show us there the love of God and give us certainty of endless joy.
>
> For we truly see there that though we have sinned grievously in this life, we were never of less value in his sight; for enduring and marvelous is his motherly love which cannot and will not be broken because of offenses.

And so Julian encourages sinners:

> When we are so much afraid and greatly ashamed of ourselves that we scarcely know what to do, our courteous

Mother does not wish us to flee away. But he wants us to behave like a child who when distressed runs quickly to its mother, calling to its mother with all its might saying, my kind Mother, my gracious Mother, my beloved Mother, help me. I have made myself filthy and unlike you, and I cannot make it right except with your help and grace. . . . And then the flood of mercy which is his dear blood will flow plentifully to make us fair and clean. Yes, the blessed wounds of our Savior are open to rejoice and heal us. The sweet gracious hands of our Mother are always ready and diligent about us.

Stretching this theology of motherly love to include the whole world, Julian concludes:

Let us lament our sins to our beloved Mother, and he will sprinkle us all with his precious blood, and heal us most gently, for his own glory and our joy. And from this sweet and gentle operation he will never cease or desist until all his beloved children are born and brought to birth.

It might seem strange to speak of Jesus' cross in this motherly way. Not only is there a contrast of genders, for he is male and mothers are female, but such speech also takes the physical act of childbirth, traditionally judged by patriarchal thought and law to be unclean, and uses it as a symbol of the loving mystery of God's saving work. As the complex metaphor plays out, we are subtly led away from a notion of the cross as a necessary act required by a displeased God in payment for sin. Rather, Jesus' suffering, freely borne in faithful love, is precisely the way our gracious God has chosen to enter into solidarity with all those who suffer and are lost in this violent world, in order to bring new life. Divine participation in suffering brings about new life beyond sin, misery, guilt, and death. It is, in some sense, a very motherly work.

In a graduate class at Fordham University where we were studying these texts, one of my students announced that her daughter-in-law was even now in labor. The baby would be this student's first grandchild. After class she hurried to the hospital and, according to hospital policy, was admitted to the delivery room where a healthy little boy had been born a half-hour before. As she along with the other delighted grandparents held the baby and welcomed him into their family, she noticed a sheet stained red with blood, witness to the price of the birth. It was the brightest red she had ever seen. Her glimpse was only a brief moment of awareness amid the general rejoicing. An aide soon quietly and efficiently scooped it up for laundering. The next morning this new grandmother attended Mass to thank God for the safe delivery. During communion, a moment of revelation struck. "Body of Christ," yes, Amen. But when she was handed the cup with the words "Blood of Christ," the vision of that sheet red with the blood of a young woman who had brought forth life riveted her to the spot. Stunned with realization, she wept and could scarcely drink. Mother Jesus, indeed. Jesus' death on the cross is part of the larger, cosmic mystery of pain-for-life, of that struggle for the new creation, evocative of the rhythm of pregnancy, labor, and birthing so familiar to women of all ages.

Our text reminds us: "God showed his love for us in that while we were yet sinners, Christ died for us." In the middle of this Lent, let us individually and as a community be drawn ever more deeply into the liberating mystery of how Jesus' suffering born of active love can lead to life, by the gracious power of God. Yes, there is Mother Jesus' agony. There is also the promise that rings from Easter morning. In Julian's words, "All shall be well, and all manner of thing shall be well." Let us cling to this hope, ever so haltingly but gratefully. For "this hope does not disappoint us, because the love of God has been poured into our hearts through the Holy Spirit who has been given to us."

Adapted from a homily at Lenten Vespers, Corpus Christi Church, Manhattan, 2000. Citations from Julian of Norwich, Showings, *ed. Edmund Colledge and James Walsh (New York: Paulist Press, 1978), 293–305.*

13

Resurrection
Promise of the Future

At the very center of the Christian faith lives a source of hope, namely, the crucified Jesus alive in God and graciously, vigorously present through the power of the Spirit within the suffering world. At its deepest level Christian faith is a response to this presence or it makes no sense at all. Returning to this center offers a profound antidote to discouragement. For the sake of hope, this article will explore the theological meaning and spiritual power unleashed by the resurrection of the crucified.

No one actually saw Jesus rise from the dead. While the gospels describe the empty tomb, none attempt to explain exactly how it got that way. "Christ rose in the silence of God," wrote Ignatius of Antioch. At the outset we must caution ourselves that ordinary language is inadequate to the event being described, which goes beyond history and human experience. None of us yet knows what it is like to live beyond death in the glory of God.

That being said, theology does dare to seek some understanding. One of the preferred categories frequently pressed into service is that of transformation. For Jesus himself, the resurrection brings about the transformation of his whole human, historical life now alive in glory with God. This is not simply belief in the immortality of the soul; Jesus does not shuck off his humanity like a suit of clothes and rise heavenward as a purely spiritual being. Rather, his whole person in all its dimensions is pervaded by the vivifying Spirit and made whole in a completely new way.

To highlight this understanding, it is helpful to contrast this model of transformation with two other ways of thinking about the risen Christ.

At one end of the spectrum, a basically literal interpretation of the Bible holds the resurrection to be a physical event similar to the resuscitation of a corpse. In this view the risen Jesus' body still has the same qualities as our own, only with more powerful control. It is taken as obvious that the original appearances of the risen Jesus were objectively tangible events in time and space, events which even a neutral bystander could have observed. Many stained glass windows and Easter cards depicting Jesus coming forth from a bright grave wrapped in a winding sheet and carrying a flag of victory are imaginative expression of this point of view.

At the other end of the spectrum, a historically skeptical approach to the Bible interprets the resurrection as a purely internal experience of the disciples, equivalent to the rise of Easter faith in their hearts. In their grief and discouragement they began to see the importance of Jesus' death on the cross: he died "for us." They then came to realize that his cause was not finished but they were being called to promote it with their own lives. The resurrection really means, in the famous expression of Rudolf Bultmann, that "Jesus rose into the kerygma." It would not matter if we found his bones.

Currently the majority of Catholic theologians hold to a more centrist, transformationist position, neither purely external and objective like the literalists' position nor completely internal and subjective like that of the existentialists. In this view, both the Easter proclamations such as "he is risen" and the Easter stories of empty tomb and appearances point to God's living Spirit acting on behalf of the crucified Jesus, transforming him to new life in glory. This is made known to his disciples still living in history through a revelatory experience of faith.

This is not a naively physical belief: Jesus has truly died and passed from this world as a historical, embodied person. But neither is it an overly spiritual belief that would grant eternal life only to his spirit while his body corrupts in the grave. Rather, Jesus as a whole person, in all his dimensions and relationships, is transformed and alive with God. There is continuity: notice the wounds. But there is also discontinuity: the disciples do not recognize him.

While this event is frankly unimaginable, the oldest text on the resurrection does shed some light. Responding to questions from the church in Corinth, Paul sends metaphor running after metaphor in order to describe the indescribable. What is the risen body like? First he appeals to agriculture: you do not plant the full body that you eventually harvest, but a seed which has to burst and die before it comes to life. Next he draws attention to the different types of bodies that God has already created: bodies of animals, birds, and fish; bodies on earth and bodies in heaven; the sun, the moon, the stars. With this appeal to nature as a background, he moves into the heart of the matter:

> So it is with the resurrection of the dead. What is sown is perishable; what is raised is imperishable. It is sown in dishonor; it is raised in glory. It is sown in weakness; it is raised in power. It is sown a physical body; it is raised a spiritual body. (1 Cor 1:42–44)

A spiritual body! What a contradiction in terms. Paul has stretched language to the breaking point. But his efforts nevertheless point us toward the basic truth: the crucified one is the living one, his whole person in all dimensions, transformed.

Today some would also appeal to the wonder of a caterpillar becoming a butterfly. The little furry, crawling creature spins a chrysalis about itself, the equivalent of a tomb. Its caterpillar organs and tissues break down. If we were to open a chrysalis at this stage, we would observe total disintegration. But already the creature's genes have triggered adult structures, so that its dying caterpillar cells are refashioned into new organs. What emerges is a beautiful, colorful creature who can fly. What continuity, what discontinuity, what transformation!

Still, the resurrection of Jesus is more unlike than like this or any other organic example from the natural world. For it is not by any inbuilt mechanism of human nature that a deceased person lives again, but only by the gracious power of God. The resurrection starts on earth with Jesus dead and buried and ends up in

God, with Jesus the Living One, transformed by the power of the Spirit. Alive in God, his presence is no longer bound by earth's usual limits but partakes of the omnipresence of God's own love. The disciples became aware of this not through objective sight or inner visions only, but though revelatory religious experiences which may indeed have had a physical component but point to a deeper reality. They "see the light" and know his "presence" through the power of the Spirit with the eyes of faith. From now on they recognize him in the approach of a wise stranger and the breaking of the bread (Emmaus); in the peace of forgiveness (the upper room); in her name uttered to a weeping woman (Mary Magdalene); in a catch of fish and someone cooking breakfast on the shore (John's lovely scene). Christ can also be recognized whenever two or three gather in his name, and in the boldness of speech that accompanies the community in mission. True to the pattern of his ministry, he also approaches, mysteriously revealed and concealed, in the hungry, the thirsty, the sick, the homeless, those in prison, the very least of those in need. Ultimately, through the power of the Spirit, Jesus is with the whole community of disciples though every hour, until the end of time.

To sum up: theologically, the resurrection refers to the act of God that transforms the whole historical reality of the crucified Jesus into new life in glory through the power of the Spirit, thereby releasing his presence throughout the world.

To underscore the obvious, it was not just any person who was raised from the dead but Jesus of Nazareth who was crucified under Pontius Pilate. In a basic and dramatic way, therefore, the resurrection reverses the direction of the human religious and political judges who found the words and deeds of his ministry deserving of death. It makes clear that in God's eyes the victim of capital punishment was right in his message, his actions, his very person. In the teeth of authoritative rejection, it signals God's yes to Jesus of Nazareth and everything he stands for: "to preach good news to the poor, to proclaim release to the captives, recovery of sight to the blind, to set at liberty those who are oppressed, to proclaim the acceptable year of the Lord" (Lk 4:18–19).

Historically, Jesus' death is a consequence of the hostile responses of religious and civil rulers to the style and content of his ministry, to which he was radically faithful with a freedom that would not quit. But, contrary to this judgment of the powerful against him, the resurrection discloses that in and through and beyond his death, God's loving power and wisdom are winning through. Crucified for his ministry, Jesus is now confirmed as the very Word of God, Wisdom of God, Emmanuel, God with us. This disclosure about Jesus is pivotal for his relation to the community of disciples. It reveals him as truly God's anointed, the Messiah. Without it, Christian faith is in vain.

Through what it discloses about Jesus Christ, the resurrection of the crucified also reveals, even defines, the true character of God. Despite all appearances to the contrary, it turns out that God did not abandon Jesus on the cross after all. Rather, when human beings had done their worst and there was no future left for this victim of unjust state punishment, then the vivifying Spirit of God quickened him to life. Instead of dying into nothingness, Jesus dies into the living mystery of God. Thus is disclosed God at God's most typical: full of *hesed* and *emeth*, abounding in loving kindness and fidelity. The God in whom Christians believe is powerful enough and loving enough to do this.

Logically speaking, faith in God who raised Jesus from the dead is not some weird belief, let alone a peculiar supplement to some more essential truth. Rather, it expresses faith in God the Creator in a powerful way. "In the beginning" the Spirit of God moves over dark chaos and God speaks the word of creation: "Let there be." In the resurrection, the Spirit of God moves again over the body of death and God speaks the same word anew: "Let there be life." Original creation and new creation: it is the same loving power of God. The Nicene Creed is utterly logical in the way it begins with God who creates heaven and earth, affirms at the mid-point that on the third day Jesus rose again from the dead, and concludes with belief in the resurrection of the body and the life of the world to come. It is one and the same God, "who gives life to the dead and calls into being the things that do not exist" (Rom 4:17).

The resurrection of Jesus did not end the suffering of the world. Crosses keep on being set up throughout history, and agony perdures. But Christ crucified and risen discloses the truth that divine justice continuously leavens the world, and does so in a way different from the techniques of dominating violence. The victory is won not by the sword of a warrior god but by the power of compassionate love that brings the living God into solidarity with those who suffer in order to heal and set free. The resurrection, then, discloses in a profound way the character of divine mystery: compassionate, faithful, powerfully loving, close even in darkness and failure, bringing forth the new.

The significance of this event for all of humanity cannot be overestimated, for Jesus' resurrection is the beginning of the resurrection of all the dead. Indeed, we are dealing here with an event of the future that has arrived in advance of the last day. In one school of first-century Jewish expectation, the end of the world was going to entail all the dead arising from their graves. The early disciples used this expectation to interpret their experience of the risen Christ, but with a new twist: only one has been raised, not all; and the world has not ended but keeps on its historical way. Yet the fact that one has been raised discloses our common future, and even more importantly, it inserts that future as a reality already here in the struggling world.

Like the first tomato that ripens in a garden, bringing the promise of the harvest to come, "Christ has been raised from the dead, the first fruits of those who have died" (1 Cor 15:20). We see now that the future will be on a universal scale what has already happened in him. Just as the living mystery of God enveloped Jesus at the end of the darkness of death, we too can trust that God will have the last word in our lives as indeed God had the first, and it is the same word: Let there be life.

This is a deep encouragement for men and women who face the reality of their own death. But in a particular way it is profoundly good news for persons who are poor, denigrated, oppressed, struggling, victimized, falsely accused, disappeared, questing for life and the fullness of life. The crucified victim of state injustice is not abandoned forever. God's pure, beneficent, people-loving Spirit seals him in unimaginable life as pledge of a future for all the violated and the dead. Henceforth, his cross becomes the flashpoint that discloses how God participates in the suffering of the world in order to save.

This is the deepest ground of Christian hope and the source of all mission. Formed in the power of the Spirit, the community of disciples keeps alive the dangerous memory of Jesus' life, death, and resurrection as the promise of a blessed future for all, and cooperates with the Spirit to make this redemptive wholeness present in fragments, in an anticipatory way, even now as the struggle of history goes on.

If the Easter event is good news for all human beings, it is equally so for the whole natural world, the cosmos itself. Since Jesus is risen in all his dimensions including the bodily, then matter and all the life systems that develop from it are also destined to become a new heaven and a new earth. Karl Rahner pens a telling phrase: in the risen Jesus a piece of this earth, real to the core, is now forever with God in glory. Since everything is connected with everything else, the future will be on a cosmic scale what has already happened in him. In that sense, Easter is the festival of the future of the earth.

If Christian spirituality and theology had kept this truth clearly in view, they most likely would not have developed the severe world-denying attitudes and practices that mark so much of subsequent religious history. But early Christian theology soon intersected with Hellenistic thought, adopting ancient Greek dualism in its strong form. Hence a strict distinction was made between matter and spirit, with the latter valued more highly because it was thought to be closer in essence to the divine. The basic dualism of spirit over matter with its separate but unequal valuation played itself out in a host of ways: in soul over body, reason over feelings, the permanent over the transitory, heaven over earth, and not incidentally, the masculine over the feminine principle. To be holy was to identify oneself with the first member of these pairs and to flee the second as inferior.

The Easter mystery, however, discloses the sacred value of matter, of the body with its feelings, of what is transitory, and therefore of the earth and the whole universe which is destined for glory. Therefore, to teach or pursue an a-cosmic spirituality is to be profoundly mistaken about the God of the Bible. In the light of the resurrection, those who seek to conform their heart to God's heart will love matter, bodies, the earth, and engage in creative deeds to cherish these in cooperation with the pervasive presence and purpose of the vivifying Spirit.

Christians today may well find themselves dealing with the same emotions and disappointments as the two disciples on the road to Emmaus. They may suffer the "we had hoped" syndrome. The resurrection of the crucified, however, already raises up the pledge that the future is in the hands of the living God who will be victorious in, through, and beyond all suffering and dying. To live imbued with this hope, believers need to be attuned to the presence of Christ in word and sacrament, in those in need, and in the love and community they share. As the Emmaus story makes clear, they also need to attend to the stranger met on the road. Who might be the unrecognized bearer of the presence of Christ? Is it the person of a different culture, a different economic class, a different generation, a different race, a different gender, a different sexual orientation, a different philosophy of life, even a different religious experience of the holy and therefore a different faith tradition? Who are the people with whom we need to dialogue, and what roads are we willing to walk on to meet them? It is entirely possible that such encounter, engaged from the standpoint of faith, may bear the seeds of new, as yet unimagined life.

At the present moment, we have no magic key that will unlock the future. We have only the gracious presence of the living God, searched for in the tangle of our lives and the shadows of our troubled world. We live in faith that the blessing of redeemed wholeness which appeared in Jesus Christ will continue to come in the fragments of personal and social integrity that are a foretaste of future life. Borne up by this transforming hope, we can look into the heart of suffering in our day, not pretending that things are other than they are, but discovering the God of life at work even in the depths of pain. Only in this way can we be energized to cooperate with the Spirit of Jesus the Living One who is moving us into the future, promised but unknown.

*Adapted from an address to the Leadership Conference of Women Religious;
published in* Sisters Today *67 (November 1995): 404–11.*

14

Wisdom Was Made Flesh
and Pitched Her Tent among Us

At a university symposium entitled "Christology in Women's Voices," held at an American university one spring weekend, women and their crosses were very much in evidence. To decorate the auditorium women were invited to display a cross that belonged to them and to describe how this religious symbol connected with their lives. Around the walls of the large meeting hall each artifact was mounted on a colorful scarf with an explanatory card attached. There were marriage crosses with two rings emblazoned at the top; religious profession crosses worn smooth from repeated kissing and handling; crosses taken from the coffin of parents at funerals; Mexican crosses made of straw; Jerusalem crosses received on pilgrimage; multicolored peasant Salvadoran crosses acquired during missions of accompaniment; crosses with the female form of Christa; Celtic crosses and African crosses; a cross given to a woman by her friend before he died of AIDS; ordinary, garden-variety crosses mass-produced in the United States.

Walking the great hall and perusing the meaning of each specific cross in a woman's life left one with a profound sense of wonder. No woman had gone out and bought herself a cross. Each replica of the central Christian symbol had been given and received in the context of a relationship, at the crossroads of great and small events in life. Assembled together, they were a text that told the story of women's ongoing relationship with Jesus Christ. The display witnessed to women's generous practice of true discipleship, the heart of the matter of Christian faith. For women have consistently connected, passionately and practically, with the mystery of Christ despite traditional patriarchal barriers that regularly stand in the way.

Feminist theology is the endeavor that brings this situation, both the faith experience of women and the patriarchal barriers that block their full participation in the church, to explicit, critical reflection. As *theology*, it is an act of "faith seeking understanding" (Anselm), or reflection on God and all things in the light of God (Aquinas), with the goal of moving the heart to love and the whole community to praxis. As *feminist*, it seeks understanding from women's perspective with the same goals, expressly including the flourishing of women. One of its guiding criteria is this: the full humanity of women.

Christian feminist theology works with a threefold method. First, it deconstructs, seeking to uncover readings of the religious narratives, symbols, doctrines, and structures that have traditionally functioned to privilege men and to relegate women's concerns to secondary status. Unfortunately, it discovers that of all the doctrines of the church, christology is the one most used to exclude women. Next, feminist theology looks for buried or neglected alternative interpretations. Is christology hopelessly patriarchal, governed by the rule of the father, or kyriarchal, controlled by the rule of the lord? Or are there other possibilities that could shape a christology of healing and liberation? Third, this theology reconstructs. With critical analysis and alternative options in view, feminist theology speaks anew about Jesus Christ in the liberating light of the gospel, to practical and critical effect. The goal of this way of doing theology is a transformed community and a transformed world, where women's full human dignity is respected in mutuality with that of men, in union with the whole community of life on earth.

This kind of theology is being done on every continent by women of different races, classes, cultures, and churches.[1] They form a mounting chorus of new interpretation arguably more coherent with the original Spirit-inspired impulse of the Christian gospel than is the patriarchal construal that has become so dominant.

From an African-American perspective, Jacqueline Grant analyzes how poor black women are marginalized not only by sex but also by race and class. Drawing upon the experience of some of these women, she describes how they interpret Jesus as their co-sufferer, divine friend, and the only one who knows the trouble they've seen. Since Christ is in solidarity with the "least of the people," he stands with black women in their everyday struggles, affirming their basic worth and inspiring active hope to resist dehumanization. The resurrected Christ, whose Spirit can be seen in the faces of black women, empowers their hope of liberation.[2]

Articulating the experience of women in Korea and the Philippines who bear the mark of colonized people in addition to sexist discrimination, Chung Hyun Kyung and Virginia Fabella write of how the question is not "who" is Jesus Christ but "where" is Jesus Christ for Asian women. In community with his Spirit, women find the seeds of life rather than death, order rather than chaos, friendship rather than isolation. As healer, exorcist, consoler, and friend, and even as mother and shaman, Jesus is an empowering source for women's dignity amid the wider struggle for the full humanity of all those who cry to be liberated from spiritual impoverishment as well as from the suffering of an unjust society.[3]

Amid the exploitation of women in a Latin American culture pervaded with *machismo*, Nellie Ritchie rereads the story of Jesus' immersion in the life of the poor in order to bring them the good news of the kingdom of God. As once he said to women in the gospel, so he says now: Woman, don't cry; stand up; go in peace. The cross will inevitably come, but a new world is being born in the resurrection. "That is why we, Jesus' sisters, do not fold up our banners, nor are we afraid to join the struggle." Instead we employ women's creative, nurturing, and courageous powers to build a world of freedom.[4]

Noting that Christ was a refugee and a guest of Africa, Elizabeth Amoah and Mercy Amba Oduyoye write of the mutuality between African women and Jesus Christ. They seek to extend hospitality to him so that the whole household of the continent may feel at home with him. At the same time, he is their friend and companion who honors and liberates them. As the midwife and farmer named Afua prays, "Yesu, who has received the poor and made us honorable, our exceedingly wise friend, we depend on you as the tongue depends on the jaw...We take shelter under you, the great bush with cooling shade, the giant tree who enables climbers to see the heavens."[5]

For all of these writers and the women whose faith experience they interpret, the ministry, death, and resurrection of Jesus Christ are not simply stories, symbols, doctrines, or religious beliefs, but the impetus that sparks an empowering way of life. As part of this worldwide conversation among Christian women, I write in my own voice, which is that of a white, middle-class, educated, American, Catholic woman. (Note: to respect diversity, feminist theologians refuse to make claims that are universal. In mutual dialogue, we draw strength and insight from our differences.) In this context, this essay traces one pattern of feminist critique, explores one alternative in the Wisdom tradition, and reconstructs one understanding that leads persuasively to the praxis of justice.

CRITIQUING PATRIARCHAL TRADITION:
DISTORTING THE CHRIST

A basic problem presents itself. The church has interpreted Jesus Christ within a patriarchal framework, with the result that the good news of the gospel for all people has been pervaded by the bad news of patriarchal privilege. Historically, as the early church became inculturated in the Greco-Roman world, it adapted its own structures to the model of the patriarchal household and imperial empire. In the process the gospel image of Jesus, the Galilean prophet and healer, was changed into the image of the male head of household and society. He became the absolute ruler, the Pantocrator, whose heavenly reign legitimates the earthly rule of the male head of family, empire, and church. Intellectually the church also adapted its thought patterns to the dualistic philosophy of the day which identified spirit, kin to reason and the divine, with the male principle in the cosmos, while matter, subject to passion and decay, became associated with the female principle. It then seemed proper to interpret the crucified Galilean prophet mainly in male images as the Son of the heavenly Father, or as the incarnate *Logos*, both symbols connected with rationality and thus with the ruling male. Coopted into a model of patriarchal dominance both politically and cognitively, the powerful life of the liberating Jesus lost its subversive significance.

Liberation theologians who are men have vigorously analyzed this development in terms of how it has marginalized the poor. But feminist theology makes clear that the imperial and philosophical traditions that assimilated christology are precisely patriarchal in character. They value male over female reality, arranging both in a hierarchical social order and assigning the highest value and pride of place to men. Let me be very clear about what is at issue here. This is not a criticism of men in general; there are tremendous human beings both inside and outside the church who are men. Nor does this stance question the fact that Jesus of Nazareth was a man, that is, a male human being. His maleness is constitutive for his personal identity, part of the perfection and limitation of his historical reality, and as such it is to be respected. His sex is as intrinsic to his historical person as are his race, class, ethnic heritage, culture, his Jewish religion, his Galilean village roots, and so forth. The difficulty arises, rather, from a thought pattern that privileges men within a structure of church governance from which women are excluded. In this situation, Jesus' sex, unlike other particulars, is singled out and made essential for his being and function as the Christ. Whether this happens consciously or unconsciously, his maleness receives an interpretation that blocks women from participating in the fullness of Christian identity. Consider these distortions.

❖ Jesus' maleness functions to support men's superiority over women in the belief that a particular honor, dignity, and normativity accrue to men because their sex was chosen by the Son of God himself. Indeed, thanks to their sex, men are said to resemble the image of Christ more than women are. This is the iconic argument still mounted against women's ordination by Vatican teaching. For this mentality, the idea the Word might have become female flesh is not even seriously imaginable.

❖ Jesus' maleness is also used to reinforce an exclusively male image of God. If Jesus as a male is the revelation of God, so the implicit reasoning goes, then this points to maleness as an essential characteristic of divine being itself. At the very least it indicates, if not an identification, then more of an affinity between maleness and divinity than is the case with femaleness. This idea is reinforced by the almost exclusive use of father-son metaphors to interpret Jesus' relationship to God. The unwarranted idea develops that there is a necessary ontological connection between the maleness of Jesus' historical person and the maleness of *Logos* as male offspring and disclosure of a male God.

❖ In addition to casting both the human race and God in an androcentric or male-centered mold, yet another distortion jeopardizes women's salvation. The early Christian axiom "What is not assumed is not redeemed, but what is assumed is saved by union with God," sums up the insight that Christ's solidarity with all of human nature is what is crucial for salvation. *Et homo factus est,* "and became a human being": thus does the Nicene Creed speak inclusively using the Latin word *homo.* But if in fact what is meant is *et vir factus est,* "and became a man," with stress on sexual manhood, if maleness is essential for the christic role, then women are cut out of the loop of salvation, for female sexuality is not taken on by the flesh of the incarnate Word. Female humanity is not assumed and therefore not saved. In this case the logical answer to the searching question "Can a male savior save women?" can only be "no."[6]

These and other distortions add up to a christology in which Jesus is a male representative of a male God whose key representatives can only be male. What self-respecting woman would want to be part of such a religion? Given the sharp character of the feminist critique, impinging as it does on the person of the Savior, one might wonder if there is any possible retrieval of a tradition that has grown so hardened against women. And yet, "something more" has always gone on in the existential and religious lives of women in the Christian community, as that array of crosses in the university hall attests.

SEEKING AN ALTERNATIVE: DISCOVERING WISDOM

The early Christian communities were enormously creative in interpreting the meaning and message of Jesus. To describe what a
blessing he was in their lives, they gave him names and told his
story over and over again in a multitude of frameworks. Their exuberant efforts led them to comb through their Jewish religious
tradition and, in time, the Hellenistic heritage for titles, images,
and other elements that could be used to interpret his meaning.
In the process, they named him the Messiah, Christ; they named
him Son of Man, Lord, Lamb of God, Word of God, Son of God.
In every instance, the long pre-history of these iconic terms fertilized the Christian imagination. The meanings they had in Jewish
and Hellenistic usage flooded into Christian understanding of
Jesus. There they interacted with his particular history to shape
the community's confession of faith, and the praxis that flowed
from following a person named in just this way.

Early Christians also pressed the biblical wisdom writings into
service with their central figure of Wisdom, *Hokmah* in Hebrew,
Sophia in Greek. The biblical picture of Sophia is a composite one,
formed of differing presentations in Job and Proverbs (books common to all users of the Bible), and in deutero-canonical books such
as Sirach, Baruch, and the Wisdom of Solomon (books considered
canonical by Catholic and Orthodox but not by Protestant and Jewish communities). Intertestamental literature such as Enoch also
contributes to her depiction. Portrayed as sister, mother, bride,
hostess, female beloved, woman prophet, teacher, and friend, but
above all as divine creating and redeeming Spirit, Sophia's portrait
has its roots in the Great Goddess of the ancient Near Eastern
world. Overall, there is no other personification of such depth and
magnitude in the entire Scriptures of Israel.

Scholarly debate on how to interpret this figure abounds, not
least because various biblical books interpret her in different ways,
so that no one interpretation can be applied to every verse where
Wisdom appears. Thus the arguments: Wisdom is the personification of cosmic order. No, she is the personification of the

knowledge sought and learned in Israel's wisdom schools. No, she is a personified way of speaking about God's own divine wisdom and knowledge. No, she is a hypostasis, a sort of mediator who operates between the transcendent, inaccessible God and those on earth. No, she is the personification of the mystery of God's own self in graceful, powerful, and close engagement with the world.

Early rabbinic commentators favored this last interpretation, arguing that biblical wisdom texts must be read within their historical context, which was and remains monotheism. The writers of wisdom texts took popular female imagery of the divine and used it in a different religious narrative to talk about the God of Israel. Wisdom texts affirm that Sophia is the fashioner of all things, that she delivered Israel from a nation of oppressors, that whoever finds her finds life, that she overcomes evil. These are all divine actions. Unless one thinks that the Jewish community broke with its faith in one God when writing and receiving wisdom literature, Sophia's functional equivalence with Yahweh requires that she be interpreted as a powerful female symbol of the one indescribable God. The Wisdom of God in late Jewish thought is simply God, revealing and known.

This is the meaning that was to bear fruit in christology. At first, early Christians saw Jesus as a wisdom teacher, speaking sage words in parables, beatitudes, and evocative sayings. More than this, they depicted him as an envoy sent by Wisdom, one of her prophets uttering oracles and laments in the pattern of her speech, and offering consolation and knowledge of the intimate ways of God. He does her deeds. When Jesus does "the deeds of the Christ" (Mt 11:2) that enable the blind to see, the lame to walk, and the lepers to be cleansed, the gospel affirms that "Wisdom is vindicated by her deeds" (Mt 11:19).

In time the identification of Jesus with Holy Wisdom becomes so intense that he himself comes to be seen as personified Wisdom, indeed, the incarnation of Sophia herself. The prologue to John's gospel, which more than any other scriptural text influenced subsequent development in christology, actually presents the pre-history of Jesus in terms lifted right from the story of Sophia: present with God in the beginning, an active agent in creating the world, a radiant light that darkness cannot overcome, one who descends from heaven to pitch a tent among the people, rejected by some, but giving life to those who receive her (Jn 1:1–18).

It is a matter of some dispute why the gospel's final redactor substituted the symbol of Logos or Word for Sophia or Wisdom in the prologue. At least one reason would seem to lie with the gender issue. As patriarchal tendencies grew stronger it became unseemly to interpret the male human being Jesus in terms of a powerful female symbol of God. To give but one example of this view: Wilfred Knox argues that the fact that the Logos is masculine makes it a convenient substitute for "the awkward feminine figure."[7] Whatever the reason for the change, in John's prologue the Logos is a symbolic male surrogate for Wisdom, there being no similar personification or sustained story of the Logos in the Scriptures of Israel. This is borne out in the way the rest of John's gospel is simply suffused with wisdom themes: seeking and finding, feeding and nourishing, revealing, making people friends of God, showing the way to life, the play of light and darkness.

From Paul, who identifies Jesus as the Wisdom of God (1 Cor 1:24), to Matthew, who puts Sophia's words in Jesus' mouth and has him do her compassionate deeds, to John, who presents Jesus as Wisdom incarnate embodying her way, her truth, and her life, the use of Wisdom to interpret Jesus had profound consequences. It enabled the fledgling church to attribute cosmic significance to the crucified Jesus, relating his historically provincial life and death to the creation and governance of the world. It deepened understanding of Christ's saving deeds by placing them in continuity with Wisdom's saving work throughout history. It also fertilized developing insight into Jesus' ontological relationship with God. The title Son of God did not mean divinity in the original Hebrew sources; neither did Christ, or Son of Man, or (at first) Lord. But Wisdom did. "Herein we see the origin of the doctrine of incarnation," concludes James Dunn, with long-reaching influence on trinitarian doctrine.[8] Connecting Jesus with Sophia encouraged the idea that Jesus is not simply a human being inspired by God but must be related in a more personally unique way to God. It is a key move that sets the church's feet on the road to Nicea. Without the strength of New Testament wisdom christology, the christological doctrine that we have inherited is barely conceivable.

Jesus is the human being Sophia became. Over time this tradition faded, as official christology was increasingly cast in terms of Son of God, Word of God, and Lord. But Wisdom left a deep imprint on the heart of the early church's interpretation of Jesus.

TRANSFORMING THEOLOGY: JESUS THE WISDOM OF GOD

The rediscovery of the wisdom tradition offers one tool for feminist discourse about Christ. It is not the only tool, and is not even a perfect tool, given the misogyny of much of the wisdom literature. Indeed some of the most vicious biblical statements about women are found in wisdom's pages. So long as only men interpreted these texts, their patriarchal assumptions were scarcely noticeable. But as women today join the conversation, the habit of patriarchy to think symbolically by way of woman is thrown into confusion. For women cannot relate to themselves symbolically as men do, idealizing or vilifying as "other" whatever is identified as female. Thus we must look critically at every text, discerning the oppressive dynamics within it and spotting clues to liberating motifs that more truly reflect what we hope is the word of God.

With that caution operating, the figure of personified Wisdom offers an augmented field of female metaphors with which to interpret the saving significance and personal identity of Jesus the Christ. And metaphors matter. The female gender symbolism of Sophia not only casts Jesus into an inclusive framework with regard to his relationships with human beings and with God, removing the male emphasis that is by now engraved with domination. But, the symbol giving rise to thought, this symbolism also evokes Sophia's characteristic gracious goodness, life-giving creativity, and passion for justice as key hermeneutical elements in speaking about the mission and person of Jesus. In what follows, observe one way that using wisdom metaphors allows for retelling the gospel story of Jesus and transforming the doctrinal symbol of Christ to beneficial effect.

Retelling the Story

The gospel can be proclaimed as the good news of Jesus, a prophet and child of Sophia, sent to announce that God is the God of all-inclusive love who wills the wholeness and humanity of everyone, especially the poor and heavy burdened. He is sent to gather all the outcast under the wings of their gracious Sophia-God and bring them to shalom. This envoy of Sophia walks her paths of justice and peace and invites others to do likewise. Again and again in imaginative parables, compassionate healings, startling exorcisms, and festive meals he spells out the reality of the renewing power of the reign of Sophia-God drawing near. New possibilities of relationships flower among the women and men who respond and join his circle. They form a community of the discipleship of equals.[9]

Then they crucified him. Jesus' death included all that makes death terrifying: public condemnation, physical anguish, betrayal by some close friends, even abandonment by God. Historically, this death is a consequence of the hostile response of religious and civil rulers to the style and content of Jesus' ministry to which he was radically faithful with a freedom that would not quit. The friendship and inclusive care of Sophia are rejected as Jesus, preeminent in the long line of Sophia's murdered prophets, is violently executed. *Ecce homo:* Christ crucified, the Wisdom of God (1 Cor 1:24). Faith in the resurrection witnesses that this crucified victim of state violence is not abandoned forever. Sophia's characteristic gift of life is given in a new, unimaginable way. Her pure, beneficent, people-loving Spirit seals him in life with God as pledge of the future for all the violated and the dead. This same Spirit is poured out on the circle of disciples drawn by the attractiveness of Jesus and his gracious God, and they are missioned to make the inclusive goodness and saving power of Sophia-God experientially available to the ends of the earth. Here in the resurrection of the crucified the feminist theme of the preservation of the bodily integrity of each, even the most violated, is inscribed at the very center of the Christian vision.

Along with other forms of political and liberation theology, feminist theology repudiates an interpretation of the death of

Jesus as required by God in repayment for sin. Today, such a view is virtually inseparable from an underlying image of God as an angry, bloodthirsty, violent, and sadistic father, reflecting the very worst kind of male behavior. Rather, Jesus' death was an act of violence brought about by threatened human beings. It was a sinful deed, and therefore against the will of God. What comes clear in the event, however, is the willingness of the gracious Sophia-God of Jesus to enter into solidarity with all those who suffer and are lost. The cross in all its dimensions—violence, suffering, and love—is the living parable that enacts Sophia-God's participation in the suffering of the world.

This makes clear that the victory of shalom is won not by a kind of spiritual military might but by the awesome power of compassionate love, in and through solidarity with those who suffer. The unfathomable depths of evil and suffering, entered into in friendship with Sophia-God, become a path to life. Guided by wisdom categories, the story of the cross, rejected as passive, penal victimization, is re-appropriated as heartbreaking empowerment. The suffering that accompanies such a life as Jesus led is neither passive nor useless nor divinely ordained, but is linked to the ways of Sophia forging justice and peace in an antagonistic world. Let it be noted that at the moment of final crisis Mary Magdalene, Mary the mother of James and Joseph, Salome, and "many other women" disciples (Mk 15:41) kept vigil at the cross, their presence a sacrament of God's own fidelity to the dying Jesus. Their faithful friendship bore witness to the hope that he was not totally abandoned.

When the story of Jesus is told in this way, a certain appropriateness accrues to the historical fact that he was a male human being. If in a patriarchal culture a woman had preached compassionate love and enacted a style of authority that serves others and washes feet, she would most certainly have been greeted with a colossal shrug. Is this not what women are supposed to do by nature? But from a social position of male privilege Jesus preached and acted this way, and herein lies the summons. In this view, the crucified Jesus embodies the exact opposite of the ideal of the kyriarchal lord and master. The cross stands as a poignant sym-

bol of the "kenosis of patriarchy," the self-emptying of male dominating power-over, in favor of the new humanity of compassionate service and mutual love. On this reading it becomes clear that
the heart of the problem is not that Jesus was a man but that more
men are not like Jesus. They have not followed his footsteps, insofar as patriarchy has defined their self-identity and relationships.

Reading the gospel through the lens of the wisdom tradition
makes it possible to affirm that despite subsequent distortion,
something more than the marginalization of women is possible.
Jesus-Sophia's story of ministry, suffering, final victory, and new
community signify love, grace, and shalom for everyone equally,
and for the outcast, including marginalized women, most of all.

Transforming the Christ Symbol

Theology speaks not only of the story of the historical Jesus but
also of his saving significance and rootedness in God. Here again
Wisdom comes into play in a beneficial way. An ancient christological title, inscribed in prayer and the name of churches, calls
Jesus the Wisdom of God. This appellation relieves the monopoly
of the Father-Son metaphor and destabilizes the patriarchal imagination. Whoever espouses a wisdom christology is asserting that
Sophia in all her fullness was in Jesus so that in his history he embodies divine mystery in creative and saving involvement with
the world. Augustine in his treatise on the Trinity put it this way:
"But she was sent in one way that she might be with human beings; and she has been sent in another way that she herself might
be a human being."[10] Such a way of speaking breaks through the
assumption that there is any necessary connection between maleness and God, leading to the realization that even as a human
man, Jesus can be thought to be revelatory of the graciousness of
God imaged as female.

Divine Sophia incarnate in Jesus addresses all persons in her
call to be friends of God and can be truly represented by any
human being called in her Spirit, women as well as men. Not incidentally, wisdom christology subverts the typical stereotypes of
masculine and feminine, since female Sophia represents creative

transcendence, primordial passion for justice, and knowledge of the truth, while the male human being Jesus incarnates these divine characteristics in an immanent way relative to bodiliness and the earth. The creative, redeeming paradox of Jesus-Sophia points the way to a reconciliation of opposites and their transformation from enemies into a liberating, unified diversity.

In the end gender is not constitutive of the symbol of the Christ. Nor does gender affect the identity of the Christian person as *imago Christi*. Through baptism, the whole community participates in the dying and rising of Christ to such an extent that it too has a christomorphic character: "Now you are the body of Christ and individually members of it" (1 Cor 12:27). This includes women. The identification with Christ is not accomplished by a literal duplication of the historical Jesus' physical features in a kind of naive physicalism. If that were the case, elderly men, black men, Gentile men, and so forth would not bear a "natural resemblance" to Jesus. Rather, the image of Christ occurs when the pattern of his love is inscribed in one's life by the power of the Spirit. The baptismal tradition that configures both women and men to the living Christ, and the martyrdom tradition that recognizes the face of Christ in those who shed their blood, have always borne this out. Maleness does not constitute the essence of Christ, but, in the Spirit, redeemed and redeeming humanity does. In a word the story of Jesus the prophet and friend of Sophia, indeed Sophia incarnate, anointed as the Christ, goes on in history as the story of the whole Christ, *christa* and *christus* alike, the wisdom community.

Theology will have come of age when the particularity it highlights is not Jesus' historical sex but the scandal of his option for the poor and marginalized, including women, in the Spirit of his compassionate, liberating Sophia-God. This is the scandal of particularity that really matters, aimed as it is toward the creation of a new order of justice. Toward that end, feminist theological speech about Jesus the Wisdom of God shifts the focus of reflection off maleness and onto the whole theological significance of what transpires in the Christ event. Jesus in his human, historical specificity can be confessed as Sophia incarnate, revelatory of the liberating graciousness of God imaged as female. Women, as friends of Jesus-Sophia, share equally with men in his saving mission throughout time and can fully represent Christ, being themselves other Christs. This has profound implications for reshaping the theology of the church in the direction of a community of the discipleship and ministry of equals.

CONCLUSION

The wisdom tradition with its figure of personified Sophia and its sapiential christology is still a largely untapped resource for speaking about Jesus Christ. Connecting it critically with women's struggle for full human dignity and reading it with a liberation hermeneutic allows a beneficial field of metaphors, concepts, and values to emerge with which to articulate the meaning of Christ for the church and the world. Think again of that great hall with women's crosses covering the walls. At this historical moment, our task is to redeem the very name of Christ—to redeem it from patriarchal interpretations and for the healing and wholeness that is God's saving intent. By retelling the story of Jesus in an egalitarian framework and transforming the symbol of Christ in wisdom and friendship categories, feminist theology calls the whole church to conversion, away from sexism and toward a community of the discipleship of equals, for the sake of Christ's mission in the world.

Adapted from a lecture at Tübingen University, Germany, 2004; published in Evangelische Theologie *66:2 (2006): 142–55.*

Notes

1. Ursula King, ed., *Feminist Theology from the Third World: A Reader* (Maryknoll, NY: Orbis Books, 1994); Linda Moody, *Women Encounter God: Theology across the Boundaries of Difference* (Maryknoll, NY: Orbis Books, 1996); Teresa Berger, ed., *Dissident Daughters: Feminist Liturgies in Global Context* (Louisville, KY: Westminster/John Knox, 2001).

2. Jacqueline Grant, *White Woman's Christ, Black Woman's Jesus: Feminist Christology and Womanist Response* (Atlanta: Scholars Press, 1989); and

Diana Hayes, *And Still We Rise: An Introduction to Black Liberation Theology* (New York: Paulist Press, 1996).

3. Chung Hyun Kyung, "Who Is Jesus for Asian Women?" in her *Struggle to be the Sun Again: Introducing Asian Women's Theology* (Maryknoll, NY: Orbis Books, 1994), 53–73; and Virginia Fabella, "A Common Methodology for Diverse Christologies?" in *With Passion and Compassion: Third World Women Doing Theology*, ed. Virginia Fabella and Mercy Amba Oduyoye (Maryknoll, NY: Orbis Books, 1988), 108–17.

4. Nellie Ritchie, "Women and Christology," in *Through Her Eyes: Women's Theology from Latin America*, ed. Elsa Tamez (Maryknoll, NY: Orbis Books, 1989), 95; and Maria Pilar Aquino, *Our Cry for Life: Feminist Theology from Latin America* (Maryknoll, NY: Orbis Books, 1996).

5. Elizabeth Amoah, "The Christ for African Women," in *With Passion and Compassion*, ed. Virginia Fabella and Mercy Amba Oduyoye, 42; and Mercy Amba Oduyoye, *Introducing African Women's Theology* (Sheffield, England: Sheffield Academic Press, 2001).

6. Rosemary Radford Ruether, *Sexism and God-Talk: Toward a Feminist Theology* (Boston: Beacon Press, 1983), 116–38.

7. Wilfred Knox, *Paul and the Church of the Gentiles* (Cambridge: Cambridge University Press, 1934), 84.

8. James Dunn, *Christology in the Making* (Philadelphia: Westminster, 1980), 212.

9. Elisabeth Schüssler Fiorenza, *In Memory of Her: A Feminist Theological Reconstruction of Christian Origins* (New York: Crossroad, 1983), 118–59.

10. Augustine, *The Trinity*, 4.20.27.

15

Torture

"You did it to me"

There once was a prisoner, seen as a threat to the state, who was tortured while being held under guard. The story of his torment comes to us in four versions. It starts with his arrest and interrogation before public officials and ends with his being put to death. In between these two bookends we glimpse, in snippets of phrases, how he was hurt and humiliated as a prisoner. The narrative of his torture rings down the centuries to challenge consciences today.

In the twentieth century the practice of torture has been declared illegal by international law. According to the Geneva Conventions, prisoners must be treated in a way that respects the integrity of their body, as befits human persons. In addition to its illegality, torture is also immoral, transgressing ethical standards of right behavior on the part of those who inflict the pain. These moral norms took centuries to develop. For a long time the church itself used torture as a punishment or means of extracting information until, as with slavery, both church and society came to see the practice as gravely wrong. The atrocity of torture is inhumane to an intense degree, violating the basic human rights of the victim while at the same time tearing the moral fabric of the society that condones it.

Breaching both law and morality, our nation now practices torture. In recent years the United States government has drawn up a blueprint, approved it, authorized it for use, illegal and immoral though this be. The venues differ. From the clandestine network of so-called "black sites," admittedly run by the Central Intelligence Agency, to established detention facilities and military prisons, to places in other countries to which the government ingeniously outsources torture after secretly transporting detainees there, torture in

211

its many forms is state-sponsored. Official sanction allows the practice to trickle down to the lowest ranks of the military. We have seen the photographs from Abu Ghraib. Yet there is little sustained criticism from the public, people being intent on the daily pressures of their own lives. We are looking the other way.

For Christians, called to love God with all our heart, mind, soul, and strength and our neighbor as ourselves, there is another dimension to the practice of torture. Besides its illegal, immoral, and inhumane character, torture is profoundly irreligious. Slow, prayerful meditation on the treatment of the one prisoner mentioned above brings this to light.

Between his public hearing before officials and his very public death, this is what happened while he was in custody:

> *They spat in his face and they struck him.*
> *Some slapped him, saying, "Prophesy for us, Messiah: who is it*
>   *that struck you?"*
> *(The governor had him scourged.)*

Then the soldiers of the governor took him inside the praetorium and gathered the whole cohort around him:

> *They stripped off his clothes.*
> *Weaving a crown out of thorns, they placed it on his head.*
> *Kneeling before him they mocked him.*
> *They spat upon him.*
> *They took the reed and kept on striking him on the head.*
> *And when they had mocked him, they stripped him of the cloak,*
>   *dressed him in his own clothes, and led him off to crucify him.*

That is Matthew's account. To this scene of soldiers having cruel sport, Mark adds another scene of earlier abuse at a hearing before the elders:

> *Some began to spit on him.*
> *They blindfolded him and struck him and said to him, "Prophesy!"*
> *And the guards greeted him with blows.*

Luke's version includes an extra scene where the prisoner was sent off by the Roman governor to the Jewish king. Herod and his soldiers treated him contemptuously.

They mocked him.

Following this, Pilate decided to have him flogged, beaten to a pulp. Then,

He handed Jesus over to them to deal with as they wished.

In John's recounting, the prisoner is hit while under interrogation:

When he had said this, one of the temple guards standing there struck Jesus.

The scene unfolds as we have come to dread:

Then Pilate took Jesus and had him scourged. And the soldiers wove a crown of thorns and placed it on his head, and clothed him in a purple cloak, and they came to him and said, "Hail, King of the Jews," and they struck him repeatedly.

After some more ineffectual maneuvering, Pilate yields:

Then he handed him over to them to be crucified.

There is a deep theological connection between the prisoner Jesus of Nazareth and prisoners tortured while in U.S. custody today. Pope John Paul II's first encyclical, *Redeemer of the Human Race*, drew the connection with compelling clarity: "By his Incarnation, he, the Son of God, in a certain way united himself with each human being." Consequently, though we are disfigured by sin, "human nature has been raised in us to a dignity beyond compare." When we grasp this redeeming truth, we are filled with "deep wonder at ourselves" and "deep amazement at the worth and dignity of every human person."

The pope declares that this dignity is the basis for vigorous care for human rights. When these rights are violated, Christ again is personally involved. The encyclical underscores this teaching in a series of rhetorical questions: In the course of so many centuries, of so many generations, is it not Jesus Christ himself who has made an appearance at the side of people judged for the sake of the truth? And has he not gone to death with people condemned for the sake of the truth? Does he ever cease to be the continuous spokesman and advocate for such persons?

The answer to these rhetorical questions, should they need one, comes to light in a well-known parable told by Jesus while he was still alive and well. As recounted in Matthew, the scene is Judgment Day when the sheep and the goats will be separated, the former to inherit the kingdom, the latter to depart into eternal fire. The criterion of judgment is treatment of one's neighbor who by turns may be hungry, thirsty, without shelter, naked, sick, or in prison. Note the inclusion of those in prison. Meeting the needs of the neighbor in prison receives a startling word of praise and appreciation: "Whatever you did to one these least brothers or sisters of mine, you did for me" (25:40). By contrast, not caring for the prisoner is tantamount to scorning Christ: "What you did not do for one of these least ones, you did not do for me" (25:45).

There is no mention in this parable of abuse, only beneficial activity or neglect. But the point of the parable, Christ's solidarity with each person in need, extends beyond the two scenarios to situations of actual mistreatment.

As the church meditates on the passion of Jesus during Lent, the torture of prisoners by U.S.–approved methods ("coercive interrogation") should not be far from our conscience. It is still being done in the name of us citizens, supposedly to enhance national security. Apart from the debate over whether torture is effective in this regard or not, Christ's words, amplified by his own graphic suffering, mandate an end to this reprehensible brutality: "You did it to me."

Adapted from America *196 (February 26, 2007): 14–16.*

16

Jesus and Women
"You are set free"

SHE STOOD UP STRAIGHT

There is a powerful scene in the gospels that shows in a flash how life-giving the encounter between Jesus and women can be. As Luke tells the story:

> Jesus was teaching in one of the synagogues on the sabbath, and a woman came in who had been crippled by a spirit for eighteen years. She was bent over and could not straighten up at all. When Jesus saw her, he called her forward and said to her, "Woman, you are set free from your infirmity." Then he put his hands on her, and immediately she stood up straight and began to praise God. (Luke 13:10–13)

Notice the setting: a holy place where the community gathers on the sabbath day. Notice, too, the position of Jesus: front and center, the famous teacher instructing the group. It is a solemn moment. The woman slips in quietly. She is nobody important. For almost two decades she has moved through the world stooped over, crippled by a terrible handicap, a pitiful figure in the eyes of her neighbors. Unless she makes a great effort, all she sees as she goes about her life is the ground or the floor. Now on this sabbath she just wants to listen and pray. But Jesus notices. He could have gone on with his teaching, but, as we are told in other stories, a feeling of compassion wells up in his heart. He stops mid-stream, turning full attention her way. In front of the whole assembly he calls her forth, reaches out, and his powerful words and healing touch bring strength to her twisted spine. "Woman, you are set free!" Imagine how it felt to stand up straight, to lift up her head, to look around and see faces instead of the ground. A new way of life opens before her. And this woman knows whom to thank. She praises God for showing her such tender mercy through the kindness of this prophet and teacher, Jesus of Nazareth.

Christian women today read this story as a revelation of what their relationship with Jesus can still bring about. Bent over by many forces, they find his powerful compassion a spur to liberation, enabling them to stand up straight. Women scholars are discovering that there are many scenes like this in the New Testament that show Jesus' love for women, his concern for their well-being, and his freeing effect on their lives. But over the centuries the power of these stories has often been ignored because the men who preach and teach usually do not appreciate the suffering that women bear. What are some of the burdens that cripple women?

BURDENS

Society: Consider these United Nations statistics: women, who form 1/2 of the world's population, work 3/4 of the world's working hours; receive 1/10 of the world's salary; own 1/100 of the world's land; form 2/3 of illiterate adults; and together with their dependent children form 3/4 of the world's starving people. To make a bleak picture worse, women are subject to domestic violence at home, and are raped, prostituted, trafficked into sexual slavery, and murdered by men to a degree that is not reciprocal. Regarding education, employment, and other social goods, men have advantages simply by being born male. Racial and ethnic prejudices add further disadvantage to women, as does class privilege which disrespects women who are poor. Every culture has different dynamics. But it is always women who are regarded as of lesser value.

This situation, called *sexism,* or prejudice against women because of their sex, is rampant on a global scale. To point this out is not to make women into a class of victims. But it is to underscore statistics that make clear the struggles women face in society because of their gender. In no country on earth are women and men yet treated in an equal manner befitting their human dignity.

In 1995 the United Nations held a conference on women in Beijing, China. A historic event, it was the first gathering attended by women from every nation in the world. On that occasion Pope John Paul II wrote a *Letter to Women* strongly supporting the conference's agenda of social equality:

> As far as personal rights are concerned, there is an urgent need to achieve real equality in every area: equal pay for equal work, protection for working mothers, fairness in career advancement, equality of spouses with respect to family rights, and the recognition of everything that is part of the rights and duties of citizens in a democratic state. This is matter of justice, but also of necessity. (*Letter to Women at the Beijing Conference,* July 1995, par. 4)

This was a most welcome letter, putting the Catholic Church squarely in league with women's struggle for justice. The movement to obtain equality for women in law and culture is actually a movement for social justice in accord with Catholic social teaching. This in turn is based on the truth that women, like men, are created in the image and likeness of God, and should live with the dignity befitting all human persons.

However, there are problems in the church itself that the pope did not address.

Church: Christianity took shape in the culture of the Roman Empire where elite men held power over lesser men, women, children, and slaves. This social structure, called *patriarchy* (rule of the father), is a pyramid-shaped arrangement where power is always in the hands of dominant man or men at the top. As the church grew and became established, its leaders adopted this pattern for its own internal life. Within this system, women are of necessity placed in predetermined subordinate roles. Men teach and decide; women listen and obey.

The church reflects this inequality in all of its aspects. Sacred texts, religious symbols, doctrines, moral teachings, canon laws, rituals, and governing offices are all designed and led by men. Even God is imagined most often as a powerful patriarch in heaven ruling the earth and its peoples. In turn, this sacred patriarchy justifies the rule of men over women in family and the wider society.

While the histories are different, a similar pattern afflicts all the world's religions.

THEOLOGY IN WOMEN'S VOICES

In view of these burdens, women today are discovering how liberating an encounter with Jesus of the gospels can be. His words to the first-century woman echo down through the centuries: "Woman, you are set free." A newly educated group of women theologians is exploring the meaning of this promise and the ways in which it might become reality. The fact that there are such scholars noticing this at all is a startling development. For two thousand years almost all Christian theology has been done by men. After the Second Vatican Council (1962–1965) opened the study of theology to Catholic laypersons in the church, many women began to be educated in this field. The work of theology, as Anselm of Canterbury famously defined it, is "faith seeking understanding." The goal of theological thinking is to shed light on faith's meaning so it can be lived more vibrantly, more lovingly. Women bring to this work a new perspective, asking questions that arise from the suffering and life experiences of women. This type of theology is commonly called *feminist* theology, from the Latin *femina*, meaning woman. It sees faith with women's eyes. It sees what is wrong or missing in the way faith has been presented insofar as that presentation has ignored or burdened women. And it searches the tradition for powerful liberating elements that can transform life today.

The vision that guides feminist theology is the one that Jesus preached, centered in his frequent use of the symbol "the kingdom of God." This reign of God brings about a new form of community where people live in mutual respect with each other and the other living creatures of the earth. The goal is not reverse discrimination, a community where women dominate men; this would just continue injustice in a new form. Rather, women dream of a new heaven and a new earth, with no one group dominating and no one group being subordinated, but each person cherished and participating according to his or her own God-given gifts, in genuinely reciprocal relations. With this hope, the work of feminist theology today emphasizes a new appreciation of the meaning of Jesus Christ for human beings who are women. Consider these few highlights.

JESUS' LIFE, DEATH, AND RESURRECTION

Studies of Jesus' relationships during his public life reveal his lack of fear of women and a strong interest in their flourishing. No word of disparagement passed his lips, nor did he see women as a lesser class of human being. Treating them with grace and respect, he healed, exorcized, forgave, and restored women to *shalom*, being particularly attentive to those most in need: the newly dead little girl, the widow whose son had just died, the impoverished widow who gave all she had to the temple, the adulterer about to be stoned. Jesus learned from women; after some witty wordplay a non-Jewish woman from Syria gained healing for her daughter in an encounter that cast light on the need for him to widen his ministry beyond the lost sheep of the house of Israel. Known for his particular concern for people on the margins of life, this prophet saw the worth of prostitutes, even telling the religious leaders that such women would enter the kingdom of heaven before they did (Mt 21:31). Personally, women were counted among his friends; the sisters Martha and Mary, for example, hosted him in their home and received his teaching. Trying to sum this up is next to impossible, but Pope John Paul II caught the essence:

> When it comes to setting women free from every kind of exploitation and domination, the Gospel contains an ever relevant message which goes back to the attitude of Jesus Christ himself.... Jesus treated women with openness, respect, acceptance, and tenderness. In this way he honored the dignity which women have always possessed according to God's plan and in his love.... It is natural to ask ourselves how much of his message has been heard and acted upon. (*Letter to Women at the Beijing Conference*, July 1995, par. 3)

In addition to his actions, Jesus' preaching is inclusive of women. He never sets out one way of acting for men and another for women. Note and be startled by the fact that the Sermon on the Mount is addressed to all; whatever is right for men to do is right for women to do too. In a radical way the vision of the kingdom of God that pervades his teaching overturns unjust relations: the last shall be first and the first last, so that in the end a new kind of community may form.

The parables Jesus told also honor women by pointing to their human reality as worthy symbols for the living God. In the Jewish Scriptures, the all-holy God is spoken of with female images in moving and beautiful ways, as a pregnant woman, nursing mother, midwife, caregiver carrying the young, as Lady Wisdom (*Sophia*) governing the world sweetly and mightily. Influenced by this his own biblical heritage, Jesus, too, spun out female images in his preaching. The reign of God is like leaven that a woman kneads into dough so that the whole loaf rises: here is the bakerwoman God, working the yeast of the new creation into the world until all is transformed (Mt 13:33). Even more startling, perhaps, is the parable of the woman searching for her coin. She has lost one of her ten silver pieces (are they her dowry? insurance for old age?), and she turns the house upside down until she finds it. Then she calls friends and neighbors to rejoice with her, because she has found what was lost (Luke 15:8–10). Here we have a marvelous image of God the Redeemer searching high and low for the sinner. The parable is one of a pair, the other being the good shepherd who searches for his lost sheep. Both parables reveal the extravagant love of God for those who get lost. While the Christian imagination has favored the shepherd, the homemaker is there to reflect how women's everyday life offers up images for God. So do female animals: Jesus once referred to himself as a hen, wishing he could gather the people of Jerusalem within his arms as a mother hen gathers her chicks under her wings (Mt 23:37).

Besides healing women of their infirmities, enjoying their friendship, and speaking of God in their image, Jesus went further and invited women into the circle of his close followers. They left their families and homes to join him on the road in Galilee. They absorbed his teaching and were present with him at joyful community meals where there was a foretaste of the coming kingdom of God. The wealthy among them bankrolled his ministry, providing for the needs of the community out of their own pocket:

> Soon afterward he went through cities and villages, preaching and bringing the good news of the kingdom of God. And the twelve were with him, and also some women who had been healed of evil spirits and infirmities: Mary, called Magdalene, from whom seven demons had gone out, and Joanna, the wife of Chuza, Herod's steward. And Susanna, and many others who provided for them out of their means. (Lk 8:1–3)

The names of these and other women ("many others"! "with him!") are given several times in the gospels but have become a forgotten part of the story.

Women's discipleship during the ministry of Jesus did not cease at the end of his life. They accompanied him up to Jerusalem, becoming the moving point of witness to the passion. Each of the four gospels recounts that while the male disciples ran and hid when Jesus was arrested, the women kept vigil with him at the cross. In fact, the only person named by all four gospels as having stood by the cross is Mary Magdalene. Because it was the women who stayed, they knew where his tomb was, and they were the first to discover it empty when they went to finish anointing his body on the first day of the week. There they encountered Christ risen and were commissioned to "Go and tell" the others. Mary Magdalene, whom the church later called the "apostle to the apostles," and the other women did so, though the men did not believe them, thinking they were just being hysterical women. Nevertheless, Scripture shows that both in his earthly life and risen life Jesus Christ included women in his community, not as subordinates to men but as sisters to their brothers and, in the case of the resurrection proclamation, even as those first entrusted.

Through the lens of women's experience, the crucifixion of Jesus mounts a tremendous critique against patriarchy. Here is the very "Word made flesh" (Jn 1:14) brought to a tortured death by state power, pouring himself out in self-sacrificing love. This event is the exact opposite of the exercise of male dominating power. In light of the cross, feminist theologians reflect that sociologically it was probably better that the incarnation happened in a male human being. For if a woman had preached compassion and given the gift of herself even unto death, it would not have made a great impression. People expect women to serve. But for a man to live and die like this in a world of male privilege is to challenge the patriarchal ideal of male domination at its root. The cross is the *kenosis*, the self-emptying, of patriarchy.

In the resurrection, the Spirit of God fills Jesus with new life beyond death. Present in the community in a new way, Christ Jesus becomes the cornerstone of the new community which is his body, the church. On Pentecost women as well as men are in the upper room when tongues of fire signal the outpouring of the Spirit: "and they were all filled with the Holy Spirit and began to speak in other tongues" (Acts 2:4). Early Christians adopted the initiation rite of baptism. Unlike the gender-specific Jewish ritual of circumcision open only to males, baptism is administered by immersion in water and so is given the same way to persons of both genders. Paul's letter to the Galatians contains an early Christian baptismal hymn that shows what this practice means. As the newly baptized come up out of the water wearing white robes, they sing, "now there is no Jew or Greek, slave or free, male and female, but all are one in Christ Jesus" (3:28). All divisions based on race, or class, or even gender are transcended in the oneness of the sanctifying Spirit. The power of the risen Christ becomes effective to the extent that this vision becomes reality in the community.

In the early decades of the church there is strong evidence for a vigorous ministry of women spreading the gospel as colleagues with men. From the Acts of the Apostles and letters of Paul we get the picture of women as missionaries, preachers, teachers, prophets, apostles, healers, speakers in tongues, and leaders of house churches. They are co-workers with Paul and the other men, gifted with all of the charisms that were given for the building up of the church. Scholars are now trying to piece together what forces brought this public ministry of women in the early church to a diminished state. But that Phoebe, Prisca, Junia, Persis, and many other women preached the gospel in the early days of the church there is no doubt (see especially Paul's letter to the Romans, chapter 16).

CONCLUSION

Theology in women's hands has discovered Jesus Christ as compassionate friend, liberator from burdens, consoling friend in sorrows, and ally of women's strivings. He brings salvation through his life and Spirit, supporting women's efforts to realize how beloved they are in the eyes of God. The blessing that women find in their relationship with Jesus is not simply private and spiritual, though it is certainly that. But it also affects their life in public and social domains, inspiring the struggle for liberation from structures of domination in every dimension of life. In Christ's name, society and church are called to conversion of hearts, minds, and structures so that the reign of God may take firmer hold in this world. This is a challenging view. But the liberating words have already been spoken: "Woman, you are set free from your infirmity." Stand up straight, praise God, and get on with the work of healing the world.

Adapted from Svjetlo Riječi *(2012): 26–28; written for this Franciscan journal in Sarajevo. The friars were putting out a special issue on the meaning of Jesus Christ in their pluralistic, multi-religious society (Catholic, Orthodox, Muslim, atheist), and requested an article on Jesus and women. Translated into Bosnian, the piece appeared as "Isus I Žene: Uspravite Se!" in the special issue entitled "Isus iz Nazareta: U Perspektivi Medureligijskog Dijaloga."*

IV

KINDLE IN US THE FIRE OF DIVINE LOVE: CHURCH MATTERS

17

Remembering the Holy Spirit
Love Poured Out

If you ask the average woman or man in the pew the question "Who is God?" I wager most would answer by referring to God the Father (and/or Mother, if they were concerned with inclusive language) or to Jesus Christ. It would be the rare person who would call the Holy Spirit to mind. True, there are some exceptions. In the years after Vatican II the charismatic movement put exceptional focus on the Spirit. And the Spirit comes in for special attention during preparation for confirmation and on the feast of Pentecost. But beyond that it is probably safe to say that the Spirit is not, in a conscious way, a significant part of the ordinary life of faith. The Holy Spirit is the forgotten God among Catholic Christians in the West.

This causes great impoverishment to our everyday sense of God's presence and activity in the world today, for the Holy Spirit is nothing less than God's own loving self, present and active in the world. The Holy Spirit is God, present and active to vivify, renew, and bring new life to all peoples and the whole of creation.

Awakening to this truth can greatly enrich the life of faith. As an aid to renewed awareness, consider these questions: Where do we encounter the Holy Spirit? Why has the Spirit been so overlooked? And, in light of these two questions, how might we envision the Spirit in ways that can spark our own spirits?

WHERE DO WE ENCOUNTER THE HOLY SPIRIT?

The most obvious place to begin is with religious observances, as these come most readily to mind for churchgoers. The eucharistic liturgy addresses prayer "to the Father, through the Son, in the unity of the Holy Spirit," and private prayer sometimes takes this same form. Thus we encounter the Holy Spirit in community worship and personal prayer.

But the Spirit is not limited to explicitly religious moments such as these, for the Spirit is "the Lord and giver of life," as the Nicene Creed proclaims. This means that the Spirit is first and foremost the Creator Spirit who creates, empowers, and fills the whole world with life. Therefore, we may actually encounter the Spirit everywhere. In the most basic way, the Spirit sustains every place, every moment, every creature, the whole interconnected community of creation itself.

Realizing this alerts our spirit to the possibility of encountering the Holy Spirit in many ways. A first locus of encounter can be the natural world. The Spirit of God is present and active in nature itself: in the new life of spring; in the flourishing of summer; in the harvests of autumn; in the storms of winter; in the diversity of plants and animals. Every fresh morning, every star at night, speaks of the Creator Spirit who pervades the world with creative power, giving rise to all manner of systems and species. In recent years, we have become aware that the human race with its polluting and consuming ways threatens the very survival of the Earth's life-systems of air, water, and soil along with the survival of many other fellow creatures. Remembering the Spirit makes us realize that in wasting the earth we sin against the very creativity of God, and it energizes us to be responsible stewards of this great treasure.

We may also encounter the Spirit in personal interactions and relationships, especially loving relationships. Scripture connects love with the Spirit: "The love of God is poured into our hearts by the Holy Spirit given to us" (Rom 5:5). A well-known prayer expresses this by exclaiming, "Come, Holy Spirit, fill the hearts of your faithful, and enkindle in them the fire of your divine love." Wherever human beings come together in love, the Holy Spirit is present and active in their midst. At their deepest level these human relationships mediate an encounter with the Spirit of God who is Love. Love between spouses and partners, parent and child, friend and friend, ministers and their people, those who give and receive kind service: wherever creative love enriches life, the Spirit is present and operating.

Fundamentally, the same is true when a person graciously loves himself or herself. If you enter into the love of God for yourself, appreciating your wondrousness as a creature, forgiving yourself the way God forgives, then you have an encounter with the Spirit. This type of generous self-love is a gift of the Spirit that enables you to give the gift of love to others.

Beyond individual relationships we encounter the Holy Spirit in the social world. When the same Christian prayer quoted above goes on to pray, "Send forth your Spirit and they shall be created; and you shall renew the face of the earth," it is not just the world of nature that is meant. The social world also needs to be renewed. Human groups have set up all kinds of systems and structures: economic, political, cultural. Some of these social systems are pervaded by sinfulness; they bear the sediment of previous wrong decisions. They damage persons caught in their maw. The Spirit, as the biblical prophets proclaimed so eloquently, is especially present and active whenever the poor are mistreated, when violence breaks out, when the widow and orphan are oppressed. Then we encounter the Spirit by resisting these evils in the healing work of justice and peace.

Opportunities for encountering the Spirit are as broad as the world itself. We cannot confine the Spirit to sacred moments or sacred places. To be sure, the Spirit is present there as well. But the Creator Spirit pervades all of life, creating goodness and beauty and burning in the midst of suffering and death to inspire hope. We are dealing here with the presence of God.

NEGLECT OF THE SPIRIT

Given the reality of the Spirit, it is all the more surprising how little attention theology has paid to the subject. The fact that the Spirit has been neglected in Western theology and spirituality cannot be denied. In colorful language theologians now describe the woeful result. "The Spirit among Catholics is faceless, some-thing shadowy" (Walter Kasper). "The Spirit in most people's minds is something ghostly" (John Macquarrie). "The Spirit is a vague something or other" (Georgia Harkness). "Of all three di-vine persons the Spirit is the most anonymous, indeed the poor relation of the Trinity" (Norman Pittenger). "The Spirit is the half-known God" (Yves Congar). "The doctrine of the Spirit ap-pears to be watered down from its biblical presentation" (Wolf-hart Pannenberg). Finally, "The Holy Spirit is the Cinderella of theology" (G. J. Sirks of Harvard University).

One factor that might help explain this neglect can be traced to the polemical atmosphere of the Reformation in the sixteenth century. Fierce arguments flew between the churches over how we are saved: by faith alone, which would be due solely to the Spirit's gift of grace (the Protestant position), or by faith and good works, which would entail grace plus a human response (the Catholic position). Each side pressed the Spirit into the shape of its own position. Protestant theology tended to privatize the Spirit, finding the Spirit's work primarily in the justification and sanctification of the individual. The song "Amazing Grace" cap-tures this position beautifully. By contrast, Catholic theology tended to institutionalize the Spirit, tying the Spirit very tightly to church office and the teaching of the magisterium. Both neglected the broader tradition of the Spirit's pervasive presence through-out the human and cosmic world.

Two examples may serve to clarify the Catholic pattern. In the 1930s the German theologian Karl Adam wrote: "The struc-ture of the Catholic faith may be summarized in a single sen-tence: I come to a living faith in the triune God through Christ in the Church. I experience the action of the living God through Christ realizing himself in the Church. So we can see that certi-tude rests on the sacred triad God, Christ, Church." This theolo-gian was not alone in substituting the institution of the church for the divine reality of the Spirit.

When Catholics did not substitute the church for the Spirit, they substituted Mary. Yves Congar, the French theologian who wrote a three-volume work entitled *I Believe in the Holy Spirit*, gives interesting examples of this tendency. Catholic devotional materials state that "Mary is spiritually present to guide and inspire"; that she "forms Christ in believers"; and that she "links believers to Christ." A common expression urges believers "To Jesus through Mary." She is called the intercessor, the mediatrix, the helper. The Bible, by contrast, gives these roles and titles to the Spirit. Pope Leo XIII, who wrote twelve encyclicals on the rosary, provides another example. In one encyclical he wrote, "Every grace granted to human beings has three degrees in order: from God it is communicated to Christ, from Christ it passes to the Virgin, and from the Virgin it descends to us." Here, as Congar observes, is a precise substitution of Mary for the Spirit in the trinitarian communication of grace to the world.

Several other factors besides the Reformation are often mentioned as responsible for the eclipse of the Spirit. Raging disputes in the early Christian centuries over the identity of Jesus Christ would be one. Was Jesus truly God? Was he truly human? How can he be both in one person? Up until the fifth century these debates focused the church's attention on issues concerning the second person of the Trinity and his relationship with the Father. After some controversy the Nicene Creed confessed that the Spirit "together with the Father and the Son is to be worshiped and glorified," but it seems that affirmation of the Spirit never interested theologians the way the divinity of Christ did. Some have also argued a psychological reason, seeing that to begin with the Holy Spirit is harder to latch onto as a person compared to a father or a son, about whom we can at least summon up a basic idea.

More recently women scholars have suggested that a similarity between the functions of the Spirit and traditional roles of women may be another such factor. In Scripture the Spirit's work includes bringing forth life, nurturing that life, and constantly renewing what the ravages of sin and time break down. This is parallel to the work women have long done in home, church, and countless social situations. These functions, while crucial, are seldom noticed or valued the way men's traditional public roles have been. Today's women's movement suggests that the theological neglect of the Spirit and the social marginalization of women seem to have an affinity, at least symbolically, and may well go hand in hand.

Whatever the reasons, bringing a theology of the Holy Spirit back into streaming focus can serve to enrich the life of faith in our day.

HOW TO ENVISION THE SPIRIT

According to Christian teaching the Holy Spirit is the third person of the blessed Trinity. For most people, the usual discussion of the mystery of the Trinity itself makes their eyes glaze over; the language of scholastic categories limps. More helpful is a return to Scripture and to the rhetoric of the first centuries of the church. There we find poetic expressions that awaken the heart.

Throughout the Bible several metaphors taken from nature are often used to refer indirectly to the presence and activity of the Spirit. These include wind, fire, and water.

Wind: The Spirit frequently appears in wind-blown events: the wind blowing back the sea during the exodus; the wind blowing through the valley of the dry bones, reconnecting them and breathing life back into them in the vision of Ezekiel; and the wind blowing through the house where the men and women disciples were gathered at Pentecost.

One of the Bible's best descriptions of the Spirit as wind is in John's gospel (3:8). Speaking to Nicodemus, Jesus likens the Spirit to wind. We do not know where the wind comes from or where it goes. We can't see it but we know it's passing by when we feel it or see its effects. In other words, Jesus is saying that the Spirit is present among us, invisible and not under control, but able to be glimpsed when we experience its divine influence.

Fire: Like wind, fire has no definite shape. It is always changing, not able to be touched. While essential for human life on earth, for cooking and warmth, it is essentially a dangerous element. It appears in the sky as lightning, as the sun, as other stars, but even a candle's flame is deeply mysterious. Moses received his call to lead the Israelites out of Egypt from the voice in the burning bush, on fire but not consumed. At Pentecost, in addition to the sound of a mighty wind, tongues of fire appear over each person's head and all are filled with the Spirit.

The biblical notion of fire as a symbol for the Spirit shows up again and again in later Christian writings. In one beautiful instance from the fourth century Cyril of Jerusalem wrote, "If fire passing through a mass of iron makes the whole of it glow, so that what was cold becomes burning and what was black is made bright, so too the power of the Spirit transforms hearts and minds, and indeed the clay of creation itself, so that what was cold and dark becomes bright and glowing." Note here that the coming of the Spirit doesn't damage or violate the creature, but transforms it into something more alive.

In reflecting on the biblical use of fire as an image for the Spirit, I am struck by the fact that contemporary science now uses the expression "the Big Bang" to describe the primeval explosion that ultimately developed into the universe. Some Christian writers now want to say, in referring to this original fireball, that the act of creation was itself already a Pentecost, the first sparking of the Spirit's energy in wind and fire.

Water: Like wind and fire, water has no definite shape, but unlike them it is the nourishing matrix of all. Life on earth began in the seas; human life begins in the water of the womb. There is sap in the trees, blood in our veins, wine in our vessels, and rain on the earth. Water, and these liquids which are largely water, can serve as symbols of the active presence of the Spirit vivifying all things and gladdening our hearts.

Speaking through the prophet Ezekiel, God promises that the suffering people will be renewed in the Spirit as if by a refreshing shower: "I will sprinkle clean water upon you and a new spirit I will put within you. And I will remove from your body the heart of stone and give you a heart of flesh" (Ezek 36:25–26). A fleshy heart is one that is alive, one that can feel.

Frequently, Scripture talks about the Spirit being poured out the way water flows from a pitcher. God says, "I will pour out my spirit on all flesh; your sons and your daughters will prophesy, your old men shall dream dreams, and your young men shall see visions. Even on male and female slaves I will pour out my spirit" (Joel 2:28–29). The New Testament account of Pentecost quotes this prophetic passage to proclaim what was indeed happening: the Spirit was being poured out (Acts 2:17–18).

Many post-biblical writers also speak of the Spirit as water. Irenaeus, a second century bishop and theologian, used this image to refer to the Spirit's working in the people of the church.

He wrote, "Just as dry wheat cannot be shaped into a cohesive lump of dough nor a loaf of bread be held together without moisture, so in the same way we many could not become one bread without the water that comes down from heaven. As dry earth bears no fruit unless it receives moisture, so we also were originally dry wood, and could never have borne the fruit of life without the rain freely given from above. We have received this rain through the Holy Spirit." Here the water of the Spirit is involved in two homely activities, making bread and bearing fruit. Both are helpful, I think, for understanding how the Holy Spirit works in our lives.

Cyril, bishop of Jerusalem, in talking about the dialogue between Jesus and the Samaritan woman, says: "Why did Christ call the grace of the Spirit water? Because by water all things subsist. Because water brings forth grass and living things. Because the water of the showers comes down from heaven. Because it comes down in one form but works in many forms: it becomes white in the lily, red in the rose, purple in the violets and hyacinths, different and varied species. It is one thing in the palm tree, yet another in the vine; and yet in all things the same Spirit."

These are wonderful images for the Spirit, the Spirit who is one and yet brings forth many varied gifts. Paul makes the same point when he says, "Now there are varieties of gifts but the same Spirit" (1 Cor 12:4); we, though many, are united because "we were all given to drink of the same Spirit" (1 Cor 12:13). The point, whether in Irenaeus, Cyril, or Paul, is that magnificent diversity as well as cohesive unity in the church, indeed in the entire cosmos, is the gift of Holy Spirit.

The Spirit is like wind, fire, water. The Spirit is none of the above in reality, yet all of these metaphors set up an impression. Each one points to the nearness of God to each one of us and to the whole creation. They symbolize in a poetic way that God is intimately involved with the world, so intimate that, as Augustine wrote, God is nearer to us than we are to ourselves. To summarize, ponder some of the lustrous images that Hildegard of Bingen uses to talk about the Spirit. The Spirit, she writes, is the life of the life of all creatures; the way in which everything is penetrated with connectedness and relatedness; a burning fire who sparks, ignites, inflames, kindles hearts; a guide in the fog; a balm for wounds; a shining serenity; an overflowing fountain that spreads to all sides. The Spirit is life, movement, color, radiance, restorative stillness in the din. The Spirit pours the juice of contrition into hardened hearts; makes dry twigs and withered souls green again with the juice of life; purifies, absolves, strengthens, heals, gathers the perplexed, seeks the lost. The Spirit plays music in the soul; awakens mighty hope, blowing everywhere the winds of renewal in creation.

Hildegard's rhetoric puts me in mind of the encouragement offered in the fourth century by Basil of Caesarea in his great work on the Spirit. Let us not be afraid of being too extravagant in what we say about the Holy Spirit, he writes; our thoughts will always fall short.

The Spirit is simply God's self-communication in grace, present and active everywhere, pervading the world. This basic but profound reality bears repeating today, because so many do not experience God's nearness but think of God as distant or even unreal. This is most unfortunate. Through the Spirit, the risen Christ is universally present in the world everywhere and in every moment, as pervasive as the air we breathe, as the sun or the rain that comes down on us, as the wind that blows around us, as the life that flows with our every breath.

CONCLUSION

Rediscovering places of encounter with the Spirit, realizing why Western theology has neglected the Spirit in the first place, and reimagining the Spirit's play in the world using biblical images are all small steps toward restoring a robust theology of the Spirit for our day. The stakes are high, for individual believers and for the church as a whole. What awaits is a new vitality.

18

Coming in from the Cold
Women Envision the Church

At one point in her life, the Caribbean American poet Audre Lorde switched from wearing eyeglasses to using contact lenses. Her poem reflecting on the experience has a poignant closing line. Once she lived behind thick walls of glass without much peripheral vision. Now her eyes are more exposed, risky, open: "I see much/ better now/and my eyes hurt." Metaphorically speaking, multitudes of women in the church have traded in their eyeglasses for contact lenses. They see much better now where problems in the church's teaching and praxis regarding women lie, and their eyes hurt. They don't stop there, however, but also see what the church could be in a more just time to come. After first identifying what gives women the right to dream in this way, this article highlights three sets of ambiguities that bedevil teaching about women's equality in the following of Christ. Grasping the measure of these equivocations makes it clear that envisioning the church women want is a courageous work of hope.

SPEAKING WITH AUTHORITY

Christianity took shape in a Mediterranean culture where elite men held power over women, other men, children, and slaves. As the church grew and became more established, its leaders adopted this pattern, called patriarchy (rule of the father) or kyriarchy (rule of the lord), for its own internal life. Through the centuries the church remained patriarchal, as did society. In fact the church's teaching and governing style gave religious authorization to such a pattern of organization in the wider society. Let me emphasize that we are talking about a structural system here, a pattern of relationship that predetermines the roles men and women play. Within this system, some men are humanly mature, spiritually advanced, respect women and may even love them. Analysis of patriarchy is not male-bashing. But the undoubted fact remains that the church over time evolved a top-down, hierarchical governing structure. Designed by men, the ruling positions in this overall design are held exclusively by men. Quite apart from personal virtue or merit, this places men and women in unequal roles. The church reflects this inequality in its sacred texts, its religious symbols, the way it carries out ritual, makes decisions, and creates laws. As a result, for most of its history, women have been silent and invisible in the public square of the institutional church.

It comes as a shock to some who are comfortable with this patriarchal structure that some women and men wish it were otherwise. When a book I edited entitled *The Church Women Want: Catholic Women in Dialogue* was published in 2002, one critic told me it should have been called "the church Jesus wants" (as if Jesus did not warn his disciples against lording it over each other like the Gentiles; as if he did not wash feet). Others argued that men should be envisioning the church too, which of course they should. But the main criticism came from those who said that women have no right to say what they think the church should be. They should practice the godly virtues of loyalty and obedience to what the men in charge decide is right and true. To justify the endeavor of dreaming the church anew, therefore, it is imperative to begin by establishing the source of women's right to engage the question. Drawing from baptismal theology and the history of spirituality, Mary Catherine Hilkert provides an excellent guide in three points.

First and most important, women are gifted with the Spirit of God in their baptism. This sacrament consecrates a girl profoundly to God. Her whole being, body and soul, is blessed and made holy with God's own life. With her name linked publicly to Jesus Christ and her body covered in the white robe of resurrection, she becomes a member of the body of Christ, a branch on the vine alive with the sap of the Spirit. Henceforth she is called to share in the prophetic, priestly, leadership work of Christ, prophet, priest, and king. The baptismal dignity of the laity is one of the great themes to emerge from the Second Vatican Council (see the Constitution on the Church, chapters 2 and 5). Graced by the Spirit of God, women are called and gifted. This is the theological foundation of their right to speak with authority.

Then, through their actual experience of living through all the vagaries of Christian life, women gain insight into the ways of God with the world. Through practices of contemplation and prayer, commitment to their responsibilities, ethical decisions of conscience, service to others in need, efforts to pass on the faith, loving God and neighbor with all their hearts, they garner personal knowledge. One could say they grow in wisdom and grace along with age. A great range of experiential knowledge allows them to discern the truth of what works and what doesn't to promote the coming reign of God.

In a particular way through their suffering women gain knowledge of the power of sin. Their negative experience teaches them by contrast what is needed for life to flourish. They come to know what precisely needs to be done to heal and redeem life, for themselves and for others who weep.

The sacrament of baptism, the experience of living a mature spiritual life, and the pain of suffering: each of these deeply connects women in the church with the power of the Spirit who consecrates them fully into the life of Christ, crucified and risen. Here is the source of women's power to speak with authority. They speak as persons of faith with the authority of their vocation as disciples of Jesus. Conversely, it can be argued that the growing strength of women's voices about religious matters in our day is an immense blessing for the church and the world.

From this standpoint, women discover elements that block what would be a more just church as well as elements that give their vision clear direction.

A PERVADING AMBIGUITY

A strong ambiguity about women runs through the Christian heritage. On the one hand there are sacred texts and laws that are patriarchal, relegating women to a subordinate role as if by divine decree. These sources are appealed to today by those who wish to maintain the status quo. On the other hand there are points of light that challenge this arrangement, calling for greater justice. Such sources focus on the solidarity of God with the poor, the dispossessed, and those considered of less importance, including women. Let us call this the prophetic strand in the tradition. Far from supporting the dominance of any one group over another, the prophetic pattern aims at a transformation of the church into a community of the discipleship of equals, living by mutual regard.

Both patriarchal and prophetic impulses are present in the Christian tradition. *Sic et Non*, yes and no, to cite the title of a famous medieval book by Abelard. The ambiguity itself opens interesting possibilities. Why? Because it makes clear that patriarchy is *not* all there is to Christianity. Something more is possible. Let us consider three important loci.

Scripture

The creation story that opens the Bible makes a major beneficial claim. On the sixth day "God created humankind in his own image; in the image of God he created them; male and female he created them. And God blessed them..." (Gen 1:26–28a). Note how simply this text establishes that women and men together and equally, as human beings, are created in the image and likeness of God. One does not dominate over the other, but both receive their lives with their gendered specificity as a divine gift. The New Testament inherits this teaching and gives it a Christian twist. An early baptismal hymn had the Christians in Galatia singing: "For as many of you as were baptized into Christ have put on Christ. There is no more Jew or Greek, slave or free, male and female, but you are all one in Christ Jesus" (Gal 3:27–28). Note how simply this text teaches that baptism clothes human beings with Christ without distinctions based on race (Jew or Greek), or economic class (slave or free), or gender (male or female), because they have all drunk of the one Spirit. The usual ways in which humans divide themselves no longer apply.

These are points of light. However, they are dimmed by law and cultural custom. Paul himself is terribly ambivalent. Weighing in on whether or not women should wear veils, he denies them the dignity of being created in the image of God, writing, "A man ought not to cover his head, since he is the image and reflection of God. But the woman is not so, but is the reflection of man...that is why a woman ought to have a veil on her head" (1 Cor 11:7, 10). Later Christian writers insisted that the equality in Christ due to baptism is only spiritual and should not affect the social order. "Wives be subject to your husbands" (Eph 5:22), and "slaves be obedient to your masters" (Eph 6:5), the household codes instruct. The letter to Timothy roots this in woman's role as portrayed in Genesis: "Let woman learn in silence with all submissiveness. I permit no woman to teach or have authority over men; she is to keep silent. For Adam was created first, then Eve; and Adam was not deceived, but the woman was deceived and became a transgressor. Yet woman will be saved through bearing children" (1 Tim 2:11–15). There you have it: woman was created second and sinned first, and the redemption wrought by Christ doesn't seem to make a bit of difference.

How are the people of God to sort this out? We can quote texts back and forth, patriarchal ones vs. prophetic ones. But how to discern the essence of what Scripture is conveying? The Second Vatican Council provided a terribly important criterion in its Decree on Revelation. Discussing how today's scientific and historical findings seem at times to contradict statements in the Bible, the Council taught that such texts in Scripture need not be taken literally. The Bible does not set out to teach science or history, but the gracious love of God come to redeem the world. Thus the criterion for discernment: what needs to be believed in Scripture is "that truth which God wanted written down for the sake of our salvation" (#11). The good news of salvation is the norm. Outdated science need not be considered the inspired word of God. Neither should legendary history. Applying this criterion with even more cogency, women can see today that texts reflecting oppressive cultural traditions are another category that need not be taken as divinely revealed. The church has already made this judgment with regard to biblical teaching on slavery and contempt for the Jews. The evils of sexism need to be treated to the same judgment.

The criterion of salvation receives concrete embodiment in the words and deeds of Jesus. Biblical scholars today point out that Jesus called both women and men to be his disciples; that women left their homes and responded to his call; that he received from women not only financial support (they bankrolled his ministry), but also encouragement and instruction about his own mission; that when Jesus was arrested the men deserted but the women remained faithful witnesses at the cross and at the tomb; that the risen Christ chose them to be the first recipients of the good news of the resurrection and gave them the apostolic mandate to "go and tell" the others, which they did, even in the face of ridicule. Reading the gospels with the gender question in mind, British writer Dorothy Sayers observed, "there is no act, no sermon, no parable in the whole gospel that borrows its pungency from female perversity. Nobody could possibly guess from the words and deeds of Jesus that there was anything 'defective' about woman's nature. But we might easily deduce . . . it from his church to this day."

After Jesus' death and resurrection, biblical texts as well as archaeological inscriptions give evidence that women functioned in the early church as apostles, prophets, teachers, healers, preachers, missionaries, deacons, and leaders of house churches. Scholars today point out, furthermore, that Jesus' inclusive table fellowship, his solidarity with the marginalized, his criticism of oppressive leaders, and his mandate that leadership must be exercised as the service of washing feet, all combine to prevent his community from setting up a system where one group lords it over another.

The prophetic interpretation of Scripture is peering through the fog of centuries to glimpse women's participation in founding the church. Over time male leaders opted for a patriarchal path, suppressing female leadership in the developing orthodox ecclesial community. But it can be argued that the alternative is more in line with Jesus' own practice and design. *Sic et Non*? Interpreted with a prophetic vision, Scripture nourishes hope. What was past may nourish the future.

Tradition

The same ambiguity about women found in Scripture perdures throughout subsequent tradition. Christianity was committed from the beginning to woman's capacity to be redeemed, to be baptized equally with men, and to attain eternal life. At the same time, a terrible bias against the dignity of women's full humanity plagued even the most influential of men thinkers. Recall Tertullian's teaching that women are the second Eve: just as she "softened up with her cajoling words he whom the devil himself could not attack," so too all women are "the devil's gateway." Recall how Augustine allowed that women's souls were capable of being the image of God equally with that of men; but precisely as female, that is, sexual in her body, woman is not in the image of God, but can be considered such only when taken together with man who is her head. Recall Thomas Aquinas's definition of woman as a "defective male," misbegotten when the male seed at conception is not up to full strength. Recall Martin Luther's view about why women had to live under the power of their husbands: "This punishment springs from original sin.... The rule remains with the husband, and the wife is compelled to obey him by God's command. He rules the home and the state, wages wars, defends his possessions, tills the soil, builds, plants, etc. The woman, on the other hand, is like a nail driven into the wall. She sits at home, looking after the affairs of the household, deprived of administering affairs outside or that concern the state. In this way is Eve punished."

Centuries of theologians drew from and contributed to the classical Christian doctrine of women's inferiority and their need to be subjected to men. As with any prejudice, once this is repeated it begins to be taken for granted. Over time women internalize the self-image that the oppressive system feeds them and instinctively think of themselves as less than worthy. Not all women have done this; there have always been feisty women who refuse that definition. But it becomes a pervasive idea that affects us all in some way.

In a contrasting development, women's movements throughout Christian history have hung on to or rediscovered the liberating framework of equality that subverts this patriarchal view and offers a radical alternative. In patristic and medieval periods, some women rejected patriarchal marriage to form monastic communities where they could pursue their relationship to God and one another undeterred. Some women were mystics who experienced a God who is beyond gender though able to be imaged as both male and female. In Julian of Norwich's famous visions, she affirms that "God all Wisdom is our kindly Mother; yes, as truly God is our Father, so truly is God our Mother." Her writings are the flowering in medieval women's mysticism of this fluid and gender-inclusive understanding of God. Some women remained outside convent walls, becoming involved in church reform by sheer dint of their fidelity to a call from God. Catherine of Siena, for example, gave strong directions to the pope. At one point she wrote to Gregory XI rebuking his choice of pastors and cardinals, saying that they were "stinking weeds, full of impurity and avarice, and bloated with pride," whereas the church deserved pastors who would be true servants of Jesus Christ with care for the poor (and she is a doctor of the church!).

Of course, in addition to singular women, there have always been "anonymous," the millions of unnamed women who have ignored the definition of their inferiority and built up the living Christian tradition through their quest for God, their creative initiatives, their prayer, their service, and their love. Again, the ambiguity perdures. *Sic et Non.* There is an alternative prophetic stream in the patriarchal tradition, this time not in theory so much as in practice.

Teaching of the Magisterium

In this era of the civil push for women's equality and the increasing stigmatizing of crimes against them, the official church has shifted away from the traditional teaching of women's inferiority. Vatican II sounded the new drumbeat loud and clear. Its teaching can be found in general statements filled with implications (the *whole* church is called to holiness; Christ is present in the *whole* assembly gathered in prayer), as well as in explicit statements such as this from the document on the Church in the Modern World: "With respect to the fundamental rights of the person, every type of discrimination, whether social or cultural, whether based on sex, race, color, social condition, language, or religion, is to be overcome and eradicated as contrary to God's intent" (29). Perhaps nowhere has this been more strongly articulated than in the encyclicals of Pope John Paul II. Rather than repeat the old canards, he vigorously maintains the equality of women and men in creation and redemption. In his 1988 encyclical "On the Dignity of Women," for example, he writes: "Both man and woman are human beings to an equal degree, both are created in God's image." And again, "A human being is a person, man and woman *equally* so, since both were created in the image and likeness of the personal God." The whole letter is filled with this affirmation, which can now also be found in the *Catechism of the Catholic Church*. Clearly, the ambiguity that saw women's human dignity as less worthy than men's is being cleared up in theory.

However, this does not lead the magisterium to posit equality in the social structures of church life, the clearest example being the ordination of women to the ministerial priesthood. In 1976, acknowledging that the reasons given in the past are inadequate (based as they were on the idea of women's inferiority), the Vatican document *Inter Insignores* brought forth three new reasons why the church cannot ordain women: (1) the example of Jesus, who ordained only twelve men, (2) the unbroken tradition of the church, and (3) the iconic argument which holds that the priest has to look like the male Jesus in order for the sacrament of the Eucharist to have its natural symbolic value. These reasons are buttressed by a view of human nature based on complementarity, which sees masculine nature fitted with rationality and the ability to lead in the public realm, while feminine nature is essentially oriented to love and nurturing the vulnerable in the private realm.

As an aside, let me note that these reasons have been analyzed as not accurate either historically or theologically. They have proved so consistently unconvincing to scholars and the church at large that twenty years later the Vatican issued another statement saying that women cannot be ordained, *period*, that this is authoritative teaching, and that the discussion is ended. It is a good example of the depth of patriarchal resistance to women's equality. Officials of the church are less willing to sit down and discuss baptized women's ordination in an open, collegial, and rational manner, than they are to sit down with other Christian churches to discuss contentious issues about the real presence of Christ in the Eucharist, the divinity of Christ, or even the inner life of the trinitarian God, all of which are subjects of ecumenical dialogue.

Looking at official church teaching in the post-conciliar decades, there is repetition of patriarchal ideas, some in new guises. But there is also startlingly strong affirmation of prophetic ideas about women's equality and human dignity. The tension between them is not tenable over the long haul. *Sic et Non*? Which one accords with what God desires "for the sake of our salvation"?

In Scripture, tradition, and the teaching of the magisterium, there is perduring ambiguity on the subject of women both in theory and practice. This makes the tradition open today to both patriarchal and prophetic interpretations. The good news is that there is light from our heritage for envisioning a church where women can flourish.

ENVISIONING THE CHURCH

Let us take the authority of women to speak and the ambiguity of the Christian heritage and draw them into the present task of envisioning the church that would embody a liberating form of community.

Coming into the present does not remove us from ambiguity. The present moment is shaped by two powerful forces on this subject: the movement for women's equality with men, and the resistance to that movement from entrenched male interests structured according to patriarchy. These forces first arose in civil society but were quickly mirrored in the church, because we do not live schizophrenically, one half of ourselves in society, the other half in the church. The twentieth century saw the rise of the women's movement in Western nations, and it swiftly became an issue of global importance. What made it start at this time? Education that increased female literacy; medical technology that allowed women control of their own fertility; and access to the workplace that allowed women a measure of economic independence. Above all it was impelled by a swelling of political, cultural, and psychological consciousness in the twentieth century that challenged sedimented patterns of colonialism and control.

Women themselves took the lead in this consciousness-raising, lifting up their voices to have this equality written into law.

Around the world women of color, of different racial and ethnic identity, women of different sexual orientations, and women of poorer economic status have all insisted that in addition to gender, all other aspects of women's concrete lives must be accorded respect. This equality of women with men changes the landscape of our imagination, with concrete ethical consequences. It demands rights and assigns responsibilities based on the dignity of the human person. The movement for women's equality is, at root, a movement for social justice on a global scale.

In light of Vatican II's teaching about baptism and recent revisions in theological anthropology, it can be seen that the church has embraced this issue. As a result new sociological facts have taken shape on the ground. Today many thousands of Catholic women are involved in church ministry. More than 80 percent of the ministry done in parishes today is carried out by women who are the majority of catechists, teachers, directors of religious education, charitable service workers, and volunteers of all kinds. Women serve in liturgical roles as lectors, eucharistic ministers, cantors. They function as parish administrators where priests are unavailable and lead communion services that include preaching at the liturgy of the word. They work as diocesan chancellors, judges in marriage tribunals, seminary professors, and professional staff in church agencies. Along with laymen, they increasingly lead the three great areas of Catholic contribution to American society: hospitals, schools and colleges, and social service agencies. Their spiritual wisdom flows in columns, books, and blogs; their work as spiritual directors and retreat leaders affects thousands of people in their relationship to God. As scholars they are active in fields of biblical research, church history, systematic theology, ethics, liturgy, and spirituality, bringing women's wisdom to bear on the whole range of Christian doctrines, symbols, ethics, and rituals.

At the same time, despite and indeed because of their participation, women report enormous tension in themselves due to their ongoing experience of exclusion. They note that doctrinal teachings, laws, and ethical mandates are still handed down from a council of men without the participation of women, even when this affects women most intimately in their own sexual bodies. Barred from presiding at Eucharist, they note that women's spiritual experience ordinarily never interprets the word of God in preaching, while the rite itself works like all good sacraments do: it effects by signifying. In this case it signifies women's unworthiness to represent Christ, despite their fidelity in following Jesus and what might be characterized as their prayerful, loving communion with the triune God. Eucharistic liturgy remains a presiding symbol of the church's reluctance to include women fully in the mysteries of salvation.

Into this fraught situation where the immovable object of patriarchy is encountering the irresistible force of women's desire for equality and full participation in the life of the church, into this situation, like a bomb, have dropped multiple scandals. Misuse of the financial resources of the church has been made public, with some bishops appropriating monies for luxurious living and the Vatican Bank using church monies for shady dealings. Horrific revelations of the sexual abuse of children by a small percentage of Catholic priests are outweighed, if possible, by news of the failure of a greater percentage of bishops to protect the innocent from harm. Reports of episcopal inaction and active cover-ups have simply undermined people's trust in the hierarchical church. Its structures are hemorrhaging their traditional authority. We now have what one writer has called "a perfect storm": lay people are scandalized and outraged; good priests are demoralized; many bishops are profoundly compromised; and an increasingly reactionary Vatican bureaucracy seems clueless about the seriousness of what is happening. The responses of competent laity calling for reform are met in many episcopal quarters with fear and disdain. Is it any wonder that hundreds of thousands of people have just walked or drifted away?

It is worth noting that since its beginnings in the 1960s feminist theology of the church has continuously analyzed the dark side of hierarchical patriarchy, where a male clerical elite has power without accountability and operates according to its own in-house norms. While often overlooked, this analysis has become piercingly relevant in the light of the current crisis. That same scholarship has also identified prophetic streams in Scripture and tradition, streams that make possible the dream of a different kind of church. When coupled with the human capital of women today who claim their baptismal identity and the men who stand in solidarity with them, a community of the discipleship of equals comes into view, one that is filled with the fire and wind of the Spirit to make God's compassionate, liberating love known in a world rife with poverty, hunger, war, and ecological devastation and in need of healing of all kinds.

CONCLUSION

The church is the redemptive community called to follow Jesus in serving the coming of the kingdom of God into this world. Again and again it fails and becomes a collaborator in domination, within and without. But the power of the Spirit, Holy Wisdom, at work in the community empowers us to rise, again and again. I believe we are living in such a moment. And what is new about it is that, for the first time in Christian history, women are silent and invisible no longer. Envisioning the church women want is, I believe, the work of the Spirit of God. And She will not be quenched.

Adapted from an address at the "Envisioning the Church Women Want" confer-ence at Boston College, 2004; published in Boston College Magazine *64:3 (Summer 2004): 20–22, 26–28.*

Resources

Audre Lorde, "Contact Lenses," *The Black Unicorn, Poems* (New York: W. W. Norton & Company, 1978), 94.
Mary Catherine Hilkert, *Speaking with Authority: Catherine of Siena and the Voices of Women Today* (New York: Paulist Press, 2008).

19

Interpreting Scripture through Women's Eyes

Recall a Jewish story: Under the heel of the powerful pharaoh of Egypt, the Hebrew people led lives bitter with slave labor. One day, worried that their number was increasing too rapidly, the pharaoh called into his presence two Hebrew midwives, one named Shiphrah and the other Puah. He gave them orders to kill every male baby that they delivered. What a dilemma: the might of the state came into conflict with their religious conscience. They risked their own lives if they did not sin. "But the midwives feared God, and did not do as the king of Egypt commanded them, but let the male children live." Summoned back into his fearsome presence, they glossed over their dissenting behavior with praise for the vigorous health of Hebrew women who gave birth before the midwives could arrive. "And the people multiplied and grew very strong," leaving the pharaoh no choice but to order all of his own people to do the murderous dirty work against the male babies. Subsequently, one male child was rescued through the combined efforts of his imaginative mother, his quick-thinking sister Miriam, herself still a child, and the pharaoh's own daughter, who named him Moses. He grew up to become the leader of the people out of the land of oppression. (Exodus, chapters 1–2).

The story of the exodus thus begins not with the heroic individual Moses but with the collaboration of women: two midwives who risked personal danger to obey God by disobeying an unjust, though authoritative, command; three other women who bonded across barriers of age, ethnicity, class, and religion to save a child. Without them, Moses would never have had his chance.

Recall a Christian story: Traveling through the district of the Samaritans, a people alienated from the Jews, a weary Jesus sat down by a well and asked a woman for a drink of water. Verbal sparring led to theological conversation, which climaxed in Jesus' personally revealing his messianic identity: "I who speak to you am he." The encounter was broken up by the return from town of the food-bearing disciples, who "marveled that he was talking to a woman." She (we do not know her name) returned to the city and, daring to face neighbors who had no great opinion of her virtue, began to proclaim Jesus as the Messiah. "Many Samaritans from that city believed in him because of the woman's testimony," and they prevailed upon him to remain for a few days. In the end, many more believed after listening to Jesus himself, knowing for themselves that he was the Savior of the world (Jn 4:1–42).

Jesus' ministry thus meets with success in a most unlikely and unexpected place through the ministry of a woman. In spite of the way Christian preachers have lingered over her sexual misconduct (five so-called husbands), what is really present here is the story of an early Christian missionary, a woman whose preaching had such power that it brought many folk in a Samaritan city to faith in Christ.

What is going on when biblical texts are interpreted this way? What is happening when long-forgotten women are once again remembered by name (Shiphrah and Puah), and when women whose stories have been long distorted are seen for their actual contributions to the history of salvation (the Samaritan woman as preacher and missionary)? Technically, these are instances of feminist hermeneutics, from the Latin *femina,* woman, and the Greek *hermeneia,* interpretation. They are examples of interpretation of Scripture done from a perspective that explicitly prizes and advocates the full human dignity of women. In this article, I propose to make a broad reconnaissance of this developing field of biblical interpretation. After a brief look at its historical background, we will consider various models currently in use and, opting for one in particular, examine some of its strategies. Christian imagination as it is expressed in prayer, catechesis, and preaching stands to be transformed by the result.

BACKGROUND

In the United States, the beginnings of women's efforts to interpret the Bible on behalf of their own agency date from the second quarter of the nineteenth century. As a wave of abolitionist activity swept the country, women became publicly involved in the struggle against slavery. Some traveled to give speeches in different cities. However, using the Bible as their authority clergy resisted women's speaking in public and attempted to silence female abolitionists. In a move of counter-resistance these women began to argue for an interpretation of the Bible that would validate their public speaking against injustice on an equal par with men. As they grappled with the texts, an insight was born: Jesus is the emancipator of women as well as of the slaves.

The story of the Quaker sisters Angelina and Sarah Grimké is an illuminating case in point. Campaigning against slavery throughout the U.S. northeast, they bore the brunt of clerical critics who went so far as to denounce their audiences as "promiscuous assemblies" since both sexes were present to listen. In 1837, a group of Congregationalist clergy condemned their public efforts precisely because they were public. In a vigorous "Pastoral Letter (from) the General Association of Massachusetts to the Churches under Their Care," the ministers drew on New Testament prescriptions for the role of women to write:

> We appreciate the unostentatious prayers and efforts of woman in advancing the cause of religion at home and abroad; in Sabbath Schools; in leading religious inquirers to the pastors for instruction; and in all such efforts as become the modesty of her sex.... But when she assumes the place and tone of man as a public reformer, our care and protection of her seem unnecessary; we put ourselves in self-defense against her; she yields the power which God has given her for her protection, and her character becomes unnatural.... We cannot, therefore, but regret the mistaken conduct of those who encourage females to bear an obtrusive and ostentatious part in measures of reform,

and countenance any of that sex who so far forget themselves as to itinerate in the character of public lecturers
and teachers.[1]

In response, Sarah Grimké appealed to the teaching of Jesus.
She emphasized how his words contrasted with the clergy's insis-
tence on different spheres of responsibility for women and men.
Her "Letters on the Equality of the Sexes and the Condition of
Woman" (1838) made this judgment:

> The Lord Jesus defines the duties of his followers in his
> Sermon on the Mount. He lays down grand principles by
> which they should be governed, without any reference to
> sex or condition. . . . I find him giving the same directions
> to women as to men, never even referring to the distinc-
> tion now so strenuously insisted upon between masculine
> and feminine virtues; this is one of the anti-Christian "tra-
> ditions of men" which are taught instead of the "com-
> mandments of God." Men and women were CREATED
> EQUAL: they are both moral and accountable beings, and
> whatever is *right* for man to do, is *right* for woman.[2]

Not all nineteenth-century female reformers were so sanguine
about the existence of a liberating message for women in the Bible.
Elizabeth Cady Stanton, for one, judged the biblical text to be sexist
to its core. She spearheaded the efforts of a committee of women
authors and ordained ministers to create *The Woman's Bible* (1898).
This was comprised of commentary on all the passages dealing
with women, showing how they could be interpreted positively or
else judged negatively for their oppressive character. Whether
finding the Bible ultimately of value or not, however, a number of
nineteenth-century women publicly engaged its writings, creating a
ferment of interpretation on women's behalf.[3]

Relative quiet settled on the first half of the twentieth century.
While increasing numbers of women were trained as biblical
scholars, they were not self-consciously feminist but pursued
their discipline according to accepted methods. It was not until
the 1960s that the silence was broken. Biblical scholar Margaret
Brackenbury Crook was one who sounded the call:

A masculine monopoly in religion begins when Miriam raises her indignant question: "Does the Lord speak only through Moses?" Since then, in all three of the great religious groups stemming from the land and books of Israel —Judaism, Christianity, and Islam—men have formulated doctrine and established systems of worship offering only meager opportunity for expression of the religious genius of womankind.... If a woman born and bred in any of these faiths takes a comprehensive look at the form of theology best known to her, she discovers that it is masculine in administration, in the phrasing of its doctrines, liturgies, and hymns. It is man-formulated, man-argued, man-directed.[4]

By this time the second wave of the women's movement was afoot in civil society, and the question of feminist interpretation of the Scriptures began to flourish in earnest on the soil of women's rising consciousness.

MODELS OF INTERPRETATION

What response ensues when realization dawns that the Bible has been a major implement used to subordinate women within patriarchal institutions, both civil and religious? In biblical studies the development has been so diverse and so rapid, and debate between proponents of different approaches so vigorous, that it is difficult to survey the whole landscape. Carolyn Osiek has introduced a note of order by proposing that there are five alternative types of feminist interpretation that are currently being utilized.[5] While these methods are for the most part mutually exclusive, they have a common goal, which is so to interpret the biblical text that it will promote a blessing for women. Is there a liberating message from God in these texts for women as well as for men?

1. Rejectionist. This manner of interpretation judges the Bible to be so penetrated with sexism that it is unredeemable. Male domination is an inherent characteristic inseparable from revelation. Take away patriarchy and the biblical tradition would collapse. Thus, the Bible is to be rejected as an authoritative norm, along with the religious traditions and institutions that draw life from it. Separating oneself from the Bible is the only way to be free of its corrupt influence (e.g., Mary Daly).

2. Loyalist. The opposite of the first option, this method holds that since the Bible is the revealed and inspired word of God, it cannot by nature be oppressive. If it seems to be so, this is the fault of interpreters who may be sinful or deficient in insight. This stance presupposes that there is a divinely given order to the world, which would have people live in harmony rather than in dominating-subordinate relationships. The biblical text carries the revelation of this true order. Uncovering it through biblical interpretation is the way to promote the good of women (e.g., Evelyn and Frank Stagg; Susan Foh).

3. Revisionist. If the first model of interpretation thinks the Bible is unconvertible, and the second sees it as in no need of conversion, this third approach occupies a middle ground. It acknowledges that the biblical text is indeed shaped by patriarchy, but holds that this is a historically conditioned circumstance not intrinsic to biblical revelation. It is possible to separate out sexism from the biblical message, showing how subordinationist texts are culturally conditioned and how at many points women's contributions are valued. The tradition would survive. Moreover, it is imperative to do this work of revision, for the Bible has something vitally important to offer. Reforming interpreting of biblical texts is the best way to contribute to women's dignity (e.g., Phyllis Trible, Elizabeth Moltmann-Wendel).

4. Sublimationist. This approach goes its own unique way by idealizing the "feminine" as a category totally separate from the masculine. Working with a certain understanding of Jungian archetypes, it evaluates the life-giving and nurturing qualities of women to be so singular that women rightfully operate by a different set of rules from men. As "other," women exist in a separate, at times superior, sphere. Therefore, the question of the social equality of roles does not arise. The Bible is a source of powerful symbols of the eternal feminine, such as Israel the bride of Yahweh, the church as the bride of Christ, Mary the virgin mother. Lifting up and reflecting on these symbols is the best way to develop appreciation for the feminine in relation to the divine, and thus to enhance the dignity of women (e.g., Joan Chamberlain Engelsman).

5. Liberationist. This method of interpretation springs from a central theological insight of theology done from the perspective of the poor, namely, that the core message of the Bible is one of God's saving liberation for all people. The God of the Bible is not an oppressor. In no way does God condone the sinful situation of social injustice. To the contrary, the God of both Jewish and Christian Scriptures enters with compassionate love into solidarity with those oppressed in order to save, to set them free. This redemption is not meant solely for life hereafter but is intended to be tasted even here and now. With God the Creator and Redeemer of this world there can be no ultimate dualism between sacred and secular spheres.

This theological insight is applied to the situation of women in the actual world. Sexism past and present creates a particularly pervasive sinful situation in which one-half of the human race is subordinated to the other. Thus it is not enough simply to reinterpret biblical texts within their continuing patriarchal framework, which assumes women's subordination. Instead scholars envision a different framework for life, a new community of the reign of God in which women are valued as genuinely human subjects in a community of mutual relationship. Such vision becomes the context for understanding the meaning of biblical texts. Probing texts for their ability to release a liberating good news from God for women in social, political, economic, cultural, and religious realms is the most effective way to promote the full humanity of women (e.g., Letty Russell, Rosemary Radford Ruether, Elisabeth Schüssler Fiorenza).

While not watertight, these five alternatives do delineate major options presently available in the field of feminist hermeneutics. Arising from profoundly different assumptions about the Bible and about the nature of women, they nevertheless all seek to overcome the misogyny and devaluation of women typical of patriarchal interpretation and to promote the genuine dignity of women themselves.

PRESUPPOSITIONS OF A LIBERATIONIST READING

Of the five alternatives, the liberationist interpretation raises the greatest challenge to the churches. Its analysis of the oppression of patriarchy is as penetrating as that of the rejectionist model, but instead of abandoning the Bible, religiously committed scholars of this persuasion choose to remain and work for radical transformation of the community that employs the Bible as sacred Scripture. Having experienced the positive value of Scripture, they work so that the tradition flowing from it will be more faithful to its own best insights. Getting a grip on the basic presuppositions of this approach will enable one to appreciate the need for the strategies that are then employed. These basic assumptions include the following.

1. For the most part the books of the Bible were written by men, for men, from a male perspective, in a socio-political culture dominated by men. As a famous axiom would have it, the Bible is indeed the word of God in the words of men. The texts reflect this fact. They concern themselves primarily with the doings and experiences of men and promote male interests. Considering the male human being to be normative, they are clear examples of the androcentric mindset. Not neutral in their partiality, most biblical writings betray a vested interest in maintaining the status quo in gender relationships, since this works to the benefit of those in the dominant position. It can be painful to make the discovery of the extent of male domination in biblical texts, but honesty requires it.

2. The flip side of this assumption is that, given the male-oriented nature of the texts, they pay little or no attention to women. Regardless of the role women actually played in historical events or the insights they contributed, the texts reflect the story as told through the eyes of men. Women's experiences are marginalized, if not suppressed outright. It is this latter point which is to the fore in current discussion. Men authors have transmitted only a fraction of the women's story. Practically speaking, the existence of innumerable women and their involvement in salvation history has been erased from the public memory of the written sources. Most texts would lead us to believe that women were

not even present at the great events through which God was working salvation or, if they were, that they occupied a marginal position, except when they were producing male heirs. The texts tell us next to nothing about how the women of Israel or early Christianity discussed, debated, struggled with God, or found joy, comfort, or challenge in their developing faith understanding. We get only a glimpse of their lives, minds, and hearts behind the veil imposed by patriarchal shaping of the text.

One verse that brilliantly illustrates this state of affairs comes at the end of Matthew's account of Jesus feeding the multitudes: "And those who ate were about five thousand men, not counting the women and children" (14:21). What is usually called the feeding of the five thousand obviously included many more than this, but they were not counted; they did not count. Realizing the androcentric interest that governed redaction of biblical texts gives rise to the insight that these texts as they stand are not a reliable reflection of the actual story of biblical women, their deeds, and their insights.

3. In addition to recognizing the fact that the Bible has a patriarchal stamp and marginalizes or erases the presence of women, the liberationist method also keeps in view the fact that its later history continues in the hands of men within the patriarchal structures of church and society.

The formation of the canon betrays this orientation. Paul, for example, seems to have been ambivalent about women's involvement in public ministry. His authentic letters show him sometimes for, sometimes against it. Two later sets of writings crystallize each tendency. The pastoral letters (1 and 2 Timothy and Titus) opt for abolishing this ministry and placing women in a subordinate position to men in the church, while the *Acts of Paul and Thecla* decide in favor of women's evangelizing activity. There was obviously a debate going on in the community, with both sides appealing to Paul as an authority. Those against women's public involvement gained the upper hand when the pastorals were made part of the official canon of Scripture while the *Acts of Paul and Thecla* was not, although it continued to be highly influential spiritual reading into the fourth century.

Furthermore, the history of interpretation of biblical texts, public preaching on these texts, and translations of these texts have been done from an androcentric perspective. The political and social

institutions of patriarchy that formed the context for these activities ensured that such a focus on men's interests to the exclusion of
women's was considered normal.

4. One last defining presupposition of liberationist interpretation
flows logically from the above assumptions. If even some of them
are true, it becomes clear that the word of God itself needs to be
liberated. It needs to be freed from its overarching patriarchal
bias and let loose as good news for every person, regardless of
the concrete conditions of each one's existence. The liberating news
does flash out from the Scriptures in certain instances. Women are
equally created in the image of God, we read, equally redeemed in
Christ Jesus, equally filled with the gifts of the Spirit, equally destined for life in the new heaven and the new earth. This good
news for women, however, becomes generally distorted when fil-
tered through the exclusively male perspective of the biblical texts
and their subsequent interpretation. For the sake of the inclusive
salvation willed by God, the biblical word needs to be rescued
from its bondage.

STRATEGIES FOR LIBERATIONIST INTERPRETATION

Taking the inclusive impulse of Scripture as a whole to be revelatory of God's intent and therefore normative, scholars have developed strategies for reading texts that release a message of
liberation. At this stage in the development of the discipline, the
good news for women is being uncovered mainly through reclaiming the memories of our foremothers and foresisters in the
faith, their struggles, sufferings, and victories. Their historical stories, pieced together through a series of new tactics, become a key
way of mediating the religious message of God's saving liberation
for women. The interpreter becomes, in a sense, a detective. Some
strategies involve reading between the lines to discover women's
presence. Other strategies deal with more didactic texts that describe women's nature or delimit women's activities in demeaning
ways. Each tactic is a different arrow in the liberationist quiver;
particular texts are handled with one or other of them in mind.
Some of these strategies are as follows.

1. If women are in a biblical text at all, then they must have been even more powerfully present in the original event. What we are dealing with in such instances are memories so strong that they simply could not be erased even in the men-oriented retelling. This is a tip-of-the iceberg strategy. Whatever the texts report should be read as signaling even more significant activity by women at the time. An example: Mary Magdalene and other women disciples keep vigil at the cross, accompany Jesus' body to the tomb, discover it empty, are gifted with the first appearances of the risen Christ, and receive the commission to preach the good news to the other disciples. The courageous presence and initiative of these women throughout the pivotal paschal events are foundational for the church. They are the moving point of continuity between all the scenes. The significance of their presence has been vastly underestimated.

2. If women are not mentioned in a biblical text, this does not necessarily mean they were not present and active during the original event. It is not at all unusual for a dominating perspective to overlook the presence of those considered of less importance and to omit them from the retelling. We noted above how Matthew's gospel does not count the women and children who fed on loaves and fish. Mark's version, while noting the number of men, does not even mention women and children being present (6:34–44). If we had only his account we would not even see the uncounted women and children in our mind's eye. But their erasure is not necessarily historically accurate.

This strategy comes into play in interpretations of the stories of the Last Supper. Has patriarchal bias excluded the presence of women in the retelling of this story? During Jesus' ministry in Galilee women disciples were present at the many suppers he hosted. Presumably some of them even paid for the meals, given Luke's observation that many women accompanied him and provided for the group out of their own resources (8:1–3). Since they followed him up to Jerusalem, the burden of proof lies on those who would argue that they were absent from this last meal of Jesus with his disciples. At least one evangelist, Luke, seems to assume the presence of women in the way he depicts the group gathered in the supper room and in the way he recounts Jesus' teaching there, both of which imply the presence of a group of disciples larger than "the twelve."[6]

3. When male gender-specific words are used in an obviously inclusive sense, women should be read into the text. An example: "All who are led by the Spirit of God are sons (*uioi*) of God" (Rom 8:14). This text intends to describe every member of the baptized community, not just its male members. Thus women are included as sons of God. With even more cogency, therefore, women are to be understood as included in words that are not intrinsically gender-specific but rather generic. This yields a wide-ranging picture of the participation of women in the ministries of the early church. Judging from Paul's letters and the Acts of the Apostles, women functioned as apostles, disciples, preachers, prophets, missionaries, leaders of house churches, workers for the gospel. It is noteworthy that contemporary translations have restored her identity as a woman to the apostle Junia, whose name for centuries was translated as that of a man: "Greet Andronicus and Junia, my relatives who were in prison with me: they are prominent among the apostles, and they were in Christ before I was" (Rom 16:7).

4. Texts that lay down norms for women's roles should be analyzed in order to distinguish between their prescriptive and descriptive character. Oftentimes rules are made to prevent a practice only because it is already taking place. Thus the prohibition reflects the ideas of men about how women should behave, but they do not portray the actual historical reality of women themselves. Example: "Let women keep silence in the churches. For they are not permitted to speak, but should be subordinate, even as the law says" (1 Cor 14:34). This text reveals what Paul (or perhaps the male Corinthians to whose inquiries he may be responding) would wish. Interpreted with this strategy, however, it reveals that in fact women were not keeping silent in the churches. They were speaking up, preaching, prophesying, and interpreting prophecy, since they too had been inspired by the word of God. The text is prescriptive, yes. But we have no idea of how the Corinthian women responded to this dictum.

5. Texts that speak in a subordinationist way of women should be reinterpreted, if possible, to reveal a positive content. An example is 1 Timothy 13–14, which builds an argument for women's subordinate position in the domestic realm from the idea that woman was created second and sinned first. This text can be unlocked by going back to Genesis and reinterpreting the stories of creation and fall using feminist hermeneutics. Then it can be seen that Eve's creation directly by God from Adam's rib ensures her equal participation in human nature (she is not one of the animals); then it can be appreciated that her speaking with the serpent and subsequent decision reveal a lively and curious intelligence and thirst for adventure; both man and woman are equally at fault in eating the fruit of the tree of the knowledge of good and evil.

Sometimes every strategy fails. If a subordinationist text cannot possibly be reinterpreted, then the judgment simply has to be made that this is a culturally conditioned dictum, one not compatible with human dignity as our culture has come to appreciate. Hence it is not the truth that God wished to have written down for our salvation. "The books of Scripture must be acknowledged as teaching firmly, faithfully, and without error that truth which God wanted put into the sacred writings for the sake of our salvation."[7] So taught Vatican II, and unless one thinks subordination of women is according to divine will, one has latitude. As with outdated scientific and historical statements that need not be taken literally, so too socially oppressive mandates need not cramp biblical interpretation.

CONCLUSION

The strategies of liberationist interpretation are unlocking ancient texts and releasing their power to free up the flourishing of women as fully valued human persons. Taking the narrative texts as clues, we glimpse contours of the original experiences. As we rethink familiar stories and recover forgotten ones, a realization dawns: at key points in the history of Israel, in the ministry of Jesus, and in the early church, women were central figures, participating in and even leading the response of the community to God's saving gifts. Taking the texts as artifacts shaped in a culture historically privileging men, we uncover their hidden positive meaning or ultimately judge them to be not from God. In the process, another insight is born: women share a history of salvation that has not yet been told, and a promise of graced humanity lived in freedom that has not yet become reality.

As any number of feminist-minded scholars will admit, the effort to develop feminist hermeneutics is motivated not only by the desire to advance their scholarly discipline, although this in itself is legitimate. It is also undertaken as an act of survival, motivated by the desire to believe in God in the midst of a patriarchal church and society. Assuming in fact that the biblical text mediates the living word of the liberating God, feminist scholars are wrestling with the text the way Jacob wrestled all night with a mysterious angel. Like Sarah's grandson, they will not let it go until it gives them, and the whole church, a blessing (Gen 32:26).

Adapted from Chicago Studies *27 (1988): 123–35.*

Notes

1. Cited in *The Feminist Papers*, ed. Alice S. Rossi (New York: Bantam, 1974), 305–6.

2. Ibid., 16.

3. This history is documented by Carolyn De Swarte Gifford, "American Women and the Bible: The Nature of Woman as a Hermeneutical Issue," in *Feminist Perspectives on Biblical Scholarship*, ed. Adela Yarbro Collins (Chico, CA: Scholars Press, 1985), 11–33.

4. Cited in Margaret Brackenbury Crook, *Women and Religion* (Boston: Beacon, 1964), 1, 5.

5. C. Osiek, "The Feminist and the Bible: Hermeneutical Alternatives," in *Feminist Perspectives on Biblical Scholarship*, 93–105.

6. Quentin Quesnell, "The Women at Luke's Supper," in *Political Issues in Luke-Acts*, ed. Richard Cassidy and Philip Scharper (Maryknoll, NY: Orbis Books, 1983), 59–79.

7. Vatican II, Decree on Revelation, par. 11.

20

Friends of God and Prophets
Waking Up a Sleeping Symbol

Imagine a religious symbol that joins all living people around the globe who seek the face of God into a circle of mutual companions; one, furthermore, whose dynamism connects this living group with the faithful dead of all ages; one that also links them with the bread and wine of the Eucharist and through this sacrament with the whole natural world; one, finally, that embraces this totality with the outstretched wings of the creating, liberating Spirit of God who bestows on them the character of something sacred. Such is the symbol the Apostles' Creed calls the communion of saints, celebrated by Christians in the West on All Saints Day, November 1st. From every angle this symbol stretches wide to bespeak an inclusive participation in a community brought about by the Spirit throughout history and across the wide world.

Now imagine a religious symbol seldom studied in the history of theology; one, moreover, frequently reduced to referring to the dead alone and among them to only a few who have been officially canonized; one that is now mostly absent from the preaching, teaching, religious imagination, and piety of large numbers of people in advanced industrial societies. This too is the communion of saints, a doctrinal symbol that has withered to the point of oblivion or at least has gone soundly asleep in current theory and practice.

But a symbol so relational, so inclusive and egalitarian, so respectful of persons who are defeated, so praising of those who succeed against all odds, so hope-filled and so practical, such a symbol can serve to empower all people who are committed to a deeper spiritual life. I propose we wake up this sleeping symbol and allow it to begin again to exercise its beneficial dynamic. A text from the biblical book of Wisdom that speaks of the gracious work of Sophia, the Spirit of God, will ring the wake-up call:

Although she is but one, she can do all things,
and while remaining in herself, she renews all things;
in every generation she passes into holy souls
and makes them friends of God, and prophets. (Wis 7:27)

THE COMMUNITY ALIVE TODAY

In light of historic neglect, we need to be clear about this point: the communion of saints refers first and foremost to all those alive on earth today who respond to the grace of God in trying to live in accord with truth and love. While the precise term itself was coined by Christians to describe their own experience of grace, divine blessing cannot be limited to this circle. Within human cultures everywhere God's Spirit calls persons to seek truth and live lovingly and justly with others, so that holy people who are "friends of God and prophets" can be found speaking every tongue and living in every nation, and even among religion's honest cultured despisers.

The global framework serves to keep the communion of saints inclusive while we study specifically the group that originated it, the Christian community. Here it expresses a sense of blessing that arises at the heart of faith. Paul expressed the experience this way: "where sin abounded, grace did superabound" (Rom 5:20); consequently, "there is now no more condemnation for those who are in Christ Jesus" (Rom 8:1). The whole community, while composed of sinners, nevertheless is at the same time a redeemed community, a holy people of God. By virtue of belonging to this community, every baptized member is fundamentally holy. Here the holiness of the baptized is not simply an ethical matter, being holy as being morally perfect. Rather, it is a participation in divine life thanks to the free gift of God.

New Testament writers drew deeply on the Jewish tradition of being a holy people to articulate their own sense of being a holy community. The Hebrew word *holy* (*kadosh*) means dedicated or set apart. It carries the connotation of something separate, pure and clear, unmixed with evil, like a wellspring of clear running water, something rock hard in the strength of its integrity. These overtones coalesce when the theme is used to refer to God, "the Holy One of Israel" (Isa 12:6). Holiness points to God's being utterly transcendent, completely apart from what is finite or sinful, numinous, dwelling in unapproachable light. Theophanies such as the burning bush that is not consumed serve only to express the mystery. The word *holy* bespeaks the experience of God's being unlike anything or anyone else, in the face of which people are moved to fall silent, sing, dance, raise their arms, or bow down in adoration.

In biblical usage, however, the holiness of God is never used simply and undialectically to indicate divine otherness and transcendence, for God is precisely the Holy One of *Israel.* Set within the narrative framework of exodus and covenant, holiness becomes a profoundly relational term that bespeaks God's involvement with the world in creative and redeeming care. Over and over again the psalms and prophets link the active presence of divine holiness with justice, love of the truth, glory dwelling in the land, and hope in the struggle for freedom. This link is so consistently made that compassionate and challenging engagement with the world becomes the very form in which divine holiness makes itself known.

In the Hebrew Scriptures holiness is proper to God alone. But in loving kindness and fidelity God gathers a people to share in that holiness: "For I am the Lord who brought you up from the land of Egypt, to be your God; you shall be holy, for I am holy" (Lev 11:45). Liberated from bondage and chosen for covenant, this people enters into a new identity as a special community. Applied to the people, holiness now takes on the connotation of "belonging to God." This relationship is not set up because of their great achievements or merits but is offered as a free gift: "It was not because you were more numerous than any other people that the Lord set his heart on you and chose you, for you were the fewest of all peoples. It was because the Lord loved you" (Deut 7:7–8). This is a gift of inestimable generosity, abounding with ethical implications but not limited to them. Being a holy people, belonging to God, means participating in God's own way of being God. Let me underscore this key point: holiness does not consist first and foremost in ethical or pious practices, nor does it imply innocence of experience or perfection of moral achievement. Rather, it is a consecration of the very being of this people. They are imbued with a sacred quality that then of course flows into responsibility to bear witness and serve the good of the world, in accord with the world-loving dynamics of the holiness of God in which they participate.

This is a beautiful insight. But it does have a shadow side. In her insightful wrestling with the Jewish tradition, Judith Plaskow brings to critical light how within a patriarchal context holiness as "belonging to God" developed into "holiness as separation." Rather than the distinctiveness of Jewish belief and practice being interpreted in relational terms that connect, it created divisions between those inside and outside the community, leading even to intolerance and violence. The separation motif used to demarcate the Jewish people from surrounding nations also turned inward to create a graded system of holiness within the community itself, so that clean and unclean, especially in a ritual sense, tended to stratify the community into a holy elite and a deficient under-class. Socially, the subordination of women was the first and most persistent result of the hierarchical interpretation of what was more or less holy.[1]

Plaskow's own work, however, powerfully shows that this is not a necessary result of being God's holy people. Her proposal of a part-whole model rather than a hierarchical one allows the distinctiveness of a people to be honored while God is acknowledged to be at play also beyond the confines of the group. Internally, whereas both Jewish and Christian male leaders have traditionally aggrandized their position and created categories of in and out, near and far from the divine, such separations are not an essential requirement of being a holy people. Indeed, if the holiness of the people is a result of the dwelling of "the Holy One in your midst" (Hos 11:9), that is, a dwelling within the whole community and not just a part, then such hierarchical gradations of holiness can be judged to be a grave distortion. Retrieving holiness as belonging to God rather than as separation points the way to a renewed pattern of being community together where differences enrich rather than rigidly divide.

Although not a people in the same sense that the Jewish people are, early Christians drew upon the biblical theme of being a holy people to articulate their own sense of identity. Propelled by their experience of the common waters of baptism and the shared eucharistic meal, they came to realize that the power of the Spirit was forming them into a company of disciples of the crucified and risen Jesus the Christ with responsibility to bear good news into the world. As with the Jewish sense of being a holy people, their community's center of gravity was located not in their own piety or ethical perfection but in God who graciously gifted them with salvation.

To express this communal identity Christians pressed into service the Jewish term *saints*. Originally this term referred to the faithful remnant of Israel who would inherit the kingdom when the Messiah comes. Now it took on the meaning of the whole Christian community's character as a holy people. It is surprising to discover that the New Testament uses the word more than sixty times in this sense. To quote Paul's letters: "To all God's beloved in Rome, who are called to be saints" (Rom 1:7); "To all the saints in Christ Jesus who are in Philippi" (Phil 1:1); "To the church of God that is in Corinth, to all of you who are sanctified in Christ Jesus, called to be saints" (1 Cor 1:2); "All the saints greet you" (2 Cor 13:12). All together and without internal distinction, Christians gathered here or gathered there are a company of saints, each one and all together filled with the Spirit for the sake of the world.

This point is graphically portrayed by the Pentecost story. Seeking simplicity, artistic representations have traditionally depicted only thirteen people present when the Holy Spirit descended, namely, the twelve apostles with Mary in their midst. But the group numbered about one hundred twenty people gathered in prayer, including Jesus' women disciples and some of his family members (see Acts 1:15). As Luke describes the event, "And a tongue of fire rested on each of them. And all of them were filled with the Holy Spirit" (Acts 2:3–4). Here is the nucleus of the church, every single member of the community receiving the Spirit for the sake of mission to the world.

Too often theology has squeezed this inclusive meaning dry, eliminating most of the baptized from sainthood in favor of a small group of elite office-holders or canonized saints. Even today many a theologian begins discussion of the subject by acknowledging that even though the New Testament refers to the whole Christian community as saints, this will be set aside in order to consider paradigmatic figures, who then become in practice the real saints. But this strategy woefully shortchanges the breadth and depth of the gift of God who in gracious mercy forms, blesses, and sends forth the whole living community as a communion of saints.

Drawing its view of the church from the Scriptures in a renewed way, Vatican II made a remarkable contribution. It taught that God calls the whole church to holiness. Through baptism persons are truly joined to God in Christ; receiving the Spirit, they become sharers in the divine nature. "In this way they are really made holy" (*Lumen Gentium* 40). This holiness, furthermore, is essentially the same for everyone. There is not one kind of holiness for lay persons and another for those in religious life or ordained ministry. There is not one kind of indwelling of the Spirit for office-holders in the church and another for the folks. Rather, "in the various types and duties of life, one and the same holiness is cultivated by all who are moved by the Spirit of God" (*Lumen Gentium* 41). In other words, the church is not divided into saints and non-saints. Vivified by grace, every woman, man, and child, in whatever diverse circumstances and of whatever race, class, ethnicity, sexual persuasion, or any other marker that divides human beings, participates in God's holy life. The vocation to be friends of God shapes the life of everyone in the community.

If this be the case, the communion of saints emerges with an unexpected prophetic edge. It challenges those in leadership to bend every effort toward highlighting the extraordinary status of so-called ordinary women and men, often overheard to be saying "I'm no saint," but in truth called and gifted in the Spirit. The holiness of ordinary persons in the midst of ordinary time needs to be ever more strongly taught and celebrated if people are not to be robbed of their true Christian identity. A second challenge also presents itself. If the the whole community enjoys a transforming relationship with the triune God, then social relationships and structures within the community of disciples that do not embody this truth are distorted and in need of reform. Spiritual equality presses the question of social and political equality to the fore.

Forming a community of companions in grace around the globe today, living persons seek the face of God, cling to God's gracious mercy in the face of suffering and sin, and make their own contributions. Then they pass through the shattering of death into the life-giving hands of God, to be followed by the fresh young faces of a new generation of all saints.

CLOUD OF WITNESSES THROUGH TIME

Christians cling to the hope that not even death "will be able to separate us from the love of God in Christ Jesus" (Rom 8:39). Hence, early on they concluded that their community was not restricted to persons who live and breathe at the present moment but also includes those who have died. One does not leave the church by dying. Let us acknowledge at the outset that this idea presents many difficulties to contemporary minds and hearts. People in Western secular culture tend to have the experience that death truly ends life as we know it. The dead truly disappear from our world. This is certainly not true of all cultures. Mexico's Day of the Dead and African and Asian respect for ancestors express a different sensibility. But the Western empirical approach to reality demands honesty about the fact that no one knows exactly what happens after death. The future is genuinely unknown, and no empirical investigation can lift this veil. Compounding the contemporary dilemma are scientific investigations into the mind-brain connection which cast doubt on personal survival after death. Modern philosophy, too, has largely departed from a dualistic model of body and soul that can be separated at death with one part, the soul, continuing to exist. In addition, theology is acutely aware that language about what happens after death is metaphorical, so that the classical constructs of heaven, hell, and purgatory are not real "places" but need to be interpreted as evocative symbols of states of being. Even the Bible knows this holy agnosticism, writing that "eye has not seen nor ear has not heard" what things God has in store (1 Cor 2:9); thus "we hope for what we do not see" (Rom 8:25). How then can the communion of saints hold out for including the dead?

Writing a book on this subject, I wrestled with the issue in a fierce way. I explored different philosophies to see if they would " work" in assuring personal and corporate life after death. But none of them would go the distance. And so I humbly offer you the conclusion I came to as a theological opinion: since the darkness of death is final and unconquerable, the only way possible to resolve the issue of the fate of the dead is not with rational argument alone but with a reasonable, though ultimately daring, existential act of radical faith in God. Either the One who gives life to begin with can be trusted to give new life again at the end, or not.

REASONS FOR OUR HOPE

For the Christian community, the bedrock of this faith is the death and resurrection of Jesus Christ. This cruel death was a real death. It violently tore apart his whole life, no piece of him slipping through its mesh. In face of this destruction, the Easter message proclaims that the crucified one died not into nothingness but into the absolute mystery of the glory of God. Starting with Mary Magdalene, the disciples announce *Vivit!* He lives! The god-forsaken one lives forever with God as pledge of the future for all the dead. While this is utterly unimaginable and cannot be reduced to a kind of physiological miracle, it nevertheless affirms that Jesus in his whole person and in all dimensions of his historical existence has entered into a new and different brilliance of life in the embrace of God.

This belief can be rescued from designation as an esoteric oddity once one realizes the precise correlation between God's creation of the world and the resurrection of the dead. In both instances one begins with virtually nothing: no universe, no future for a dead person. Then the vivifying breath of the Creator Spirit moves over the abyss. In the case of the cosmos, this brings the world into being. In the case of the dead, this carries persons through their perishing into new life. If the compassionate power of God could bring about the existence of the world to begin with, and if the living God as encountered in the history of Israel and Jesus Christ is unshakably faithful, then that same Holy One can be trusted not to let created persons perish into oblivion but to engage in an act of new creation at the end. The wellspring of creation is also the fulfillment of the whole groaning creation, including the human race.

In the first century one stream of Jewish expectation held that all would be raised on the last day, either for judgment or blessing. In its own historical context, the proclamation that Jesus is risen simply adds the astounding twist that what Israel expected to happen on the last day to everyone has happened already and to only one person, the crucified prophet from Nazareth. The resurrection is an event of the future breaking into history in advance. Not an isolated event affecting Jesus' destiny only, it is a divine pledge of a future for all the dead: "If the Spirit of God who raised Jesus from the dead dwells in you, then he who raised Christ from the dead will give life to your mortal bodies also through the Spirit dwelling in you" (Rom 8:11). The future will be on a cosmic scale what has already happened in Christ. What awaits the world is not nothing but the vivifying touch of the Creator Spirit. Indeed, the view of God as the One who "gives life to the dead and calls into existence the things that do not exist" (Rom 4:17) becomes practically a designation of the Christian God.

There is, then, reason to hope that persons are not lost in death but are enfolded into the mystery of the gracious being of God which to us is darkness but to them is the fulfillment of their lives in the sphere of the Spirit. The loving, faithful character of God is the foundation for including the dead in the communion of saints.

If we ask after these persons in themselves, seeking where they are to be found, the only possible answer, since they do not belong to the empirical world around us, is that they abide in

God. If we seek to relate to these persons in themselves, we realize that there can be no direct, sensate communication such as was possible when they were alive in time. Even if we try to summon them and transpose them into our concrete world, something that is attempted in spiritualist séances or manipulative pieties, they appear only as we are, earth-bound, and not as they are, embraced in the light of absolute mystery. But they have passed from our circle into the hidden life of God; ultimately they are found in our experience where God is. In Karl Rahner's careful words:

> We meet the living dead, even when they are those loved by us, in faith, hope, and love, that is, when we open our hearts to the silent claim of God's own self, in which they live; not by calling them back to where we are, but by descending into the silent eternity of our own hearts, and through faith in the risen Lord, creating in time the eternity which they have brought forth forever.[2]

In other words, we meet them not by reducing their reality to our own imaginative size but by going forth to where they dwell in the mystery of the living God as the beginning of the new heaven and the new earth.

Along with those alive today the communion of saints encompasses those who have died. This company in heaven beggars description. While some few are remembered by name, millions upon anonymous millions of others are also included, people who made some personal contribution to the goodness in the world. Among these saints are those untimely dead, killed in godforsaken incidents of terror, war, and mass death. Having drunk so deeply of the cup of suffering, they call forth special mention in anguish and lament. Among the saints are also numbered some whom we know personally. Their number increases as we get older: grandparents, mother and father, sisters and brothers, beloved spouses and life partners, children, teachers, fellow students, patients, clients, friends and colleagues, relatives and neighbors, spiritual guides and religious leaders. Their lives, complete with fault and favor, have reached journey's end. Gone from us, they have arrived home in unimaginable life within the embrace of

God. To say of all these people that they form with us the company of the redeemed is to give grief a direction, affirming that in the end God graciously has the last word, which is life. In instances where persons have wrought real and lasting damage by their actions, faith holds out the possibility that at their deepest core they did not concur in diabolical evil, or if they did, that they have repented. The church's prayer is that God will be more merciful toward them than they have been to others. On their behalf, at least we have hope.

TWO MODELS OF RELATIONSHIP

Remembering all these dead is an act of the community of saints on earth that puts their finished lives in play in our midst. And here, two ways of relating to the dead are possible. One, which can conveniently be called the patronage model, imagines heaven as a magnificent throne room where the King rules in splendor surrounded by hosts of courtiers ranked in descending order of importance. Being far from the distant throne, we little people need saints as intercessors who will promote our cause and obtain spiritual and material favors that would otherwise not be forthcoming. We need friends in high places, so to speak, and we call upon them for favors. This patron-client relationship is not found in the New Testament nor in the earliest Christian centuries. It developed under the influence of the Roman Empire's civil patronage system once the church had been officially established. This pattern of relationship, so despised by the Protestant Reformers, is waning even in Catholic circles not least because its structure of power and neediness so misreads the truth of God's merciful presence in Christ to everyone. This is not to say that intercessory prayer to the saints is unwarranted, but the hierarchical framework of such prayer in the patronage model leaves much to be desired.

An alternative, more original pattern of relating to the dead can be discerned in biblical and early martyr texts. Modeled on companionship, it sees those who have died as friends and fellow travelers of the living in the one Spirit-filled community. Rather than the main action being prayers of petition from a client to a patron, the main expression of this relationship is acts of remembering that release the power of their witness into the struggles of today. As the Friday service broadcast from Temple Emmanuel in New York City prays, "May the beauty of their lives abide among us as a loving benediction." In the companionship model intercessory prayer becomes intelligible in a collegial context of mutual sharing in God's mercy.

One key example of this companionship pattern is found in the New Testament letter to the Hebrews. Here there is an extraordinary roll call of Jewish ancestors, all of whom responded to the challenge of their lives with unerring faith in God: Abel, Noah, Abraham, Sarah, the parents of Moses, Rahab, David, along with myriad others who were persecuted, suffered, and survived, but continued to have faith in God. The text reaches its dramatic highpoint with a dramatic exhortation:

> Therefore, since we are surrounded by so great a cloud of witnesses, let us also lay aside every weight and the sin that clings so closely, and let us run with perseverance the race that is set before us, looking to Jesus the pioneer and perfecter of our faith. (Heb 12:1–2)

Note how the dynamism of this passage moves from the narrative of faithful individuals (nineteen in all), to whole groups of persons in the past, and thence into enthusiastic appeal to the contemporary community. The pervasive sense of solidarity comes to a pitch in the metaphor of the cloud of witnesses surrounding the living community on earth. Biblical scholars point out that the image here is of a stadium packed with a crowd up in the stands, each of whom had once run in the race, now cheering for those on the tarmac. Here the faithful dead are proposed not as the objects of a cult, nor even as exemplars to be imitated, but as a compact throng of faithful people whose journey encourages those running the race today. It is a matter of being inspired by the whole lot of them in their wonderful witness to the living God. It is interesting that this New Testament litany of the cloud of witnesses honors figures who were important in the history of Israel but does not include Christian persons who would be equally good candidates, Mary Magdalene, for example, first apostolic witness of the resurrection, or Stephen, the first martyr. Reflecting reverence for the history of God's holy people before the Christian community came into existence, the passage sees its own audience as recipients of this tradition newly configured in Jesus, pioneer of faith, whose advent does not discredit but rather enhances the history of holiness of his own people.

In the age of the martyrs, this mutual, collegial relationship between the living and the dead came to new expression when the community drew strength from those who gave their lives in witness to Christ. The church at Smyrna, explaining the difference between Christ whom they worshiped and Polycarp their martyred bishop whom they venerated, put it eloquently: "For [Christ] we worship as the Son of God. But the martyrs we love as disciples and imitators of the Lord, and rightly so because of their matchless affection for their own king and teacher. May we too become their comrades and fellow disciples." The living were partners, comrades, co-disciples with those who had given their lives, one witnessing to the other, both graced in Christ. This same lively sense of friendship appears, even after persecution had ceased, in one of Augustine's sermons on the feast of the young women martyrs Perpetua and Felicity. Despite the weakness of their sex, as he unfortunately saw it, they had fought through to the crown of glory:

> Let it not seem a small thing to us that we are members of the same body as these. . . . We marvel at them, they have compassion on us. We rejoice for them, they pray for us. . . . Yet do we all serve one Lord, follow one teacher, attend one king. We are all joined to the head, journey to the same Jerusalem, follow after the one love, embrace the same unity. (*Sermon* 280)

Preaching on the feasts of the martyrs over many years, Augustine provides an extended vocabulary for this partnership between the living and the dead. The saints in heaven are a gift: "Blessed be the saints in whose memory we are celebrating the day they suffered on;...they have left us lessons of encouragement" (*Sermon* 273). Sometimes the lesson of encouragement is a particular one: "If we follow Stephen, we shall be crowned with the victor's laurels. It is above all in the matter of loving our enemies that he is to be followed and imitated" (*Sermon* 314). More often this great cloud of witnesses inspires us by the general tenor of their lives. They are like an open jar of ointment whose fragrance pervades our whole house. Since they did what they did by the outpouring of the grace of God, in their company we find light and warmth and direction in our struggles to be faithful: "The fountain is still flowing, it hasn't dried up" (*Sermon* 315).

The early generations of Christians deserve special appreciation, Augustine thought, for they pioneered a whole new way of life: "When numbers were few, courage had to be great. By passing along the narrow road they widened it...they went ahead of us" (*Sermon* 306). To realize as a people that we are the heirs of the faith passed on by such persons makes us grateful and rejuvenates our desire to contribute to this heritage for the next generation. Their adventure of faith opened a way for us, and now we go ahead of others in an ongoing river of companions seeking God. And when our own journey grows hard, we can draw strength from the memory of our forebears' sufferings and victories: "How can the way be rough when it has been smoothed by the feet of so many walking along it?" (*Sermon* 306). The communion of saints forges intergenerational bonds across time that sustain faith in strange new times and places.

The Second Vatican Council picked up on this model of relationship when it taught: "Just as Christian communion among wayfarers brings us closer to Christ, so our companionship with the saints joins us to Christ, from whom as from their fountain and head issue every grace and the life of God's people itself" (*Lumen Gentium* 50). Rather than be bound in a patron-client pattern, the saints in heaven and on earth become partners in memory and hope. One inspiring example of how this works can be found in El Salvador. Remembering their recent history, people of the base Christian communities recite the traditional litany of the saints and add the names of their own martyrs for the cause of justice. To each name the people respond *Presente:* be here with us, you are here with us. Oscar Romero: *Presente;* Ignacio Ellacuría: *Presente;* Celina Ramos: *Presente;* young catechists, community workers, and religious leaders of the *pueblos: Presente.* This prayer summons the memory of these martyrs as a strong, enduring power that commits the community to emulating their lives.

PARADIGMATIC FIGURES

Some people do stand out. Different times and places witness the emergence of particular persons who focus the energies of the Spirit for a local group in its own unique circumstances. When these persons are recognized by the common spiritual sense of the community, they become publicly significant for the lives of others. These are the persons traditionally called saints. Theologically they have no essential spiritual advantage over the rest of the community who are saints in the biblical sense. But the confluence of their own unique giftedness with the needs of a moment in history give them a special function among their fellow pilgrims. Their names are remembered as a benediction, an act of resistance, a call to action, a spur to fidelity, a summons to encouragement.

For the first twelve centuries, the local church with the approval of regional bishops recognized the contribution of certain holy persons by naming them during Mass and thereby entering them onto the list or "canon" of local saints. Starting in the twelfth century, however, a resurgent papacy centralized the process of canonization, with Rome demanding to have the final say. The results have been decidedly mixed. Gains in overcoming a certain fabulism and provincial limitation are offset by the nature of the list of official saints, who became an ever more elite group proclaimed for their heroic virtue and power to produce spectacular miracles; a group, furthermore, that came to mirror the face of the bureaucracy that created it, being largely clerical, celibate, aristocratic, and male; a group created in response to large investments of time and money and thus largely excluding lay and poor persons. Numerous scholars now argue that for the good of the church, the formal canonization process should be radically modified. In fact, the power of naming saints is already being reclaimed in a variety of worshiping communities. Long before the juridical process was invented, local communities, through the power of the Spirit, could recognize those persons who witnessed to the gospel in uniquely different circumstances and mediated God's presence through their life of discipleship. This power has not deserted the church.

Particular women and men are remembered for the way they distill the central values of the living tradition, making them accessible in concrete form. The direct force of their example acts as a catalyst in the community, galvanizing recognition that yes, this is what we are called to be. The uncanny integrity of their lives leavens the moral environment, luring the community ever more deeply into fidelity to God. They are like a Milky Way, a shining river of stars spiraling out from the center of the galaxy to light a path through the darkness back to that center, the divine mystery. The light of their memory encourages the creative witness of others: one fire kindles another. This is their irreplaceable role, at the same time the full meaning of what it means to be holy can be given only by the whole communion of saints.

FEMINIST THEOLOGICAL RETRIEVAL

It is precisely here that women's scholarship flags a key problem. Those who have had the power of shaping public memory in the churches have largely been men, and thus the historical witness of women has been by and large marginalized. The position of women in the public memory of the church as a result of canonization is particularly troubling. A simple head count shows that roughly 75 percent of the persons on the current roster of canonized saints are men as are three-fourths of the saints honored on the liturgical calendar, while only about 25 percent of those so recognized are women. Does this mean that men are holier than women? Of course not. But it does highlight who has the power of naming in the church. Least represented among these saints are married women who remained so for their lives (i.e., did not become nuns), reflecting the assessment that to be female is a handicap but to be a sexually active woman renders one almost incapable of embodying the sacred, the few exceptions being royal queens. As a result, the history of women's holiness has been largely deleted from the collective memory of the church. We are afflicted with a certain amnesia, ignoring what Adrienne Rich calls "the particularity and commonality of this vast turbulence of female becoming, which is continually being erased or generalized."[3]

Even when they are remembered, the lives of exemplary women are officially narrated so as to emphasize the patriarchal ideal of the "good" woman. Stereotypical feminine virtues such as obedience, submissive humility, and acceptance of suffering overshadow the history of real women's raw struggle in the Spirit. The result is a meager feast for women's souls, along with lack of impetus in the community to do justice to its women even today. For the communion of saints to function in a liberating way, deliberate attention must be paid to this history of neglect. Women's absence must be noticed, missed, criticized, and corrected. It is not just a matter of adding women to what remains a patriarchal master narrative. The challenge is to reshape the church's memory so as to reclaim an equal share in the center for women and thereby transform the community.

Providentially, an amazing resurgence of scholarship is making this task possible. Feminist biblical, historical, and theological research is developing methods of retrieving glimpses of women who, though denied power and voice, were nevertheless there, walking with their God. Recovering lost memories, rectifying patriarchal distortions, reassigning value, and breaking the silences, these methods vigorously reverse the erasure of women's lives in the Spirit. As a result of this renaissance in scholarship, hosts of neglected persons are brought to light, a lost heritage of holy lives that, once recovered, enrich the memory of the church. As diverse as situations are, parallel experiences of suffering connect the generations, spirit touching spirit, sparking women's new determination to become subjects of their own history.

We remember, for example, the story of Hagar, the Egyptian slave woman who disrupts the covenant narrative of Abraham and Sarah; who is the first person in Scripture to receive the promise of a great people stemming from her, and the first to dare to name God. We recover the truth about Mary Magdalene, who was a leading apostolic witness to the risen Christ and not a repentant prostitute as she has been made to appear in the history of patriarchal interpretation. We recoup the strength of the virgin martyrs, Agatha, Lucy, Cecilia, Anastasia, and others. They were young girls put to death not because they demeaned sexuality, but because they discovered a sense of themselves in relation to Christ; this enabled them to resist society's demands that they enter into patriarchal marriage, that is, they resisted the right of the state to dictate the terms of their humanity. And so forth. Today feminist scholars are discovering the whole host of anonymous women, marginalized and silenced women, poor women, women of color, raped and brutalized women, caring and ministering women, strong and vibrant and artistic women, sexually active women, setting-out-not-knowing-where-they-are-going women, "ordinary" women of fidelity, humor, and valor, all holy women of the world, and reading them onto the list as equal partners with men in the company of God's friends and prophets.

To discover these foresisters with their sufferings and defeats, their accomplishments and victories, and to recover their lives from the judgment that labels them insignificant is to break through a long and debilitating amnesia. The power of memory shows itself precisely here, as a historically disenfranchised group, one that ultimately includes half the human race, connects with the great cloud of witnesses who are cheering them on. Their memory is subversive, their narrative empowering, and solidarity with them in all their differences encouraging in the quest to eliminate unjust, violent structures that dehumanize persons. By connecting to generations of women who have walked faithfully on this earth until now, believing women today find a place to stand from which they can challenge the interconnected biases that continue to press down on their lives in church and society. Recognizing the play of grace in the lives of other women, women gain a more anchored appreciation of their own blessedness. Conversely, acknowledging themselves to exist as the very image of God, women become empowered to cherish and celebrate the holiness of other women and to resist whatever disparages this sacred reality. In the process, the church community itself is called to conversion.

To sum up: the dead are included in the communion of saints, by the power and mercy of God. Remembering this cloud of witnesses has a twofold prophetic edge. When practiced in the midst of a secular culture it encourages hope in an unimaginable future of life for all, thereby releasing energies for tending to this world in accord with God's compassionate justice and care. When practiced with attention to the suppressed witness of a whole group such as women, it enlists the community of forebears as allies in the struggle for equal participation in church and society: one fire kindles another.

CONCLUSION

The symbol of the communion of saints expresses a solidarity among God-seekers that exists around the world and across time itself, brought into being by the Holy Spirit who forever weaves links of graced kinship. In this sense it is a most challenging and encouraging religious symbol, for it affirms that under the outstretched wings of the Spirit of God all are connected in a community of beneficial relationships: different racial, ethnic, and cultural groups, persons with different sexual orientations, women with men, the poor and marginalized with the powerful, all of the living with the dead and the yet to be born, in a circle of grace that encompasses the earth itself. Waking this religious symbol up brings a new source of energy for the liberating practice of faith. Cheered on by the cloud of witnesses, we become ever more the friends of God and prophets in *this* generation, to the advantage of coming generations of human beings and all species upon the earth. New Zealand novelist Keri Hulme beautifully describes what is at stake:

They were nothing more than people, by themselves. Even paired, any pairing, they would have been nothing more than people by themselves. But all together, they have become the heart and muscles and mind of something perilous and new, something strange and growing and great. Together, all together, they are the instruments of change.[4]

Adapted from the Santa Clara Lecture at Santa Clara University, CA, 1998; published in Union Seminary Quarterly Review *52 (1998): 49–66.*

Notes

1. Judith Plaskow, *Standing Again at Sinai: Judaism from a Feminist Perspective* (San Francisco: HarperCollins, 1990), 96.
2. Karl Rahner, "The Life of the Dead," *Theological Investigations* IV (New York: Seabury, 1974), 353–54.
3. Adrienne Rich, "Resisting Amnesia: History and Personal Life," *Blood, Bread, and Poetry* (New York: W. W. Norton, 1986), 155.
4. Keri Hulme, *The Bone People* (New York: Penguin Books, 1983), 4.

21

Communio Sanctorum in a Cosmic Framework

At first glance the doctrinal symbol of the communion of saints appears to have a rather completely human focus, being concerned with graced persons living and dead and their companionship in the Spirit. A fascinating ambiguity in the original Latin term for the communion of saints, however, opens up this community to include the natural world. *Communio sanctorum* translates literally as communion of the holy ones. Whether these holy ones are persons or other creatures or things is not clear, however, because *sanctorum* is the plural genitive form of two nouns, the grammatically masculine noun *sancti* (holy persons) and the grammatically neuter noun *sancta* (holy things).

Let us start with persons. The phrase *communion of saints* was introduced into the Apostles' Creed in the West by the beginning of the fifth century, the last phrase to be so added. In a commentary on the creed, Nicetas, bishop of Remesiana, gives the earliest evidence that the phrase was taken to refer to human beings. He wrote:

> What is the church but the congregation of all saints? From the beginning of the world patriarchs, prophets, martyrs, and all other righteous people who have lived, or who are now alive, or who shall live in time to come, comprise the church, since they have been sanctified by one faith and manner of life, and sealed by one Spirit, and so made one body, of which Christ is declared to be the head, as the Scripture says.... So you believe that in this church you will

attain to the communion of saints.[1]

Clearly here the *communio sanctorum* stands for a graced relationship among holy people of all ages, including the whole company of heaven, which is anticipated and partially realized in the community of the church on earth. In addition to the text's recognition of illustrious persons who have died, Jewish and Christian alike, it also includes the future in a fascinating way, for generations as yet unborn also belong to this community. Similarly, the whole company is not settled in the present but moving toward the eschatological fullness yet to come: "you will attain." The whole community through time shares in the promise of hope.

In the East, meanwhile, a similar phrase in Greek was being used to refer to the Eucharist. The Greek phrase *koinonia ton hagion* (fellowship of the holy) meant the church's fellowship with sacred things, specifically the eucharistic bread and cup of salvation. The phrase with its more objective reference was translated into Latin as *communio sanctorum*. So now the identical phrase referred to two different things.

Aware of this felicitous double meaning, medieval theologians working in Latin played with both senses, the subjective and the objective, or the personal and the sacramental, thinking that there was no need to choose between them because they reinforce one another. In fact, the elusive quality of the phrase is a happy circumstance, allowing it to express a complex, multilayered reality, namely, the kinship of God's friends and prophets in a Spirit-filled company grounded in Christ and constituted by a sharing in the holy things, these being each other's lives and witness plus the eucharistic bread and wine. The double meaning of the phrase allows us to see that holy people and holy things are inextricably linked in the one Spirit of God.

Contemporary theologians are beginning to revive this double meaning and, in the light of ecological awareness, to extend the objective reference to include the whole of creation. Bread from the earth, fruit from the vine, both becoming the body and blood of Christ: this sacrament and others that use water and oil connect the people of a gracious God with the natural world. Pervaded and empowered by the Creator Spirit, the natural world itself has a sacred character. It is revelatory of the beauty, wisdom, and power of God. It is a primordial sacrament which communicates the presence of God. To say that the *communio sanctorum* includes the sacred gifts of air, water, land, and the myriad species that share the planet with human beings is to give this phrase a theological interpretation replete with ecological significance.

Holiness is the work of the Spirit. The same divine Spirit who lights the fire of the saint also fuels the vitality of all creation. The result is a holy community that includes not just human persons but the whole vibrant world: all living creatures, ecosystems, and the whole natural world itself. Jürgen Moltmann thinks this through in a beautiful manner:

> If the Holy Spirit is poured out on the whole creation, then [the Spirit] creates the community of all created things with God and with each other, making it that fellowship of creation in which all created things communicate with one another and with God, each in its own way. The existence, the life, and the warp and weft of interrelationships subsist in the Spirit.[2]

In God all things live and move and have their being. Therefore, Moltmann continues, nothing in the world exists, lives, and moves of itself. Everything exists, lives, and moves with others and for others in the cosmic community of creation in the Spirit. This many-faceted community, which includes human beings but is not limited to them, is the primordial *communio sanctorum*, or communion of holy ones, engendered by the power of the Spirit.

Opening up the communion of holy ones in this way alerts us to the fact that central biblical themes are alive with the inclusion of the cosmos. The world is God's good creation. The Spirit dwells within it and gives life. It is replete with God's generosity, beauty, playfulness, and power. Far from being a mere backdrop to the salvation history of humankind, it is intrinsically bound to covenant and jubilee, to sin and its resulting devastation, and to the messianic promise of future peace and fruitfulness. Despite later Christian suspicion of bodiliness, the gospel story of Jesus Christ affirms the incarnation of God into the very flesh of this world and the resurrection of that same flesh from the dead, and does so in a radical way that reaches out to all creation. All creation is groaning, waiting for redemption, while the good news is that Christ, the "firstborn from the dead," is also the "firstborn of all creation" (Col 1:15–20). The community of the redeemed will include the whole cosmos in glory.

Clearly, this framework imparts to the *communio sanctorum* a prophetic character that calls the church to care responsibly for all of life and to stand against destruction of the earth and its life-systems.

Including the natural world in the communion of holy ones also sets up an interesting dynamic between the doctrine's traditional hope for the dead, on the one hand, and hope for the natural world, on the other. The two become intertwined in ways that affect understanding and ethics. John Haught makes the interesting argument that human hope for something more beyond death is itself an expression of the dynamism inherent in the universe from the beginning:

> Billions of years before our appearance in evolution, [the cosmos] was already seeded with promise. Our own religious longing for future fulfillment, therefore, is not a violation but a blossoming of the promise. Human hoping is not simply our own constructs of imaginary ideals projected onto an indifferent universe, as much as modern and postmodern thought maintains. Rather, it is the faithful carrying on of the universe's perennial orientation toward the unknown future.[3]

If the universe is on an adventurous journey toward the ever-increasing complexity and beauty, then hope for the dead, encoded in the symbol of the communion of holy ones, can be interpreted as an expression of the world's own powerful impulse toward the future.

At the same time, breaking connections with the memory of the dead and losing hope for them can have deleterious effects on the human sense of ecological responsibility. It is important to ponder that those native peoples whom contemporary thinkers admire for their kinship with the land and its creatures also honor the spirits of their ancestors present upon the land. While such wisdom cannot be adapted without revision in urban and suburban communities, there is a link here that needs to be understood. Haught suggests that much current indifference to the cause of conservation stems not so much from hope for another world to which we flee at death, as was true in a previous age, but from the secular assumption that there is an unbridgeable gap between the dead and ourselves. This "broken connection" robs us of convincing reasons to care for the earth and saps our moral energy to do so. Focusing on the modern inability to imagine our connection with other generations, he writes:

> If we are unable to symbolize immortality in one way or another, we lose any sense of relatedness to the vast world that has gone before us, as well as to the generations of living beings that may follow. In breaking our connection with other generations, we understandably forfeit our responsibility to them. Stranded in a meaninglessly brief life span, and severed from communion with the perished past or the promised future, we grow ethically impotent.[4]

Consigning the dead to utter extinction undermines the basis for an ecological ethic, he argues, while healing the broken connection between the living and the dead provides sustenance for our moral commitment to care for the arth. This intriguing insight, so promising in the integrity it portends for a community that remembers and hopes, is deserving of wide study. Set within the life-giving history of God with the world which is not simply focused on human beings, the *communio sanctorum* ultimately reaches out to signify the community of all creation, past, present, and to come, sharing in the flow of life in the Spirit: holy people and a sacred earth together.

Retrieving the symbol of *communio sanctorum*, the communion of holy ones, in this way discloses the boundless creativity of the Creator Spirit continuously moving in all times and places, cultures, contexts, and peoples to awaken an amplitude of response to amazing grace. Together the living form with the dead one community of memory and hope, summoned to go forth as companions bringing the face of divine compassion into everyday life and the great struggles of history, wrestling with evil, and delighting even now when fragments of justice, peace, and healing gain however small a foothold. When people are seen together with the whole natural world as a dynamic, sacred community of the most amazing richness and complexity, then the symbol of the communion of saints reaches its fullness as a symbol of effective presence and action of the living God.

Adapted from The Living Light *35 (Winter 1998): 53–58; and* New Theology Review *12 (May 1999): 5–16.*

Notes

1. Cited in J. N. D. Kelly, *Early Christian Creeds* (London: Longman, 1972), 391; emended for inclusivity.

2. Jürgen Moltmann, *God in Creation* (San Francisco: Harper & Row, 1985), 11.

3. John Haught, *The Promise of Nature* (New York: Paulist Press, 1993), 109–10.

4. Ibid., 129.

22

Truly Our Sister

A Critical Reading of the Marian Tradition

What would be a theologically sound, spiritually empowering, and ethically challenging view of Mary, mother of Jesus the Christ, for the twenty-first century? This question has no simple answer, for the first-century Jewish woman, Miriam of Nazareth, also called *Theotokos*, the God-bearer, is arguably the most celebrated woman in the Christian tradition. One could almost drown surveying the ways the Christian tradition has honored her in paintings, sculptures, icons, music, architecture, and poetry; venerated her with titles, liturgies, and feasts; and taught about her in spiritual writings, theologies, and official doctrines. The title of a fine book by George Tavard gets it exactly right: *The Thousand Faces of the Virgin Mary.*[1]

The sought-for answer becomes even more complex in the light of recent scholarship that highlights the social-political implications of this adaptable marian image. Studies underscore, for example, the correlation between Pius IX's definition of the Immaculate Conception and his aggrandizement of papal power; or the connection between Our Lady of Fatima and Western Cold War opposition to the Soviet Union; or the alliance between Our Lady of Guadalupe and Caesar Chavez's struggle for justice for migrant workers in the California vineyards. While a historical woman obviously dwells at the root of this whole phenomenon, her image has been plastic, allowing the Christian imagination to create widely different marian symbols.

Theology today articulates the religious meaning of Mary with full awareness that the marian image is never neutral. It expresses core values of the faith community and functions to sustain a certain spirituality and praxis. How then do we, this multicultural church at this millennial time, interpret and honor her? The answer I invite you to explore in this lecture is but one among several good possibilities and it is this: Mary is truly our sister, a friend of God and prophet within the communion of saints. The approach taken here is rooted in Scripture interpreted through the lens of feminist theology: Scripture, because in these challenging times we cannot afford anything less than the core revelatory testimony of our tradition; and feminist theology, because it affords a liberating view that is beneficial to women and men alike.

Crafting this answer entails that we invite Mary to come down from her glorified counter-Reformation pedestal and rejoin us, the community of disciples, on the ground amid the graced struggle of history. The ladder enabling her to reach the ground has four steps, two negative and two positive. Walking down these steps will form the structure of this reflection.

NOT THE MATERNAL FACE OF GOD

It has become commonplace for scholars of marian history to argue that Mary embodies aspects of God best symbolized in the female form of the mother. Ample evidence for this transfer of divine character can be found in early Christian times when the Mother of God took over the titles, shrines, iconography, and power of the Great Mother Goddess of the Mediterranean. This dynamic was repeated when Christianity came to China, Africa, Mexico, and other advanced cultures where Mary once again merged with local female deities. The theology and piety of medieval and counter-Reformation Europe contains a variation of this phenomenon. In that context when God the Father became increasingly portrayed as an angry ruler exacting atonement for sin, when Christ became ever more the Just Judge, when the vivifying, indwelling Spirit faded into relative obscurity, then persons turned to Mary to gain mercy and consoling heavenly intimacy. Her gender as a woman and her historical role as a mother played no small part in this development, for what compassionate mother would let one of her children be lost? In a severely juridical context, she functioned to reveal divine love as merciful, close, interested, trustworthy, and profoundly attractive, and did so to a degree not possible when one thinks of God only as an almighty ruling male monarch. No wonder people were glad to pray, "Hail, holy Queen, Mother of mercy, our life, our sweetness and our hope," divine acclamations, all.

This analysis is helpful for understanding some of the exaggerations of marian theology and devotion. It makes clear that the marian symbol developed divine qualities to *compensate* for an overly patriarchal theology of God. Well and good. But a problem arises when theologians want to maintain this state of affairs forever, as seen for example in Leonardo Boff's treatise on Mary, *The Maternal Face of God*.[2] For one thing, Mary is not and never will be divine but remains thoroughly human. For another, keeping female images of God attached only to Mary implies that such images, based on women's reality, are somehow inadequate for use in speech about God's own holy being and saving deeds. But if women are truly created in the image of God, then female images can be used to refer to God in as adequate and inadequate a way as traditional male ones. Indeed, using female and cosmic names prevents the male image from turning into a false idol. The mystery of the living God deserves no less.

The marian tradition is a fruitful source of female imagery for God, such as maternity with its nurturing warmth and fierce protection; love with unbounded compassion; power that sustains, heals and liberates; and all-pervading immanence. These divine qualities migrated to Mary because of deficiencies in theology of God, christology, and pneumatology. It makes no lasting sense to keep this as a permanent status quo, using Mary as a cover-up for defective notions of the divine. Rather, this female imagery should be allowed to travel back to its source. Let God have her own maternal face. Australian theologian Patricia Fox demonstrates this movement in her address, "Mother of Mercy: A Title Reclaimed for God," as do Julian of Norwich, John Paul I, and myriad other Christians today who dare to name God in female form.

While a twenty-first century theology critically deconstructs Mary as the maternal face of God, there is one insight we can carry forward from this whole long confusion. The fact that divine mercy and power have indeed been successfully carried in the image of Mary reveals the power of women to represent God. Not just Mary's face but the face of every woman is created *imago Dei*. Not just Mary's vocation but that of every woman—and man —is to partner Holy Wisdom in bringing about the reign of mercy and peaceful justice. Relieved of her historic burden as complement to the patriarchal divine and positively signaling the depth of women's dignity vis-à-vis God, Mary becomes free to rejoin us in the communion of saints.

NOT THE IDEAL WOMAN

A second fallacy that has dogged mariology interprets Mary as the ideal woman or the embodiment of the so-called "eternal feminine." As such, she functions as a role model for all other women. Those who take this approach invariably take sexual differences between women and men as the single most important element of a person's identity. This implicitly elevates sex to an ontological principle that defines two types of human nature. On the one hand masculine nature, characterized by intelligence, assertiveness, independence, and the ability to make decisions, is destined for leadership in the public realm. On the other hand feminine nature, marked by relationality, gentleness, nurturing, a non-assertive, non-competitive attitude, and the giving of service and reassurance, is fit for the private domain of childbearing, homemaking, and care for the vulnerable.

Hans Urs von Balthasar takes this approach, arguing that in the church there is a marian principle of holy obedience complementary to the petrine principle of orderly hierarchical rule. This marian principle indicates that women ought to divest themselves of self-will in order to be obedient to the word of God as articulated by male authority figures. A prime example is Mary at Cana, who noticed the lack of wine and turned to Jesus for help. Comments Balthasar, "As a woman she has her heart where it ought to be and not in her brain."[3]

Perhaps the most widely heard proponent of this view has been Pope John Paul II. In his encyclicals on the "Mother of Redemption" and on the "Dignity of Women" he links the virtues of Mary with the vocation of women, writing, "It can thus be said that women, by looking to Mary, find in her the secret of living their femininity with dignity and of achieving their own true advancement." Like Mary, he continues, all women are oriented toward giving love without measure once they have received it (note that final phrase). Like Mary, all women are to be mothers, either physically or spiritually (virgins). In Mary, women see mirrored the highest virtues to which they are called, which the pope delineates as "the self-offering totality of love; the strength that is capable of bearing the greatest sorrows; limitless fidelity and tireless devotion to work; the ability to combine penetrating intuition with words of support and encouragement."[4]

As these examples demonstrate, the notion of Mary as the ideal feminine inevitably leads to the subordination of women and the privileging of men politically, psychologically, and spiritually. The rigid definition of the feminine, when applied to social roles, blocks women from functioning in the public order. In addition, much of women's negative reaction to this image of Mary stems from the realization that this feminine ideal functions as an obstacle to personal growth, preventing women from developing a critical intellect, capacity for righteous anger, and other characteristics of a mature personality. Living "femininely" can even be dangerous to one's health and life, inculcating passivity in abusive and violent situations.

African American and *mujerista*/Latina theologians raise the further criticism that this concept of the feminine is shaped by the privilege of race and class. Women of racial minorities and women who live in poverty have neither the possibility nor the opportunity to live lives defined by this ideal. Sojourner Truth put her finger on this racist and classist underbelly of the notion of the feminine when she argued:

> That man over there says that women need to be helped
> into carriages and lifted over ditches....Nobody ever helps
> me into carriages or over mud puddles, or give me any best
> place. And ain't I a woman? Look at me! Look at my arms! I
> have ploughed and planted and gathered into barns, and
> no man could head me! And ain't I a woman? I could work
> as much and eat as much as a man—when I could get it—
> and bear the lash as well. And ain't I a woman? I have

borne thirteen children, and seen them most all sold off to slavery and when I cried out with my mother's grief, none but Jesus heard me! And ain't I a woman?[5]

Indeed, we ask today, what is a woman? And who gets to decide?

An adequate theology of Mary for the third millennium must be clear on this point: there is no eternal feminine; there is no objective, essential feminine nature; there is no ideal woman. The very notion of the feminine is a product of patriarchal thinking intended to keep women in their so-called proper "place." In contrast to dualistic anthropology that so separates head and heart, a liberating view of Mary grows out of an egalitarian anthropology of partnership. In no way does this stance negate differences between women and men, but it refuses to make sex the sole primary marker of personal identity or to use sex to stereotype a person's characteristics. We all exist as human persons with multiple differences, and we should be allowed to function according to the gifts we have received.

Relieved of the burden of being the ideal feminine woman, Mary can be simply herself. A poor woman singing her *Magnificat* about the downfall of tyrants and full bellies for the hungry, she takes another step toward rejoining us in the communion of saints.

YES, TRULY OUR SISTER IN THE COMMUNION OF SAINTS

Bringing Mary into the community of the saints may seem strange at first hearing, even though the name "Saint Mary" graces many churches, schools, and hospitals. But this in fact is what the gospels do as they weave the Mary story into the historical, earthy story of Jesus and his disciples. It is also the pattern followed by Vatican II which deliberately wrote marian teaching into the Constitution on the Church (*Lumen Gentium*) rather than craft a separate document that emphasized her glories. In the creed the communion of saints is the belief that all God-seekers, including the living and the dead, are joined into a sacred community by the power of the Spirit. Since Mary was a first-century Jewish woman of faith, and since she has obviously also died, she belongs in this company of grace.

Once we admit Mary into our company, the question of how to relate to her arises. In the patronage model that has dominated the tradition, the church envisions Mary as a mediator of blessings. Because she is the Mother of the Lord, Mary is the most powerful intercessor for those at a distance. She obtains gifts, even salvation, that would otherwise be denied. This pattern of relationship projects the patriarchal family into heaven, with the mother compassionately obtaining benefits for the children from a strict, commanding father, or father and son.

A more ancient pattern of relationship can be discovered in biblical and early Christian texts. Modeled on companionship, it names those who have died as a great "cloud of witnesses" who accompany the living through the encouragement of their remembered lives (Heb 12:1). Within this vast cloud of witnesses, particular persons emerge who witness to God's promise in special ways. When these persons are recognized by the common spiritual intuition of the community, they become publicly significant for the lives of others. Such a person, I suggest, is Miriam of Nazareth, the first-century Jewish woman of faith who mothered Jesus. Thus the last step enabling her to reach the good ground of our community raises the question: how shall we remember her?

YES, A JEWISH VILLAGE WOMAN OF FAITH, FRIEND OF GOD AND PROPHET

The first thing we need to be clear about as we engage in the work of remembering is that we know very little about Miriam of Nazareth as an actual historical person. In this she is in solidarity with the multitudes of people through the centuries, especially poor women and men, whose lives are not considered worth recording. We also must be respectful of her historical difference from us in time, place, and culture. Indeed, it is precisely from the contours of her concrete strangeness that her powerful contribution can be made.

In addition, we must be mindful that the New Testament witness is quite diverse. Each evangelist portrays Mary in accord with the theological framework of his gospel. Mark's negative view of Jesus' mother and brothers as *outside* his circle of followers corresponds with the anti-familial ethic of the rest of the gospel. Matthew's genealogy of the Messiah locates Mary in a line of four other women who take initiative in dubious sexual circumstances outside the patriarchal marriage structure, thereby becoming unexpectedly God's partners in a theology of promise-fulfillment. Luke describes Mary as a woman of faith, overshadowed by the Spirit at Jesus' conception and at the beginning of the church at Pentecost, the first to respond to the glad tidings and to hear the word of God and keep it; she is a pictorial example of this gospel's theology of discipleship. John's highly stylized portrayal of the mother of Jesus at Cana and at the cross accords with his own vision of the response of discipleship to the Word made flesh, manifest and glorified. As with gospel portraits of Jesus, these diverse interpretations cannot be harmonized but each is instructive in its own way.

To glimpse the actual woman behind these texts in any kind of full and adequate way is impossible. There are new studies of the fabric of first-century Palestine, however, that enable us to fill in aspects of her life in broad strokes. Much of this knowledge has resulted from the quest for the historical Jesus, but it serves equally well for a quest for the historical Miriam of Nazareth. As it feeds our religious imagination we can shape the marian symbol with concrete historical awareness.

Let us remember our foremother Mary as a Jewish village woman of faith.

Jewish: As a member of the people of Israel, Mary inherited the faith stemming from Abraham and Sarah onwards in one living God, a God who hears the cries of the poor and frees the enslaved into covenanted relationship. Given Jesus' clear knowledge and practice of the Jewish faith, it is reasonable to assume that Mary with her husband Joseph practiced this Jewish religion in their home, following Torah, observing the festivals, reciting prayers, and going to synagogue according to custom in Galilee. This suggests a lovely image: Mary lighting sabbath lamps as Joseph blesses the bread and wine to begin the sabbath meal.

Luke depicts Mary in her older years as a member of the early Jerusalem community, praying with one hundred twenty women and men before the coming of the Spirit at Pentecost (Acts 1:13–14). She participated in this community along with Mary Magdalene, a primary witness of the risen Christ, and many other women and men who had followed Jesus. In light of the death and resurrection of Jesus, this gathering believed that the Messiah had come. In no way did they think this was a cause to leave their religion. Rather, they continued to worship in the temple while preaching the good news first to their fellow Jews and then to the Gentiles. Mary's presence in this group signals her solidarity with these Jewish disciples rather than her being on an isolated journey of faith. To use a term coined in scholarship, Mary was a Jewish-Christian, one who lived before the split between synagogue and church. It does no honor to bleach her of her Jewishness not only ethnically, by turning her swarthy complexion into blond hair and blue eyes, but religiously, by turning her deeply rooted Jewish piety into that of a latter day Catholic.

Village woman: This Jewish woman lived her adult life in a rural village, Nazareth, peopled largely by peasants working the land and craftsmen who served their basic needs. Married to the local *tekton* (a worker in wood and stone), she was ordinarily taken up with the life-giving, hard, unrecompensed work of women of all ages to feed, clothe, and nurture their household. Most such women at the time were unlettered. The economic status of this family is a matter of some dispute, with scholars such as John Meier placing them in the blue collar working class, with others such as John Dominic Crossan assigning them to the peasant class desperately struggling under the triple taxation of Temple, Herod, and Rome. Either way, the times were tough. This village was part of an occupied state under the heel of imperial Rome; revolutionary resistance made the atmosphere tense; violence and poverty prevailed.

We owe a debt to third-world women theologians who have noticed the similarities between Mary's life and the lives of so many poor women even today.[6] Look at the parallels. In Roman-ruled Palestine with its native puppet kings, Mary and Joseph's journey to Bethlehem for the census accords with displacement from ancestral homes because of debt and taxation. The narrative of flight into Egypt reflects movements of refugees who flee to avoid being killed by military action. Loss of a son by unjust state execution parallels the disappearance and murder of beloved children under dictatorial regimes. Mary is sister to the unchronicled lives of marginalized women in oppressive situations. It does her no honor to rip her out of her conflictual, dangerous historical circumstances and transmute her into an icon of a peaceful, middle class life robed in royal blue.

Woman of faith: The concreteness of her life in a Mediterranean Jewish peasant society provides compelling background for interpreting Miriam of Nazareth as a woman of faith. As depicted in Scripture, she walked by faith not by sight, asking questions, pondering in her heart again and again what God might be doing. Her freely given consent to the call to mother the Messiah put her in league with God's redeeming intent in the world, and she remained faithful even when grief stabbed her to the heart. In those days, the expectation of an anointed king was part of a larger hope for liberation from oppressive rule. This aberrant woman and her child conceived outside the patriarchal family structure begin the fulfillment of the divine promise.

Mary's faith-filled partnership with God in the work of liberation comes to dramatic expression in the gospel story of the wedding feast at Cana (Jn 2:1–11). A typically poor family in the small village of Cana in Galilee hosts a wedding banquet. Amid the dancing and the singing, the wine gives out. Miriam of Nazareth notices. And she acts. "They have no wine," she says to Jesus. Despite his hesitation, she persists and gets results: six water jars filled with excellent wine. The wedding feast and the banquet are often used in the Bible to symbolize those heart-stopping moments when the reign of God arrives as a fulfilling blessing. In the theology of this gospel, the wine—more than one hundred gallons of it—signifies the abundant gift of salvation being joyfully poured out by the presence of Christ. But Mary's action here is dangerous.

First, because she behaves counter to traditional definitions of the ideal "feminine" person. Contra Balthasar, far from keeping silent, she speaks. Far from being passive, she acts. Far from being receptive to the wishes of the leading man, she contradicts and persuades him otherwise. Far from yielding to a grievous situation, she takes charge, organizing matters so that a bountiful abundance soon flows to those in need.

Second, because her words still call out prophetically in criticism and in hope. Hearing her words, "They have no wine," people in need continue her observation, which is also a judgment and a plea: no food, no clean drinking water, no housing, education, or health care, no employment, no security from rape, no human rights. Mary stands among the marginalized people, herself a member of the group without wine, and speaks the hope of the needy. Her strong impulse to call for relief corresponds to God's own compassionate desire to spread the hospitality of life on the earth. Just as her words propelled Jesus into action at Cana, her challenging words address the conscience of the church, the body of Christ in the world today. Even though people in wealthy nations might prefer not to be informed, her voice reverberates through the centuries saying, "They have no wine . . . you have to act."

The encouraging power of Mary's faith receives yet another critical edge when we remember her as poor, female, and endangered in a historically violent society. Then the vital memory of this woman awakens courage for the struggle for the reign of God, that is, for a just and peaceful world in which all humans and the earth can flourish. Consider how this works as we remember Mary standing near the cross (Jn 19:25–27).

The subject of countless works of art, this event conjures all the anguish and desolation a woman can experience who has given birth to a child, loved that child, raised and taught that child, even tried to protect that child, only to have him put to death in excruciating torment. There is no speaking this racking sorrow. One never really gets over the pain when someone loved is a victim of violence. *Mater Dolorosa* is not a theological concept nor a symbolic image nor an archetypal experience, but a real woman who one day had to come to grips with the terrible fact that her firstborn was dead by state execution.

Mary's grief for her dead son places her in the company of her contemporaries in Galilee whose children also fell victim to the imperial power of Rome, and to their descendants. This particular, unappeasable pain places her in solidarity with mothers of children dead by state violence everywhere, for it remains horrifically the case that the life given from women's bodies keeps on being taken away by brutality, war, and terrorism.

In the light of the Nazi holocaust, one Jewish writer has observed, "She belongs to the countless Jewish mothers who lament their cruelly murdered children.... It would not be such a bad Mariology that did not forget these sisters of Mary in the flesh."[7] Latin American women theologians speak of the "shared Calvary" women suffer with Mary in the civil wars and political repression that feed on their own children's lives. Palestinian, Bosnian, Afghani, and Congolese women, mothers of criminals executed in the United States, surviving mothers of Cambodian and Rwandan genocides, the mothers and grandmothers of Argentina's Plaza de Mayo still demanding to know the fate of their disappeared loved ones—all drink from the same cup of anguish. Like them, Mary suffered the affliction of not being able to save her child from the hand of torturers and executioners. The fact that Christian imagination can picture Mary standing with desolated people under all the crosses set up in the world is due to the history of her own very real grief.

This memory finds its liberating effectiveness when it enables grieving mothers, wives, daughters, and sisters to find strength and consolation in their bitter struggle against personal despair. Its danger functions publicly when it empowers the church's women and men to say, STOP IT. No more killing of other people's children! No more torture or war! This is, of course, a hope for a world shaped by the reign of God, which would be a world with no more sorrowing mothers. On the way there, the memory of Mary near the cross abides, inspiring non-violent action to stop the violence as a profoundly compassionate expression of faith in God.

Time does not permit further development of the memory of Mary, but we can begin to see the potential latent in other gospel scenes. Interpreting this Jewish village woman as herself a person of faith who walked with God through the joys and troubles of life raises up her dangerous memory to encourage our own lives.

CONCLUSION

We began by asking what would be a theologically sound, spiritually empowering, and ethically challenging view of Mary, mother of Jesus the Christ, for the twenty-first century. Our answer leads along the path of remembrance in the communion of saints. To relate to Miriam of Nazareth as a partner in hope in the company of all the holy women and men who have gone before us; to reclaim the power of her memory for the flourishing of suffering people; and to draw on the energy of her memory for a deeper relationship with the living God and stronger care for the world: these results of a critical reading of the marian tradition are of immeasurable benefit. When the Christian community remembers like this, she becomes truly our sister, a woman in the cloud of witnesses cheering on the people of God today.

Adapted from the John Courtney Murray Lecture, 2000; and from America *182:21 (June 17–24, 2000): 7–13.*

Notes

1. George H. Tavard, *The Thousand Faces of the Virgin Mary* (Collegeville, MN: Liturgical Press, 1996).

2. Leonardo Boff, *The Maternal Face of God* (San Francisco: Harper & Row, 1987).

3. Hans Urs von Balthasar, *Mary for Today* (San Francisco: Ignatius Press, 1987), 74.

4. John Paul II, *Redemptoris Mater*, in *Origins* 16:43 (April 9, 1987): 762 (par. #46).

5. Sojourner Truth, "Ain't I a Woman?" in Anne Clifford, *Introducing Feminist Theology* (Maryknoll, NY: Orbis, 2001), 158.

6. Ivone Gebara and Maria Clara Bingemer, *Mary Mother of God, Mother of the Poor* (Maryknoll, NY: Orbis Books, 1989); Chung Hyun Kyung, "Who Is Mary for Asian Women?" in her *Struggle to be the Sun Again* (Maryknoll, NY: Orbis Books, 1994), 74–84.

7. David Flusser, "Mary and Israel," in Jaroslav Pelikan, David Flusser, and Justin Lang, *Mary: Images of the Mother of Jesus in Jewish and Christian Perspective* (Philadelphia: Fortress Press, 1986).

23

Hearts on Fire

A Revolutionary Song

Woven through the saving history recounted in the Scriptures, one startling theme emerges. This is the peculiar way the God of Israel has of siding with vulnerable persons considered of no account. Freeing slaves from Egypt; protecting the widow and orphan; making known through the prophets that divine glory will be revealed only when justice is done; making known through Jesus that the last will be first in the kingdom of God; raising that crucified victim of state violence from the dead; this is not the way the powerful Creator of the world might be expected to act. But to ignore this is to be ill-informed about the God of the Bible.

One unexpectedly beautiful text that carries this revelation comes near the beginning of Luke's gospel. A woman sings out her joy that God's revolutionary manner of acting is to show mercy to the lowly, starting with herself. The woman is Mary of Nazareth. Her canticle is commonly called the *Magnificat*, from its opening word in the Latin translation (Lk 1:46–55). In this reflection we will consider first the speaker, a woman with her heart on fire; second, the setting; next the prayer itself; and finally how singing this might spark a fire in our own hearts today.

THE SPEAKER

Miriam of Nazareth who proclaims these words is a young, first-century Jewish woman from a farming village in Roman-occupied Galilee. Economically, she knows what it means to be poor;

302

Roman land practices and taxation policies are exploiting village people, tipping many into destitution. Politically, her society is turbulent, wracked by violence let loose by an occupying foreign army. Socially, this young woman inhabits a low rung on the cultural ladder, probably uneducated as was the case with peasant women of her time and place. In a word, Mary is simply a nobody on the world stage. Poor women today who struggle to live a dignified life against vast odds, whether in rural or urban settings, understand where she is coming from. Both dwell in poverty due to structural injustices; both inhabit worlds organized around the idea of masculine superiority and the inhibition of women's gifts. Indigenous women suffer added indignities due to their racial heritage and culture. If you want to know something about the speaker of this canticle, look to the lives of such women.

This insignificant young woman is pregnant. Immediately preceding the scene in which the Magnificat is proclaimed, Luke's gospel tells of how she became that way (1:26–38). The story of the annunciation has all the earmarks of a vocation story, structured as it is according to the five elements of the call of Moses and the prophets in the Old Testament. The voice of God through the angel Gabriel invites (you will conceive and bear a son); the person being address is troubled and objects or asks questions (how can this be, since I do not know a man?); divine assurance is given (the Holy Spirit will overshadow you); a sign is given (your cousin Elizabeth in her old age has also conceived a child); and the person being called finally agrees (here I am, the servant of the Lord; be it done to me according to your word). The singer of the Magnificat is a woman of faith who has stepped up to the plate, convinced that nothing is impossible for God.

The significance of the Spirit overshadowing Mary is profound. Christian imagination has sometimes made this into a sexual event, but such is not its meaning in the gospel. The figure of the overshadowing Spirit shows up first in the Genesis creation story where the Spirit of God blows/moves/hovers over the waters and the world comes into being. The figure appears again in the exodus story when the people of Israel are invited into covenant; fire and cloud overshadow Mount Sinai and lead them through the desert on the long trek to the promised land. The same figure of speech is used in the New Testament scene of the transfiguration; a bright cloud overshadows Jesus and his disciples on Mount Tabor as a voice from heaven declares Jesus to be God's beloved Son. In these and other stories the verb "overshadow" indicates not a sexual event but the approach of God to do a new thing. Whenever the Spirit overshadows, be on the alert: divine initiative is bringing a creative surprise into history.

So too in the story of the annunciation. Here again divine love is doing a creative new thing, coming personally to share the travail of sinful human beings in the flesh. Placing the life-giving powers of her female body hand-in-hand with God's invitation, Mary says yes. God's gracious gift to humankind begins to take shape within her.

Women today note that in this scene the angel of God speaks directly to Mary, the message not being conveyed through her father, betrothed spouse Joseph, or priest. In addition, she does not turn to any male authority figure to ask advice or to seek permission regarding what is to be done. Instead, this young woman of the people discerns the voice of God in her life; takes counsel with her own soul; and, in a self-determining act, commits herself.

In a church where male dominance is the rule, Mary's consent has traditionally been preached as an act of passive obedience, self-denial, and submission, which supposedly models the path of holiness women should walk. To the contrary, argues Latin American theologian Ana María Bidegain (Colombia), Mary's consent "is a free act of self-bestowal; she dares to accept the monumental undertaking proposed to her by God." In consort with other Asian thinkers, Chung Hyun Kyung (South Korea) emphasizes how this decision turned Mary's own private world upside down. "With fear and trembling she takes the risk of participating in God's plan...Jesus was born through the body of this woman, a mature young person with a mind and will of her own, capable of perseverance in her decisions." Indeed, far from the passivity imposed on women by the structures of a patriarchal society and church, Mary's stance is one of "utmost attentiveness and the creativity which flows from it, based on a listening life" (Catharina Halkes, Netherlands).

This is the speaker of the Magnificat. A woman of faith who hears the word of God, and acts upon it.

THE SETTING

Starting to swell with new life, Mary hastens through the hill country of Judea to visit old Elizabeth, herself six months into an unusual pregnancy. The moment of their meeting is the immediate setting for the Magnificat. There is something unusual about the house. Zechariah, Elizabeth's husband, has been struck dumb until she delivers their child. No other men are around. Such quieting of the male voice is highly unusual in Scripture. Within this spacious silence two women's voices resound. "Filled with the Holy Spirit," Elizabeth bursts into glorious praise of Mary's staunch faith: "Blessed is she who believed that the word spoken to her by the Lord would be fulfilled." Affirmed by this blessing, Mary, also filled with the Spirit, launches into joyful praise of God. These two mothers of redemption themselves embody the mercy of God which they now prophetically proclaim. And they do so in the context of affirming one another. We seldom think of pregnant women as prophets, yet this scene portrays them as such.

Before leaving this scene, note that the figure of Elizabeth stands as a moving embodiment of the wisdom and care that older women can offer younger ones who, brave as they are, are just starting out on their journey through life. Preceding Mary in childbirth and in theologizing, her presence assures the younger woman that she does not face the uncertain future alone. Elizabeth's mature experience helps sustain the new venture. What emerges with undoubted clarity from their interaction is women's ability to interpret God's word for one another.

THE SONG, PART I

Composed according to the structure of a traditional thanksgiving psalm, the Magnificat has two main stanzas. The first acclaims divine mercy to the speaker; the second broadens out to extol God's victorious deeds for all those oppressed. Far from being separate pieces, the two stanzas are linked by a profound sense of the odd mercy of the God of Israel who graciously chooses to be in solidarity with those who suffer and are of no account. The unity in distinction of the two stanzas, one praising God with deep personal love and the other proclaiming God's justice for those who are pressed down, expresses an insight at the core of biblical spirituality: mystical and political impulses, two loves that are one.

"And Mary said,..." The song begins with a poor woman's cry of joy. Her soul magnifies her God. In formal terms to magnify means to celebrate the greatness of someone wonderful, to sing and dance in praise of their goodness. Mary's whole self does this, her whole being, with body, mind, and strength. She is caught up, feels herself lifted up into God's good and gracious power. She flings herself Godward: "my spirit rejoices in God my Savior." This is not a superficial joy. It is a gladness written against the whole canvas of the world's pain. It is messianic joy, paschal joy, aware of the struggle unto death yet trusting that the abundance of God's love will accompany the poor person and lead to life. In the midst of suffering and turmoil, the sense of divine presence acting with compassion offers strong hope. She is glad that the Holy One is near.

Mary proclaims God's greatness because the Holy One of Israel has regarded her low estate, "poor and a serving woman." The Greek biblical term for "poor" used here describes misery, pain, persecution, and oppression; in the exodus story it describes the severe affliction of slavery from which God delivers the people (Ex 3:7). Gustavo Gutiérrez insists we notice that Mary's self-characterization in these lowly terms is not a metaphor for spiritual humility but is based on her actual social position. Young, poor, female, member of a subjugated people, she belongs to a group given a negative valuation by worldly powers. Yet it is to precisely such a woman that the living God has done great things. This is revolutionary. It is not just that God often chooses unconventional people for a task, and not just that Mary is among the inconsequential poor of the earth like unlettered women in any poor village on this planet. It is the combination that surprises.

Her favored status, declared first by the angel Gabriel, then by Elizabeth, and now by herself, reflects God's surprising choice of what is lowly.

In his commentary on this canticle, Martin Luther notes that the gospel always involves a reversal of values, "and the mightier you are, the more must you fear; the lowlier you are, the more must you take comfort." Just as the Spirit overshadows Mary, inspiring her joy and fortitude, Luther goes on, so too the Spirit imbues us every day with rich and abundant grace to follow our own calling. The important thing to remember is that Mary had confidence in God, finding in God her Savior a wellspring of joy and comfort. "This we too should do; that would be to sing a right Magnificat."

THE SONG, PART II

What begins as praise for divine loving-kindness toward a marginalized woman grows in amplitude to include all the poor of the world. Throughout Scripture the revelation of the character of God who liberated the Hebrew slaves from bondage is expressed in texts that praise divine care for the lost. Psalm after psalm and prophet after prophet proclaim that the Holy One of Israel protects, defends, saves, and rescues these poor "nobodies," adorning them with victory and life in the face of despair. Proclaiming the Magnificat, Mary continues this deep stream of Jewish faith in the context of the advent of the Messiah, now taking shape within her. The approaching reign of God will disturb the order of the world run by the arrogant, the hard of heart, the indifferent overlord. Through God's action the social hierarchy of wealth and poverty, power and subjugation, will be turned upside down. Jubilation breaks out as the proud are scattered and the mighty are pulled down from their thrones while the lowly are exalted, and mercy, in the form of food, fills the bellies of the hungry. God has promised, sings Mary, and will be faithful.

The gospels testify that in his own lifetime Jesus preached this great reversal. Recall the beatitudes: "Blessed are you poor ... you who hunger now ... you who weep now ... But woe to you rich... who are full now... who laugh now." Through his own death and resurrection this same reversal is embodied in Jesus himself, the crucified one who becomes the motherlode of God's life-giving mercy for the world.

The history of interpretation contains many instances of thinkers and preachers who opt to spiritualize the Magnificat, to take away its political teeth, to blunt its radical tone by appeal to the justice promised for the last day. But the prophetic tradition of biblical justice will not let this ploy stand. The coming of the reign of God means flourishing for poor people in all dimensions of life *now*. In the deepest revelatory insight of Jewish and Christian traditions, there is no other God than the one who acts like this. Standing at the dawn of the messianic era, Mary is the spokeswoman of this promise. In the line of the great biblical singers Miriam, Deborah, Huldah, and Hannah, she sings of God's justice. Like the beatitudes, which Jesus proclaims for the poor and brokenhearted, her canticle rejoices in the kind of salvation that involves concrete blessings.

Thinking along these lines, Dietrich Bonhoeffer, the German theologian killed by the Nazis, preached a wonderful sermon on this canticle.

> The song of Mary is the oldest Advent hymn. It is at once the most passionate, the wildest, one might even say the most revolutionary Advent hymn ever sung. This is not the gentle, tender, dreamy Mary whom we sometimes see in paintings; it is the passionate, surrendered, proud, enthusiastic Mary who speaks out here. This song has none of the sweet, nostalgic, or even playful tones of some of our Christmas carols. It is instead a hard, strong, inexorable song about collapsing thrones and humbled lords of this world, about the power of God amid the powerlessness of humankind. These are the tones of the women prophets of the Old Testament that now come to life in Mary's mouth.

People in need in every society hear a blessing in this canticle. The battered or trafficked woman, those without food on the table or without even a table, the homeless family, the refugees, the young abandoned to their own devices, the old who are discarded: all are encompassed in the hope Mary proclaims. The church in Latin America more than any other is responsible for hearing this proclamation in a newly refreshed way. Holding that this song reveals the heart of God who acts in history, Gustavo Gutiérrez argues, "Any exegesis is fruitless that attempts to tone down what Mary's song tells us about preferential love of God for the lowly and the abused, and about the transformation of history that God's loving will implies."

This vision will not appeal to those who are satisfied with the ways things are. Even affluent people of good will have difficulty dealing with its shocking, revolutionary ring. Doesn't God love everyone? Indeed yes, but in an unjust world, the form this universal love takes differs according to circumstance. The language of Mary's canticle makes clear that divine love is particularly on the side of those whose dignity must be recovered. The point is not to reverse discrimination and thereby create a new order of injustice, but to restructure, to build up a community of sisters and brothers marked by human dignity and mutual regard. Only thus is the reign of God rendered real in history. Imagine the world according to the defiant Mary's Magnificat, invites African theologian Peter Daino. Imagine such a world: a heavenly banquet and all the children fed.

And so Mary sings her canticle. Unleashing all the energies of her heart, she praises the magnificence of the living God who is Love. This God, as classical theology puts it, is *Deus semper maior*: God always-ever-greater. Faith is an ongoing adventure into this Holy Mystery. In her canticle Mary avoids the shallows of superficial religion and launches her life into this infinite mystery, magnifying divine compassion, which is beyond all imagining.

IN WOMEN'S HEARING

This canticle finds special resonance in the hearing of women who struggle against sexism as well as against racism, classism, heterosexism, and all other injustice that demeans their humanity.

They note that this is the longest set of words placed on the lips of any woman in the whole New Testament, the most any woman gets to say. In its spirit, they draw many and varied lessons of encouragement. One of the strongest and most unusual lessons in light of traditional mariology is the right of women to say "no." Leonardo Boff makes the point well: "Men toiling in the service of male power interests represent Mary only as the woman who knew how to say yes." But here she takes on as her own the divine NO to what crushes the lowly. She stands up fearlessly and sings out that injustice will be overturned. No passivity here, but solidarity with divine outrage over the degradation of life, coupled with God's merciful promise to repair the world. In the process she bursts out of the boundaries of male-defined femininity while still every inch a woman. Singing of her joy in God's victory over oppression, she becomes not a subjugated but a prophetic woman.

Catholic women wrestle with the significance of this canticle for their own subordinate position in current church structures. With no little irony, Brazilian theologians Ivone Gebara and Maria Clara Bingemer cite the homily preached by Pope John Paul II in Zapopan, Mexico, in which he pointed to Mary of the Magnificat as a model for those "who do not passively accept the adverse circumstances of personal and social life and are not victims of alienation, as they say today, but who, with her, proclaim that God 'raises up the lowly' and if necessary, 'overthrows the powerful from their thrones.'"

If this be applied to women's struggle for full participation in the church, the reversals of the Magnificat become rife with significance. They characterize as nothing less than *mercy* God's intervention into the patriarchal social order. Theologian Susan Ross's critique spells out the implications. In many ways in the church, the mighty still occupy their thrones; the lowly still await their exaltation. "Women's very real lack of power in the church today stands as an indictment of the power structures as they exist.... Any discussion of the empowerment of women must be juxtaposed with our lack of political and symbolic power and the failure of the leadership of the church to rectify this scandal."

In addition to hope against their dispossessed status, women glean from this song a boost of encouragement for their own creative behavior. Theologian Rosemary Radford Ruether sees here an example of a woman becoming a theological agent in her own right, actively and cooperatively figuring out the direction of the Spirit. Poet and essayist Kathleen Norris treasures Mary as an original biblical interpreter, linking her people's hope to a new historical event. Noting the powerful proclamation of the Good News that issues from Mary's mouth, theologian Jane Schaberg writes, "Without an explicit commission to preach, she preaches as though she was commissioned," that is, with authority. In the struggle against sexism in the church, the great reversals roll on, their tone of judgment and promise resounding in the voices of prophetic women today.

HEARTS ON FIRE

The Magnificat is a profoundly God-centered prayer. In Edward Schillebeeckx's inimitable phrase, it is "a toast to our God." Mary stands as the maker of this toast. A poor woman of the people, she lifts up the glass of her canticle, rejoicing in God as a woman who has herself suffered and been vindicated.

In the fifth century Ambrose of Milan made a felicitous connection. He was reflecting on a text of the prophet Isaiah, which reads: "How beautiful upon the mountains are the feet of the messenger who announces peace, who brings good news, who announces salvation" (Isa 52:7). His imagination summoned up an image of Mary, hurrying through the hill country to sing her Magnificat with Elizabeth's blessing. He linked Mary's journey with the church's journey across the hills of centuries to announce glad tidings of salvation. Ambrose then exhorts, "Watch Mary, my children, for the word uttered prophetically of the church applies also to her: 'How beautiful thy sandaled steps, O generous maid!' Yes, generous and beautiful indeed are the church's steps as she goes to announce her gospel of joy: lovely the feet of Mary and the church."

Mary's canticle refuses to be relegated to the past. She sings this song not only once and not for herself alone but for all of us, to sing it with her as we walk in mission to announce the good news. Doing so places us in intense relationship to the living God along the lines of Mary's faith experience. Our own hearts catch fire with the cadences of her words. Time becomes permeable. Her passionate joy in God her Savior becomes ours. Her protest and hopeful vision of justice flow through the centuries and become ours. Rather than praising her directly, we join with her in praising God who regards suffering with utmost mercy and summons us into the struggle to build a more peaceful and just world. "And Mary said," and inspired by the same Spirit we say:

> My soul proclaims your greatness, O my God,
> and my spirit rejoices in God, my Savior.
> For your regard has blessed me, poor, and a serving
>   woman.
> From this day all generations will call me blessed,
> for you, who are mighty, have done great things for
>   me;
> and holy is your Name.
> Your mercy is on those who fear you, from generation
>   to generation.
> You have shown strength with your arm.
> You have scattered the proud in their hearts' conceit.
> You have put down the mighty from their thrones,
> and have lifted up the lowly.
> You have filled the hungry with good things,
> and have sent the rich away empty.
> You have helped your servant Israel,
> remembering your mercy,
> as you promised to Abraham and Sarah,
> mercy to their children forever. (Lk 1:46–55)

Adapted from an address at the centennial celebration of the Maryknoll Sisters, Maryknoll, NY, 2012.

V
EPILOGUE

24

Peace over an Angry Sea

Readings: 1 Corinthians 15:50–56—"O death, where is your sting?"
Mark 4:35–41—"A great windstorm arose ..."

There isn't a person in this assembly, I suspect, who has not at some point struggled with the heart-rending questions raised by suffering and death. Even young students here who may not yet have experienced personal loss had to grapple with a kind of anguish when the World Trade Towers fell in 2001. The photos of lost family members posted on walls and fences, the outdoor candle-lit vigils, the concerts and religious services, the bagpipes, the endless funerals, the knowledge that hundreds of people had simply been blown out as dust across the harbor and the city: citizens of New York were awash in grief.

Along with public tragedies, death afflicts us in an intimate, personal way when someone we love dies. We have gathered today to pray with our colleagues who have felt the "sting of death" in a particularly harsh way these last months: Leo, Donna, Larry, and Phil. The death of a beloved person in our lives, the death of our mother, our father, our spouse, is a bleak and bitter reality. It leaves us stunned, gasping with King Lear after the death of Cordelia: "Why should a dog, a horse, a rat have life, and thou no breath at all?" So much sorrow. It cannot be sugar-coated with easy consolation.

The scripture readings today invite us to reflect on the very heart of faith, a core conviction of hope that takes on profound resonance in the face of grief and loss.

In the gospel story Jesus was asleep in the stern of a boat on the Sea of Galilee. Sometime during the night a great windstorm blew up. The normally placid water grew wild with waves; the boat pitched and yawed; in short order it was swamped. Yelling their distress at the danger—did he not care that they were perishing?—the disciples woke Jesus up. First, he rebuked the wind and water: "Peace! Be still!" The wind ceased, and there was a dead calm. Then he asked his little band of followers, "Why are you afraid? Have you no faith?" The story ends with the disciples in awe, wondering what sort of man this is, that even the wind and the sea obey him.

At first glance this story could be taken as one of Jesus' nature miracles, about which there have been no end of disputes. Recall, however, that the gospels were written decades after the events they record with the intent of leading people to faith. Biblical scholars suggest that the point of this story took shape in light of the early church's reflection on the resurrection of Jesus with its promise of a blessed future for all. An angry sea whipped up by roaring winds was one of the most death-dealing elements known to first-century fishermen. Calling the disciples to faith rather than fear, Jesus calms the storm. So too, the risen Christ overcomes the untamed chaos of death. Raised to glory by the Spirit of God, he brings the peace of new life. The same call to faith rather than fear resounds.

This mystery is inscrutable. It bespeaks a new possibility in the teeth of grief and loss, a hope in resurrection because God is *God*, the Giver of life who can make a way where there is no way. Borne up by this living tradition of hope, we can affirm, even while being honest about our pain, that the Spirit of God who raised Jesus from the dead can do it again for our loved ones, for all the dead, and someday for ourselves as well. Such hope itself is a foretaste of that new life. Seized with this realization, Paul writes to the Corinthians in ecstatic terms. "Death has been swallowed up in victory. Where, O death, is your victory? Where, O death, is your sting?...But thanks be to God who has given us the victory through our Lord Jesus Christ."

In his later years, Dutch priest Henri Nouwen was fascinated by the circus and by a troupe of trapeze artists called the Flying Rodleighs. A remark by one of these trapeze artists provides a great image for the hope that I am describing. When Nouwen expressed his admiration for the artistry of one the trapeze flyers, she said, "The flyer does nothing and the catcher does everything. When I fly, I simply stretch out my arms and wait for him to catch me and pull me safely over the apron behind the catch bar. A flyer must fly, and a catcher must catch, and the flyer must trust, with outstretched arms, that her catcher will be there for her."

Confronted as we are by death's silencing of those we love, we know so little except this: Letting go, they have flown into the arms of the waiting Catcher. Hoping against hope, we affirm that they have fallen not into nothingness but into the embrace of the living God. And that is where we can find them again, when we open our own hearts to the silent calmness of God's own life in which they dwell, not by selfishly calling them back to where we are, but by descending into the depths of our own hearts where God also abides.

We gather around this table now, to share in the eucharistic bread of life and the cup of salvation. Let this memorial of the death and resurrection of Jesus Christ strengthen our hope that death, with its knock-down winds and wild waves, fierce and wrenching though it may be, is not the last word, because it was not the last word for Jesus. Then as now what is needed is faith. The storm rages. Death claims every living thing, including our loved ones and ultimately even ourselves. Fear is natural. But Jesus is in the boat.

Homily at a eucharistic gathering in a private chapel, Fordham University, for members of the Theology Department who had recently lost family members, 2002.

Index